Frank Kelleter, Alexander Starre (eds.)
Culture²

Frank Kelleter is chair of the Department of Culture at John F. Kennedy Institute for North American Studies, Freie Universität Berlin. His main fields of interest include the American Colonial and Enlightenment periods, theories of American modernity, and American media and popular culture. Select publications: *Media of Serial Narrative* (ed., 2017), *David Bowie* (Reclam, 2016), *Serial Agencies: The Wire and Its Readers* (2014).

Alexander Starre is assistant professor of North American culture at the John F. Kennedy Institute at Freie Universität Berlin. He is a former Humboldt Foundation fellow and has previously taught at the Universität Göttingen and at Brown University. Current research interests are knowledge production, literary institutions, and late 19th/early 20th-century American culture. His publications include *Metamedia* (2015), *Projecting American Studies* (ed., 2018), and *The Printed Book in Contemporary American Culture* (ed., 2019).

Frank Kelleter, Alexander Starre (eds.)

Culture²

Theorizing Theory for the Twenty-First Century, Vol. 1

[transcript]

This publication was financed in part by the open access fund for monographs and edited volumes of the Freie Universität Berlin.

Funded by the Deutsche Forschungsgemeinschaft (DFG, German Research Foundation) under Germany's Excellence Strategy in the context of the Cluster of Excellence Temporal Communities: Doing Literature in a Global Perspective - EXC 2020 - Project ID 390608380.

Bibliographic information published by the Deutsche Nationalbibliothek

The Deutsche Nationalbibliothek lists this publication in the Deutsche Nationalbibliografie; detailed bibliographic data are available on the Internet at http://dnb.d-nb.de

First published in 2022 by transcript Verlag, Bielefeld
© **Frank Kelleter, Alexander Starre (eds.)**

Cover layout: Kordula Röckenhaus, Bielefeld

Print-ISBN 978-3-8376-5787-6
PDF-ISBN 978-3-8394-5787-0
https://doi.org/10.14361/9783839457870
ISSN of series: 2747-4372
eISSN of series: 2747-4380

Contents

Humans and Other Species

Structures of Feminist Feeling and Storytelling

Cruel Optimism

Inter Disciplinary Anxieties

American Redescriptions

Works in Chronological Order

Luc Boltanski and Ève Chiapello, *The New Spirit of Capitalism* (1999/2005)
Robyn Warhol, *Having a Good Cry: Effeminate Feelings and Pop-culture Forms* (2003)
Mark McGurl, *The Program Era: Postwar Fiction and the Rise of Creative Writing* (2009)
Michael Tomasello, *Why We Cooperate* (2009)
Clare Hemmings, *Why Stories Matter: The Political Grammar of Feminist Theory* (2011)
Lauren Berlant, *Cruel Optimism* (2011)
Stefano Harney and Fred Moten, *The Undercommons: Fugitive Planning & Black Study* (2013)
David Alworth, *Site Reading: Fiction, Art, Social Form* (2015)
Rita Felski, *The Limits of Critique* (2015)
Caroline Levine, *Forms: Whole, Rhythm, Hierarchy, Network* (2015)
John Durham Peters, *The Marvelous Clouds: Toward a Philosophy of Elemental Media* (2015)
Anna Lowenhaupt Tsing, *The Mushroom at the End of the World: On the Possibility of Life in Capitalist Ruins* (2015)
Arlie Russell Hochschild, *Strangers in Their Own Land: Anger and Mourning on the American Right* (2016)
Matthew Desmond, *Evicted: Poverty and Profit in the American City* (2016)

Culture vs. Nature Culture vs. Civilization Black Culture Western Culture American Culture High Culture Low Culture Middlebrow Culture Popular Culture Queer Culture Mass Culture Counter Culture Alternative Culture Gun Culture Cold War Culture Neoliberal Culture Corporate Culture Consumer Culture Cyber Culture Conspiracy Culture Cancel Culture Protest Culture Culture Wars Culture Culture

Culture'2

Entry

Three critiques walk into a bar. Will they
(A.) give practical advice to each other,
    then pass judgment on pure reason?
(B.) tell a joke about themselves?
(C.) never leave again?

Culture²: Entry

Frank Kelleter & Alexander Starre

Does culture need a theory?

Yes, sure, why else would you teach classes on "cultural theory."

No, not as an explanation.
There is no culture that doesn't come equipped with its own theory about itself.

The matters of humanist concern—poems, television series, table manners, rap songs, or Balinese cockfights—are well aware that they're part of a culture. Technically speaking, they don't need scholars to tell them so. Conversely, much of what is branded "theory" is itself a cultural practice, producing its own reflexive loops of, about, and within academic knowledge.

Regrettably, then, labeling something with the slippery signifier "culture" doesn't tell you much about it. The word is more of a semiotic vessel that contains multitudes, sometimes platitudes. So if you go ahead and add another level of observation—as in "cultural studies"—you may well end up producing "stuff about stuff," as Michael Bérubé once quipped.[1] Despite its slipperiness, however, the word "culture" has had very distinct things to say in the writings of those who have been using it professionally. Just think of the tonal difference between W.E.B. Du Bois making a bold claim on the "kingdom of culture" in 1903 and Ruth Benedict designating culture as "a more or less

---

1   Michael Bérubé, "Introduction: Engaging the Aesthetic," in *The Aesthetics of Cultural Studies*, ed. Bérubé (Malden: Blackwell, 2005), 9.

consistent pattern of thought and action" in 1934.[2] The culture concept has performed tremendous cultural work—and it continues to do so as we enter the third decade of the twenty-first century. In fact, the recent trend toward calling any systemic groupthink behind real or imagined social problems "culture"—think "gun culture" or, in a different register, "cancel culture"—has set the American culture concept on a darker course, one that is fully aligned with, well, the culture's political situation. Seen from a more abstract perspective, the sheer proliferation of the phrase "*x* culture" points to a veritable *culture culture*—a curious way in which "our" culture observes and describes itself through the prism of "culture."

In a way, then, culture doesn't need to be squared—it squares itself.

And yet here we are with *Culture²*. Niklas Luhmann once remarked that academic talk of "culture" only subsists on the fact that we cannot do without it—however, not because "culture" is such a well-defined and useful concept but because any proposal for an alternative terminology would likely reproduce its inadequacies.[3] *Culture²* means to probe this predicament: if the loaded term "culture" is our best bad option to address, in impossible abstraction, all those behaviors, practices, forms, and ideational or ideological structures that "have been learned"—that is, the labors, arts, sports, techniques, sciences, productions, reproductions, consumptions, emotions, and daily routines of human life—then perhaps the *study* of culture is the most recursive and self-involved cultural activity of them all. The title of our volume pays homage to this intuition. It holds that what in some quarters is still called "*cultural* studies" should be taken at its word. In this spirit, *Culture²* sets out to read a number of contemporary "observations" on aesthetics, technology, literature, violence, entertainment, institutions, storytelling, capitalism, sexuality, nonhumans, the Anthropocene, etc. as the learned self-observations of a fairly coherent, historically specific, and clearly critical moment in modern thought.

In doing so, we recognize that cultural theory, broadly conceived, doesn't only think of itself through "keywords"—as in Raymond Williams's founda-

---

2   W.E.B Du Bois, *The Souls of Black Folk*, 1903 (London: Penguin, 1996), 7; Ruth Benedict, *Patterns of Culture*, 1934 (Boston: Houghton Mifflin, 2005).

3   Niklas Luhmann, *Theory of Society, Volume 2*, 1997, trans. Rhodes Barrett (Stanford: Stanford University Press, 2013), 176. The book's German title resonates well with the reflexivity stressed in the present volume: *Die Gesellschaft der Gesellschaft* (literally: "The Society of Society" or "Society's Society").

tional handbook—but also, and despite our increasingly fragmented ecosystem of scholarly communication, through individual "key works." Based on this premise, our book features fifteen essays on a selection of key works in the study of culture published over the last two decades. These essays do not speak the language of classical "reviews," encyclopedic surveys, polemical dismissals, or enthusiastic partisanship. Instead, they attempt to take seriously the implications of the project's title and enter into a respectful and responsive dialogue with their chosen interlocutors. We like to think that the chapters that follow manage to avoid the safe stance of external judgment in favor of the more tentative receptiveness, perhaps even self-consciousness and uncertainty, afforded by positions of considered con-temporaneity and third-order observation.

This is why *Culture²* is not a handbook, encyclopedia, or a "state of the field" compendium. Its goal is not to canonize "must-reads" of cultural theory but to spark productive debate through the presumptuous act of singling out individual texts that can exemplify the potentials and constraints of current modes of "doing theory."

The group of scholars assembled here represents a transatlantic network; their outlook on cultural studies is deeply informed and, at the same time, delimited by Anglo-American conversations on theory and method, while also being detached from the immediate institutional ties and political stakes of a national scholarly community. With its editors based in European American Studies (what a term), *Culture²* attempts to place the works it covers in a larger transnational conversation.

Among the "key works" discussed in the fifteen chapters are some of the most quoted books of the past twenty years (Lauren Berlant's *Cruel Optimism*, Stefano Harney and Fred Moten's *The Undercommons*, Mark McGurl's *The Program Era*, Caroline Levine's *Forms*, Rita Felski's *The Limits of Critique*) alongside several perhaps less obvious entries that reflect the interdisciplinary traffic of ideas passing through the fields of cultural and literary studies from areas such as anthropology, evolutionary biology, media studies, or sociology (by way of Anna Tsing's *The Mushroom at the End of the World*, Michael Tomasello's *Why We Cooperate*, John Durham Peters's *The Marvelous Clouds*, and Matthew Desmond's *Evicted*).[4] After collecting these one-sided dialogues, and writing

---

4   While finishing the proofs for this volume, we came across a tweet indicating that Lauren Berlant now uses the pronouns they/them. We asked Lauren Berlant to confirm, which they did. They also told us that it's fine to use she/her for a book they published

two of them ourselves, we see the gaps and omissions in this scholarly assemblage more glaringly than before. For this reason—and to underscore the provisional nature both of culture and of *Culture²*—the book is subtitled Vol. 1. If and when there will be a Vol. 2 remains to be seen. Should it come to pass, the twenty-first century will probably have moved into some post-COVID-19 era. (Several of the chapters carry visible traces of the current pandemic, as they were completed in the early days of lockdowns and social distancing in 2020.) What awaits on the other side of this watershed, no theory can predict—but chances are that, for better or worse, it will still recognize itself as culture. In this sense, too, the act of theorizing theory is a task *for* the twenty-first century.[5]

---

in 2011, which we did (see p. 182). — POSTSCRIPT. In the final stages of preparing *Culture²* for press, we learned of Lauren Berlant's death. This book is dedicated to them.

5   We would like to thank Linh Müller, Emmy Fu, and Tabea Vohmann for streamlining citations, proofreading the manuscript, and providing excellent feedback during the final editing stages. Emmy and Tabea also designed the typographic frontispiece.

Form | Critique

Auspicious strategy #47: If you feel like criticizing the temporality of other researchers (they "still" believe this, have "not yet" read that, &c.), assume that they are not left behind by your nextness claims but have moved past them already.

1.   Make the Dialectic Great Again!
On Postcritique in Rita Felski's *The Limits of Critique* (2015)

J. Jesse Ramírez

"Where is power in all of this?" When I posed the question to a speaker at a recent American Studies conference, it seemed innocuous. The speaker had used Bruno Latour's Actor Network Theory (ANT), and I wanted to know if ANT can recognize the concentrations of corporate power in the production, circulation, and reception of cultural commodities.[1] That's how I would describe at least one of the primary characteristics of US culture, which was the speaker's topic. Little did I know at the time that, by focusing on power and invoking other abstractions like "capitalism," I was being stereotypically critical. Somewhere, a postcritic yawned.

According to Rita Felski, critique has become boringly obvious. "Anyone who attends academic talks," Felski writes, "has learned to expect the inevitable question: 'But what about power?'" (17).[2] Felski saw me coming from a mile away. In *The Limits of Critique*, her postcritical manifesto, Felski argues that critique is not only an ensemble of overly familiar ideas about literary and cultural interpretation but also a pervasive and predictable mood. Critics are the deans of Paul Ricoeur's school of suspicion.[3] They read texts and other cultural artifacts as if they were police interrogating a suspect upon whose guilt they have always already passed judgment. Critics "stand back" from texts, coolly and shrewdly refusing to be duped by the beauty of a well-chosen word

---

1   "There is now very little cultural production outside the commodity form," writes Michael Denning in *Culture in the Age of Three Worlds* (New York: Verso, 2004), 104.

2   All parenthetical citations in the text refer to Rita Felski, *The Limits of Critique* (Chicago: University of Chicago Press, 2015).

3   Paul Ricoeur, *Freud and Philosophy: An Essay on Interpretation*, trans. Denis Savage (New Haven: Yale University Press, 1970), 28–36.

or identify with likeable characters. Critics also typically "dig down" into texts, excavating their political unconscious for symptoms and clues of something "unflattering" and "counterintuitive" that they cannot admit outright, which is usually this or that "complicity" with social forces that are more important than they are—capitalism, patriarchy, racism, imperialism, heteronormativity, power/knowledge, and so forth (54–55, 58). Whether standing back or digging down, critics are relentlessly negative. Consider the prefixes of critics' favorite verbs: *de*mystify, *de*bunk, *de*construct, *de*naturalize, *un*mask. And since critics treat texts as passive bearers of dominant social forces, they regard their own negativity toward texts as political resistance to the status quo. While critics may praise texts on occasion, they mostly celebrate the ones that affirm their predetermined ethical and political commitments.

To describe critique as suspicion is to "redescribe" it, since critique isn't commonly regarded as a dominant discourse or a ubiquitous mood. Felski uses the concept of redescription to distinguish her approach from what she calls the "critique of critique" (9–10). Her goal isn't to fix critique by unmasking its complicities; she wants neither to stand back from critique nor dig down into it. Instead of applying critique to demonstrate the deficiencies of critique, Felski aims to challenge the status of critique as the Swiss Army knife of literary and cultural studies. In Felski's estimation, this all-purpose tool has been too successful: it has monopolized interpretation and weakened our capacity to understand the full diversity of ways that texts mean and that readers relate to meaning. Thus, it's not a matter of banishing critique but rather of opening up its one-party system. "There is no one-size-fits-all form of thinking," Felski writes, "that can fulfill all [the] aims [of interpretation] simultaneously" (9).

In addition to its intellectual and pedagogical concerns, *The Limits of Critique* is motivated by what Felski calls the "legitimation crisis" of literary studies—and of the humanities more broadly—in the United States (14). The last decade has witnessed a precipitous decline in undergraduate enrollments and majors in the humanities, while the number of jobs published in the English and Foreign Language Editions of the Modern Language Association's *Job Information List* has fallen to historic lows.[4] "Postcritical reading" is Felski's term for a diverse assortment of rhetorics and affects that can expand understanding of our relationships with texts and cultural artifacts while providing a

---

4   Eric Hayot, "The Sky is Falling," *Profession*, May 2018, https://profession.mla.org/the-sky
-is-falling/.

positive grounding of the value of humanistic inquiry under conditions of departmental defunding. Instead of wearily standing back, the postcritical reader generously explores attachments to texts, such as "aesthetic pleasure, increased self-understanding, moral reflection, perceptual reinvigoration, ecstatic self-loss, emotional consolation, or heightened sensation" (188). Instead of digging down and discovering that the text is an effect of some predetermined social abstraction, the postcritical reader recognizes texts as agents in their own right. Drawing on ANT, Felski reframes the social nexus between texts and readers as an interdependent assemblage in which texts actively participate in eliciting attachments. Felski sums up the lessons of postcritique as follows: "*Interpretation becomes a coproduction between actors that brings new things to light rather than an endless rumination on a text's hidden meanings or representational failures*" (174). This rethinking of interpretation might renew our disciplinary methods and moods, put humanists back in touch with the everyday reading practices of students, and "inspire more capacious, and more publicly persuasive, rationales for why literature, and the study of literature, matter" (191).

The Persistence of Critique

I had enough encounters with Felski's "critics" in graduate school, where I occasionally made the mistake of using terms like "beautiful," to make me sympathetic to postcritique. But I'm also a Marxist critic, and *The Limits of Critique* left me with the impression that the problem with Felski's critics is that, to put it reductively, they aren't Marxists. Terry Eagleton, a Marxist who has critiqued aesthetic ideologies *and* written an introduction to the Gospels, reviewed *The Limits of Critique* favorably.[5] I often found myself nodding along to Felski's arguments against the fetishization of negativity and in favor of hermeneutic practices that attend to positive values like hope, joy, and love. If Marxists didn't believe in these things, their critiques would be in vain. Even Adorno, the archetypal curmudgeon, admitted that demystification and de-

---

5   Terry Eagleton, "Not Just Anybody," review of *The Limits of Critique*, by Rita Felski, *The London Review of Books*, January 5, 2017, https://www.lrb.co.uk/the-paper/v39/n01/terry-eagleton/not-just-anybody.

bunking are for the sake of something better: "Consummate negativity, once squarely faced, delineates the mirror-image of its opposite."[6]

I want to reflect on the specific location of Marxist critique in Felski's postcritical project by returning to my starting point, the postcritic's boredom with the question, "What about power?" If postcritics are bored with questions about power, that doesn't prove anything about the significance of the questions or about their object. The monotony of power may not be sexy but it's a good indicator of power's durability and thus of the continuing necessity of critiquing it. The people and institutions that wield power aren't bored enough with it to give it up. Police in riot gear aren't bored with power.

But the more I think about how boredom functions in *The Limits of Critique*, the more I see subtle instances of the dialectic and critique. What I find in Felski's boredom with the "inevitable question" about power is not an invitation to try out other, more diverse styles of interpretation, but rather a prohibition, an impatient eye-roll that asks, "Won't you please stop asking *that* question already?" Fredric Jameson, a favorite target of postcritics, observed of an earlier manifesto, Steven Knapp and Walter Benn Michael's "Against Theory," that "we are being told to stop doing something[.] [N]ew taboos ... are being erected with passionate energy and conviction."[7] Felski's invitation to postcritique also dialectically generates its opposite, a taboo. What I'm trying to identify is the dialectical form of Felski's representation of postcritique; I'm trying to understand how postcritique *disconnects* from competing theories in order to represent a new hermeneutics of connection.

The dialectical tradition tells us that the new can only be a determinate negation of the old. In other words, Felski cannot say yes to postcritique without saying no to critique; she cannot direct her reader toward postcritical styles of interpretation without simultaneously pulling them away from critique, especially if critique has as tight a grip on intellectual discourse and affect as she claims it does. A tight grip must be pried open. Felski's negativity is most apparent when she explains that the concept of postcritique isn't meant to "prescribe" and "dictate" new reading practices but to "decline" and "steer us away" from critique (173). For the championing of any new theoretical orientation must simultaneously negate competing orientations, even if

---

6   Theodor Adorno, *Minima Moralia: Reflections on a Damaged Life*, trans. E.F.N. Jephcott (New York: Verso, 2004), 247.

7   Fredric Jameson, *Postmodernism, or, The Cultural Logic of Late Capitalism* (Durham: Duke University Press, 1991), 183.

the new orientation is explicitly affirmative. To put this another way, the free-dom of a new mode of expression, as Adorno said of modernism, is undercut by the unfreedom generated by its taboo on repeating the old modes.[8]

My intention in framing Felski's rhetoric as dialectical and critical isn't to mock her as hypocritical. I take to heart her point that we can disagree with a text without accusing it of skullduggery, and for that reason I don't think Fel-ski is "repressing" the dialectic. Rather, I am insisting on the legitimacy of the dialectic as a mode of critique by showing, in a dialectical reading of Felski, that she also needs the dialectic. The terms "dialectic" and "dialectical" appear all of three times in Felski's chapters, and two of these are in quotations. The one time that she addresses dialectical thinking directly is in a parenthesis in which she brushes aside the idea that the dialectic can help critique overcome its negativity fetish (8). In Felski's view, turning to the dialectic is just dou-bling down on critique, insisting that the cure for critique is more critique. In contrast, I view the dialectic as a competitor to postcritique that already appreciates the limits of critique as one-sided negation, demystification, and debunking. The dialectical tradition is "pre"-postcritique, insofar as it antic-ipates some of Felski's core arguments, and "post"-postcritique, insofar as it can endure the decentering of what Felski means by "critique."

It's instructive to examine how Felski accommodates one of the most pow-erful counterexamples to her case against the one-sided negativity of critique: Fredric Jameson's dialectic of utopia and ideology in *The Political Unconscious*, a book that serves as a paradigm case of critique and as a disavowed cousin of postcritique. In the conclusion to *The Political Unconscious*, Jameson engages with Ricoeur's *Freud and Philosophy*, the very text that Felski draws upon to redescribe critique as suspicion. Jameson claims that the negativity of the Marxist critique of ideology is insufficient: negation must always stand in di-alectical tension with a positive utopian hermeneutic that identifies and cele-brates the traces of a more emancipatory future in the cultural production of the past and present. The Marxist hermeneutic is "the *simultaneous* recognition of the ideological *and* Utopian functions of the artistic text."[9] "The dialectic," Jameson has written more recently, "stands as an imperative to hold the oppo-

---

8   Theodor W. Adorno, *Aesthetic Theory*, trans. Robert Hullot-Kentor (New York: Blooms-bury, 2013), 1.

9   Fredric Jameson, *The Political Unconscious: Narrative as a Socially Symbolic Act* (New York: Routledge Classics, 2002), 290 (my emphasis).

sites together, and as it were to abolish the autonomy of either term in favor of a pure tension one must necessarily preserve."[10]

In order to maintain her case against the negativity of critique in the face of such claims, Felski must move the goalposts. In the case of Jameson's dialectical critique, the problem with critique suddenly isn't that it lacks a positive vision but rather that this positive vision is, first, too utopian, because it requires a total rupture with the present, and second, too Marxist, because Jameson's positive vision corresponds to the Marxist notion of classless society (64). Yet the Marxist tradition doesn't envision utopia as a complete break with the present. Ernst Bloch calls such a break an "abstract utopia" and contrasts it with "concrete utopia," a future society that builds on both the contradictions and positive potential within the present.[11] This relation between the present and the utopian future in Marxist thought is another instance of the determinate negativity that silently structures Felski's own representation of postcritique in relation to critique. And what, exactly, is wrong with classless society? Felski's advocacy for literature's power to surprise seems to mean that Jameson shouldn't already have stable ideas about what he thinks about a better society before reading literature. In other words, at the moment when Felski cannot maintain her account of critique as being bereft of positive values, she changes the criteria of critique's failure specifically to refute Marxism, whose problem is that its positive values are *too clear*. The major advantage that postcritique now seems to have over Marxism and the dialectic is that, unlike "classless society," its Latourian values sound reassuringly non-ideological and non-antagonistic. I'll return to this point later, when I come back to Felski's points about the legitimation crisis of the humanities.

Another dialectical style that pervades Felski's rhetoric is "deflation via inversion," a protocol that she ascribes to critique but ends up using herself to great effect (128). Critics think critique is a means for resisting institutional power, Felski reasons, but it's actually an institutionally validated academic discourse. Critics think critique is politically marginal, a shot at the dominant culture from "outside" or "below," but critique is in fact mainstream. Critics think they are heroically resisting disciplinary regimes, but they are really mimicking the police in their moralistic search for guilty texts. Critics think they are tearing down all conventions, but critique is itself a conventional discourse whose protocols resemble those of genre detective fiction.

10   Fredric Jameson, *Valences of the Dialectic* (New York: Verso, 2009), 65.
11   Ruth Levitas, *The Concept of Utopia* (New York: Peter Lang, 2010), 98–122.

Critics describe their projects in lofty ethical and political terms, but they are sustained by more mundane pleasures, such as the "aha" moment when a critical reading connects the dots into a satisfying whole, or the pleasure of performing expert superiority to amateurs and other uncritical readers.

To be sure, Felski's critical reversals are not *symptomatic*. "The goal," she writes, "is not to unmask critique by exposing the hidden structures that determine it" (120–121). Nonetheless, a critical strategy of estrangement pervades *The Limits of Critique*—a strategy that distances the reader from what critique appears to be and from what critics claim to be doing. If critique "seeks to wrest from a text a different account than it gives of itself" (122), then Felski is also building a case against critique that is quite different from the account that critics give of themselves. And it is this estrangement that empowers Felski's portrayal of critique, a portrayal that should strike critics as odd and fresh—and annoying—precisely because it isn't how we usually think about critique. Felski obliquely acknowledges this estrangement when, at the start of chapter 4, she briefly addresses the reader and distinguishes those who are still reading her book from those who have stopped reading in a "fit of exasperation" (117). Readers are exasperated because Felski is challenging the common-sense notion of critique in "unflattering" and "counterintuitive" ways, to use the terms she mobilizes against critique. Her critics are egotistical and self-aggrandizing, moralistic and myopic, snobby and cruel. They resemble washed-up superheroes and wannabe cops.

I'm intrigued by how Felski treats her Marxist and dialectical rivals specifically because it is allegedly *critique* that cannot abide competition. On Felski's telling, critique's hegemony is so complete that critics have corralled everything that is not critical into the deficient category of the *uncritical*. Either you're a critic or you're naïve, gullible, or politically complacent. Either you're with critique or you're with the terrorists. I'm only slightly exaggerating. Since Felski wants us to think about the affects of theory, it seems only fair that we appreciate her snarky hyperbole—a hyperbole that communicates how much Felski enjoys sticking it to critique. (Yes, I am also enjoying writing this.) Consider, for example, this wonderfully alliterative, even lyrical, passage: In the eyes of the critic, "every detail is pregnant with potential purpose, haloed with a heightened, even hallucinatory, intensity of meaning. ... [E]very literary detail quivers with a secret import; every phrase harbors a potential double meaning; any minor character can suddenly spring to the fore as a clinching proof of a text's hidden agenda" (99). There is an unmistakable pleasure in these sentences: the pleasure of exaggerating and mocking critique's own melodramatic pleasures.

In a perceptive review, Lee Konstantinou calls Felski's representation of critique a "cartoon." Konstantinou observes that "critique is certainly an important part of literary studies, but is far from being the sole or even exclusive disciplinary ethos of the profession. By contrast, Felski and other advocates of postcriticism often make it seem as if defenders of critique are a ruthless zombified horde."[12] As much as I sympathize with Konstantinou's unabashedly critical rebuttal, his point is one-sidedly negative. Yes, Felski exaggerates, but I don't see this as a simple diagnostic error. Felski acknowledges early on that she runs the risk of "unduly exaggerating [critique's] presence" and admits that while critique is "dominant," it's not the only thing we do (4). On the one hand, this admission is incompatible with colorful rhetoric that inflates critique's power. On the other hand, Felski needs a powerful adversary against which to measure the necessity and urgency of postcritique. This is how manifestos work. The justification for *The Communist Manifesto*, for example, is found in its opening invocation of the holy alliance against communism. Conversely, it's hard to imagine, say, *The Ford Pickup Truck Manifesto* or *The Cheeseburger Manifesto*. Being in a position of cultural dominance, these objects lack an antagonistic holy alliance and thus an occasion to become manifest.

Jameson anticipates Felski's problem but suggests that it cannot be solved neatly. This is how Jameson responds to the totalizing effect of Foucault's notions of discipline and power: "I have felt ... it was only in the light of some conception of a dominant cultural logic or hegemonic norm that genuine difference could be measured and assessed."[13] Jameson is foregrounding the dialectical logic of his representation of what was then a hegemonic method and mood, postmodernism. Like Felski's redescription of critique, Jameson's theory of postmodernism tends to produce a sense of totalizing closure. Jameson's solution is to underscore the dialectical relation between totalization and difference, the way that totalization provides a perspective from which difference can be more fully perceived. If we replace the term *postmodern* with *critique* in Jameson's representation of postmodernism, we get a dialectical

---

12   Lee Konstantinou, "The Hangman of Critique," *Los Angeles Review of Books*, July 17, 2016, https://lareviewofbooks.org/article/the-hangman-of-critique/.

13   Jameson, *Postmodernism*, 6.

grounding that would help to explain why critique necessarily sounds so domineering in *The Limits of Critique:*

> I am very far from feeling that all cultural production today is [critical] in the broad sense I will be conferring on this term. [Critique] is, however, the force field in which very different kinds of cultural impulses—what Raymond Williams has usefully termed "residual" and "emergent" forms of cultural production— must make their way. If we do not achieve some general sense of a cultural dominant then we fall back into a view of history as sheer heterogeneity, random difference, a coexistence of a host of distinct forces whose effectivity is undecidable. At any rate, this has been the political spirit in which the following analysis was devised: to project some conception of a new systematic cultural norm and its reproduction in order to reflect more adequately on the most effective forms of any radical cultural politics today.[14]

Felski cannot ground her dialectical representation of postcritique in this way without dislodging her non-dialectical theoretical framework, ANT. For the utility of Latour's thinking for postcritique is, on the one hand, its ontological flatness (what Jameson calls "sheer heterogeneity" and "a coexistence of a host of distinct forces whose effectivity is undecidable"), and on the other, its non-radical cultural politics.

The intellectual and aesthetic pleasure of Latour—at least in his American reception—lies in his Whitmanesque charm, the thrill of enumeration and the surprise of weird montages or "litanies."[15] The most satisfying moment in the application of ANT seems to be the sentence in which actors are indiscriminately listed and juxtaposed, as when Felski describes the literary assemblage as composed of "publishers, advertisers, critics, prize committees, reviews, word-of-mouth recommendations, syllabi, textbooks and anthologies, changing tastes and scholarly vocabularies, and last, but not least, the passions and predilections of ourselves and our students" (170). What impresses me about the list is the inequality that results from assembling unequal things equally. The politico-economic resources of publishers and advertisers—to which we should add powerful distributors like Amazon—are not equal to individual

---

14   Jameson, 6.

15   Ian Bogost, *Alien Phenomenology, Or, What It's Like to Be a Thing* (Minneapolis: University of Minnesota Press, 2012), 38–39.

passions and predilections. Disney isn't a mere partner in an egalitarian co-production.

While ANT is supposed to recognize the irreducible heterogeneity of beings and relations, it conveniently morphs into the opposite when applied to critique. In the essay from which Felski and other postcritics take inspiration, Latour's "Why Has Critique Run Out of Steam?", the postcritical litany degenerates into a means to abstractly equate and dismiss different critical theories. In Latour's view, the vast majority of critical practice follows the same rigid and predictable steps. The first move shows that a fetish object—here Latour lists "gods," "fashion," "poetry," "sport," "desire"—is nothing but a material entity onto which people have projected their idealized wishes.[16] In a second move, the all-knowing critic reveals that the source of the projected fantasies is not the individual after all, but "economic infrastructure, fields of discourse, social domination, race, class, and gender, maybe throwing in some neurobiology, evolutionary psychology, whatever."[17] The way Latour cobbles together explanatory frameworks that point to very different kinds of determination, from economics and race to discourse and biology, and ends the list with "whatever," suggests that *anything* could be added. This move elides the radical difference between arguing, for example, that class antagonisms and racism are tightly articulated in hegemonic rule, on the one hand, and that social and political hierarchies reflect biologically-encoded hatred of racial others, on the other. Any abstract homological relation that purports to show the basic similarity between these two explanations of power is trivial in comparison to their radically different ways of conceiving the social world. Yet Latour cannot acknowledge this difference because he needs all forms of critique to be essentially the same in order to exaggerate the scope of his postcritical alternative to them. On the one hand, Latour argues that one of the essential problems with critique is that it always posits vague abstractions (economics, discourse, society, race, class, whatever) behind fetish objects; on the other, this argument is itself a massive and self-serving abstraction from the concrete differences that distinguish theories from one another.

Latour's framework proves to be especially impoverished when thinking about the issues to which politically-conscious humanities scholarship and teaching are committed. There's something gravely missing in the notion that

---

16   Bruno Latour, "Why Has Critique Run out of Steam? From Matters of Fact to Matters of Concern," *Critical Inquiry* 30, no. 2 (2004): 238.

17   Latour, "Why Has Critique," 238.

the murder of unarmed Black people by police is best understood as a co-production of bullets and Black bodies, chokeholds and necks. When undocumented people and asylum seekers are deported from the United States, it's more than an assemblage of uniforms, handcuffs, guns, courts, laws, judges' gavels, chairs, desks, paper, suits, door locks, passports, and airplanes. There is something tone deaf about approaching the COVID-19 pandemic postcritically. It seems to me that ANT is inadequately critical in such cases because it's best suited to relationships that can be construed horizontally and non-hierarchically. Actor-network theory purportedly allows not only for diverse descriptions of networks but also has an ethical and democratic respect for all objects as agents. As critic Benjamin Noys observes, "the 'charm' of Latour" is his expansion and pluralization of agency and his focus on "small beauties" that "defy the snobbish and arrogant critic."[18] This is why ANT appears to be a useful language for legitimating literary studies and the humanities: it offers a *benign* theory of social connection that stands a better chance of placating more powerful critics than the ones we meet in *The Limits of Critique*.

The Crisis of the Humanities

Another way that Felski addresses the problem of exaggerating critique's hegemony is by distinguishing between two kinds of critique. There is everyday critique, which shares the stage with a range of practices of reading, writing, and teaching, especially in the undergraduate classroom; and there is critique as the dominant *metalanguage of legitimation*. The latter is allegedly too negative to provide a positive account of the value of literary and cultural studies to people outside the profession, whom Felski vaguely denotes as the "public" and "intellectual strangers who do not share our assumptions" (186). The crisis of the university is part of a larger, class-based project of bottom-to-top wealth redistribution that took off after the collapse of post-World War II prosperity in the 1970s. The widely acknowledged result is a return to Gilded Age-levels of inequality in the United States. To frame this situation in the Habermasean language of legitimation crisis, as Felski does, ignores the central dynamic of class conflict over social wealth and falsely implies

18   Benjamin Noys, "The Discreet Charm of Bruno Latour," in (*Mis*)*readings of Marx in Continental Philosophy*, ed. Jernej Habjan and Jessica Whyte (New York: Palgrave, 2014), 207.

that the struggle against the defunding of education and other public goods is principally a matter of democratic deliberation. As Wolfgang Streeck argues, economic policy is becoming ever more decoupled from democracy, one major consequence of which is the "plundering of the public domain through underfunding and privatization."[19] We will always need convincing arguments, but class power doesn't magically dissolve when elites hear a great pitch about why they should give more of "their" wealth away through forms of redistribution such as investment in education or health care. Taxes tells us more about the legitimation crisis of the humanities than the fact that many of our colleagues are critical sourpusses.

Thus, Felski's justification for decentering critique is at its politically weakest when she faults critique for hindering the articulation of the social value of literature and the humanities. Thanks to critique, we have a feeble "language of value" (5). But feeble to whom? The problem isn't that critique cannot explain the value of humanistic education to some vague "intellectual strangers" but rather that critique cannot explain this value in a way that convinces a particular coalition of plunderers of the public domain: neoliberal presidents, deans, administrators, managers, politicians, and their various allies. The plunderers will probably never be satisfied until we redescribe humanistic study in terms of nationalist self-congratulation, colorblind inquiry, and the one value that capitalist societies prize above all, profitability. Instead of racking our brains for ways to explain to them how we fit into their value system, we should build political counterforces that recognize the use value, not exchange value, of public goods. We should fight not for the scraps left over from austerity budgets but for universal free education in a society in which university funding is no longer beholden to profit. As Joshua Clover points out, "if there is to be something ahead, an emancipation of learning, it will not be discovered in the hearts and minds of administrators and legislators persuaded to see the error of their ways, but in a transformation of the society beyond the edges of campus."[20]

Within the university, the dialectic offers another alternative to postcritical thinking. As Jeffrey Nealon has argued, although it's commonplace to critique the corporate university, higher education has actually followed a differ-

19   Wolfgang Streeck, *How Will Capitalism End? Essays on a Failing System* (New York: Verso, 2016), 68.

20   Joshua Clover, "Who Can Save the University?" *Public Books*, June 12, 2017, https://www .publicbooks.org/who-can-save-the-university/.

ent trend: corporations have ruthlessly cut middle management, but the man-
agerial-bureaucratic class has *swelled* in universities.[21] This class spearheads a
discourse of scarcity that conceals their own disproportionate consumption of
budget resources. For example, an audit of the University of California Office
of the President concluded that the number of administrators and managers
has grown 60% since 2000. The number of tenure-track faculty grew by only
8% during the same period, despite a 38% increase in student enrollment. The
audit concluded that the Office's administrators and executives earned $2.5
million more than state employees in comparable positions, while the Office
also held an undisclosed $175 million in reserve that could have financed stu-
dent services.[22] In a brilliant demonstration of dialectical thinking, Nealon
recommends that we see the positive in the negative: faculty should use the
corporate logic that the corporate university celebrates against it and advo-
cate for freeing up budget revenue by downsizing the bloated managerial-
bureaucratic class, thereby returning management to its proper place, in the
hands of faculty and students.

Keep the Ladder

To her credit, Felski is remarkably lucid about some of the problems of *The
Limits of Critique*. In the book's final paragraph, she reiterates her desire to
avoid a critique of critique, but also acknowledges that she has indeed tried
to negate critique, thus falling into the "performative contradiction" of em-
ploying the very negativity from which she wants to free us (192). The end
of the book reminds me of the end of Wittgenstein's *Tractatus*, where he acknowledges that he has negated his own argument and encourages the reader
to see that argument as a ladder that took us from one mental location to the
next, and that can now be thrown away. Similarly, Felski ends by expressing
her desire not to reform critique but to get beyond it. Whatever she borrowed
from critique now seems to be just a tool to help us get through it. Having
reached the other side, we can now discard the ladder.

---

21   Jeffrey T. Nealon, *Post-Postmodernism: or, The Cultural Logic of Just-in-Time Capitalism*
      (Stanford: Stanford University Press, 2012), 66–84.
22   Patrick McGreevy, "State Audit Finds UC President's Office Paid Excessive Salaries to
      Top Staff and Mishandled Budget Money," *Los Angeles Times*, April 25, 2017, https://ww
      w.latimes.com/politics/la-pol-sac-uc-audit-20170425-story.html.

But Wittgenstein wanted to delineate not just the limits of critique but of language as such. The *Tractatus* ends with the mystical encounter with that which can be regarded only in silence. Felski, in contrast, has plenty more to say. But the question remains: if there is more left to say, why should it be said one-sidedly, in the register of positivity? There is still much in our world that deserves negation. If critique without positivity is blind, positivity without critical negativity is empty. To make the dialectic great again means to hold onto the tension between the equal validity of hope and critique—a contradiction that is grounded in an American present that we can only love *and* hate, equally.

2. Only a Matter of Form?
On Caroline Levine's *Forms* (2015)

Ulla Haselstein

When Caroline Levine's book *Forms: Whole, Rhythm, Hierarchy, Network* came out in 2015, it clearly hit a nerve. The preface indicates one reason why: it presents a condensed version of the author's CV, which may be regarded as typical for the generation of scholars who received their doctoral training in the 1990s.[1] Levine professes her enthusiasm for deconstruction in her undergraduate years, and remembers how she encountered Marxism in graduate school at Birkbeck College, University of London. Implicitly, she thus introduces her formalist approach as inspired by these camps of criticism.

Levine celebrates deconstruction for its aesthetic exuberance, characterizing it as a "kind of intellectual pyrotechnics" that creates "dazzling readings" built on "tracking subtle arrangements of words and images interwoven through literary texts" (ix).[2] In a later chapter she summarizes the aim of deconstructive readings as demonstrating how a text presents and performs meaning, but simultaneously questions and challenges it. For Levine as for many other critics before her, this insight has political consequences, as literary texts can make their readers aware that the stability of linguistic meaning is an illusion, and the reference to the real is mediated by ideology. Her discussion of Marxism or Marxist criticism is much less concrete, perhaps because of the scope of critical positions in this field.[3] In the preface, she describes her

---

[1]   For a more extensive discussion of Levine's intellectual biography, see Langdon Hammer, "Fantastic Forms," *PMLA* 14, no. 5 (2017): 1200–1205.

[2]   All parenthetical citations in the text refer to Caroline Levine, *Forms: Whole, Rhythm, Hierarchy, Network* (Princeton: Princeton University Press, 2015).

[3]   For comparisons of Levine's approach with Marxism see Marijeta Bozovich, "Whose Forms? Missing Russians in Caroline Levine's *Forms*," *PMLA* 132, no. 5 (2017): 1181–1186; with cultural studies see Angus Connell Brown, "Cultural Studies and Close Reading," *PMLA* 132, no. 5 (2017): 1187–1193.

growing awareness as a student of certain political processes of *longue durée* (primary accumulation and colonialism are her examples), and of the complex and even contradictory relation of art and literature to the social and political realities engendered by these processes. In the course of the book, she argues against ideology critique as the best way to account for this relation, and proposes her own formalist readings instead.

In contrast to traditional conceptualizations of literary form, Levine treats it neither as the embodiment of the idea of freedom nor as the shaping of language into a unique verbal composition nor as a symbolic resolution to social contradictions.[4] Nor does she understand literary form as the result of a history of breaking generic traditions and conventions as the Russian formalists did, even though—as I will argue below—she is strongly indebted to them. Instead, she uses a concept of form said to fit literary texts and social phenomena, material objects and concepts equally well: following design theory, forms are defined as configurations of elements whose materiality varies with their function. With this definition, forms can be found everywhere, adding up "to a complex environment composed of multiple and conflicting modes of organization" (16). The literary text is conceptualized as such an environment; everyday life, or institutions are other examples. Levine is not interested in aesthetic form per se, but in complexity, and argues that formalist close readings are better able to analyze it than the methods of other disciplines.[5]

In her contribution to Susan Wolfson's well-known collection of essays *Reading for Form*, Ellen Rooney lamented the "attenuation of the category of form," i.e., "the reduction of every text to its ideological or historical context," and the erosion of the ability of cultural and literary studies "to read every genre of text": "The cost is a loss of power for the politicized readings we eagerly seek to project beyond the boundaries of mere texts or disciplines, including cultural forms that are not in any sense literary or (narrowly) lin-

---

4   See Susan J. Wolfson, "Introduction: Reading for Form," in *Reading for Form*, ed. Susan J. Wolfson and Marshall Brown (Seattle: University of Washington Press, 2006), 3–24. The collection first appeared in 2000, with a slightly different set-up of contributions.

5   David E. Wellbery has distinguished between three different concepts of aesthetic form: the eidetic (in antiquity), the endogenous (in the nineteenth century) and the constructivist (in modernism): "Form und Idee. Skizze eines Begriffsfelds um 1800," in *Morphologie und Moderne. Goethes 'anschauliches Denken' in den Geistes- und Kulturwissenschaften seit 1800*, ed. Jonas Maatsch (Berlin: de Gruyter, 2014), 17–42.

guistic, such as race, the market, the immune system, democracy, virtuality."[6] It is this desire, this ambition that Levine addresses and seeks to satisfy. But instead of developing formal categories specific to different theoretical objects and assessing the relations between the respective form and the historical and political context, she proposes a generalized and abstract concept of form to fit the theoretical objects of different disciplines. As a consequence, she claims, the "troubling gap between the form of the literary text and its content and context dissolves" (2). Form vs. content, literary text vs. social and historical context: these notoriously problematic oppositions need no longer vex the literary critic, because the content and the context of a literary form can now be identified as other forms. The literary critic need not borrow a critical vocabulary from anthropology, sociology, or historical materialism to account for the cultural embeddedness of a literary text; what is required instead is a close reading of literary forms (or other social phenomena and material objects) in their interaction with other forms.

In the preface to *Forms*, the New Historicism is given short shrift as "laborious," but is also recognized for its ethical agency in addressing "power and injustice" (ix). Later in the book, Levine takes issue with the New Historicist notion of culture (116). Indeed, the New Historicist dictionary of critical terms, such as "culture," "representation," "exchange," "mediation," or "practice," is missing from *Forms*; Levine's approach entirely rests on one term only, namely "form." Angela Leighton has pointed out that "form" has at least three different opposites: form and matter, form and content, form and formlessness.[7] Matter is treated by Levine as dependent on the affordance and the function of the respective form. Content is defined as what is shaped and given identity by a specific form, namely that of a container; poems or prison cells have a content, the gender binary or the network do not. Formlessness would presumably be treated by Levine as non-existent in social reality; as for aesthetic formlessness, she would conceive of it as a particularly conflictive interaction between aesthetic and social forms.

In a review written a few years before Levine's book came out, Marjorie Levinson discussed the New Formalism as a scholarly movement of literary criticism which she described as divided by its view of "the conception, role,

---

6   Ellen Rooney, "Form and Contentment," in *Reading for Form*, ed. Susan J. Wolfson and Marshall Brown (Seattle: University of Washington Press, 2006), 25–48, here 34 and 35.

7   Angela Leighton, *On Form: Poetry, Aestheticism, and the Legacy of a Word* (Oxford: Oxford University Press, 2007), 2.

and importance of form in new historicism."[8] Identifying a call to reinstate close reading and a notion of textual complexity as common features, Levinson distinguished two camps: "a new formalism that makes a continuum with new historicism and a backlash new formalism."[9] She also noted that in the reviewed books and articles from both camps there was no effort to retheorize form.[10] Levine addresses this conspicuous lack by expanding the concept of form beyond the aesthetic and also elaborates on the notion of complexity. Most significantly, she positions her arguments as an alternative to the New Historicism of the 1980s and 1990s, which had put the study of the relations between text and social context at the center of critical practice.

The New Historicist conceptual apparatus which according to Stephen Greenblatt's well-known formula pivots on the "circulation of social energy" that produces and sustains the multiple *exchanges* between literary texts, social discourses and projected subjectivities, is replaced by Levine with a collaborative or competitive *interaction* of forms—be they political, social, religious, or aesthetic (see xi). The New Historicist term *exchange* refers to the interwovenness of the various subsystems of culture: as some semiotic material is selected for citation, combined with other semiotic material and cast into different forms of texts according to different codes, the use of this material in hegemonic discourses may be confirmed, interrogated, challenged, or subverted. Levine's term *interaction* refers to self-identical forms with different materialities and functions; brought together in a literary text, or in everyday life, or in politics, their interaction may either be resolved by the accommodation of one form to the other form, or amount to a clash of forms. These different outcomes may also occur simultaneously, since a literary text frequently consists of several literary forms which interact with several social forms. This is Levine's formula of complexity.

Obviously, there is a formal likeness between these conceptualizations. To assess its range and limits, I will begin by briefly considering the relations between literary text (not "form") and social context as put forward by New Historicists. I will rely on H. Aram Veeser's reader *The New Historicism* (1989), which collected some early programmatic essays together with critical comments.

---

8   Marjorie Levinson, "What Is New Formalism?" *PMLA* 122, no. 2 (2007): 558–569, here 559.

9   Levinson, "What Is New Formalism?," 559.

10   Levinson, 561.

1. Remembering the New Historicism

In his seminal essay "Towards a Poetics of Culture," Stephen Greenblatt made a similar if less anecdotal inaugural move as Levine would many years later. Citing Foucault as his most important inspiration and singling out *Discipline and Punish*, he turned against both Jameson's critique of capitalism as separating the fields of the social and political from the fields of art and literature in *The Political Unconscious*, and against Lyotard's idea of capitalism as an agent of "monological totalization" that collapses all distinctions between the fields.[11] With a nod to Derrida, Greenblatt proposed the term "circulation" to account for the dialectic between differentiation and totalization in American everyday life, in which political decisions, social institutions and aesthetic forms are inextricably intertwined. He quoted Michael Baxandall, who argued for a modification of the unhomologous categories of art and society so that they match, but also demanded to keep note of the modification deemed necessary as part of the information.[12] Greenblatt's modifications consisted in the introduction of the concepts of "currency" and "negotiation." He argued that art and literature are not mimetic of the social and hence not secondary to it; rather, they must be conceived of as part and parcel of the social in their exchange with various other sites of social production, attesting to the possibilities of change as much as to the cultural forces that prevent or hinder it.

A different argument and terminology were put forward by Louis Montrose. In his once widely quoted essay "The Poetics and Politics of Culture," he emphasized the cultural work of the aesthetic by pointing to its involvement in the "social networks, within which individual subjectivities and collective structures are mutually and continuously shaped."[13] His central term was mediation. With his chiastic formula of the "historicity of texts and the textuality of history," Montrose alerted his readers to the complex and partly contradictory social processes of mediation which construct the archive filled with heterogeneous and fragmentary "documents," where "so many cultural codes

---

11   Stephen Greenblatt, "Towards a Poetics of Culture," in *The New Historicism*, ed. H. Aram Veeser (New York: Routledge, 1989), 1–14, here 6.

12   Greenblatt, "Towards," 11–12.

13   Louis Montrose, "Professing the Renaissance: The Poetics and Politics of Culture," in *The New Historicism*, ed. H. Aram Veeser (New York: Routledge, 1989), 15–36, here 15.

converge and interact that ideological coherence and stability are scarcely possible."[14] He also drew attention to the historicity of the reader/critic as a subject inscribed in the social and political dynamics of her present when constructing the past. (Discussing American cultural politics of the late 1980s and pointing to an increasing sense of marginalization in the Humanities, Montrose's essay continues to speak to our present moment in the second decade of the twenty-first century.)

Like other cultural materialists, Vincent P. Pecora took a critical perspective on the New Historicism. He observed a methodological collapsing of the difference between the political and the aesthetic, engendered by a simplified notion of representation as the "performative function of cultural semiosis" and maintained that the distinction between social interaction and its interpretation—by the actors themselves, by observers, poets, or historians and anthropologists—remains crucial.[15] Pecora agreed with Greenblatt that contemporary everyday life is aestheticized to a historically unprecedented degree. But he argued for the necessity to retain a notion of mediation in order not to reconstruct political events and processes as determined by symbolic systems rather than by actors with interests and political agendas. Otherwise, he saw the risk that the same criticism that treats literature "as no more than a version of ubiquitous processes of cultural semiosis, must at the same time defend the literary both as a more revealing, and potentially as a more oppositional, version of cultural production."[16]

2.   Ordering, Patterning, Shaping

In Levine's reconstruction of the development of her scholarly work, Foucault's *Discipline and Punish* figures as prominently as in Greenblatt's. Foucault's argument that political power is invested in the creation, circulation, and validation of discourses is translated into the institutionalization of discursive *forms* endowed with the power of normalization. "Politics is a matter of imposing order on the world," Levine writes (x): since all social forms order

---

14   Montrose, "Professing the Renaissance," 22.

15   Vincent P. Pecora, "The Limits of Local Knowledge," in *The New Historicism*, ed. H. Aram Veeser (New York: Routledge, 1989), 243–276, here 244.

16   Pecora, "Limits," 271.

an inchoate and chaotic social reality, making it intelligible, iterable, manageable in the process, they are per se a matter of politics. The term "impose" indicates that there are *forces* at work—in the *application* and *enforcement* of forms, but arguably also in the *formation* of forms, since the resistances of the material—be it the materialities of social life, ordinary language, or the bodies and minds of unruly individuals—must be overcome. These forces are not given any theoretical consideration by Levine however (though they implicitly are of central importance for her argument, as I will show below). She focuses on the *power* of forms, i.e., on their imposition of (social and cognitive) order.

As the first step of her argument Levine offers some brief reflections on the conceptual history of the term "form" as used by different practices of knowledge. She does not attempt to distinguish between literary form and ordinary language or other social discourses—as the Russian formalists and the New Critics did[17]—but proposes a pared-down abstract definition of form instead: "an arrangement of elements—an ordering, patterning, or shaping" (3). The force necessary to arrange and shape the material into elements of a form goes unnoticed however. This is a major difference between Levine's work and Franco Moretti's, which is quoted a number of times in *Forms* and must be counted as one of its inspirations. "Deducing from the *form* of an object the *forces* that have been at work: this is the most elegant definition ever what a literary sociology should be," Moretti writes, and adds that these forces are both internal and external.[18]

With the second step of her argument, Levine reminds her readers that literary studies scholarship has long discussed literary forms (such as genre, rhyme, meter, plot etc.) and linked them to social structures, an implicit reference to Marxist or New Historicist efforts at historical and social contextualization. She is also interested in this link, but takes a different path by conceiving of various categories of social analysis, such as social structure, social hierarchies, but also the binaries of gender and race, as *social forms*. This relabeling is crucial, as she goes on to argue that social forms do not possess ontological priority over other forms, which is why literary forms should not be regarded as responses to social forms but as agents in their own right (16). New Historicists would have agreed with the latter proposition. But while they

---

17   See Cleanth Brooks and Robert Penn Warren, "Introduction," in *Understanding Poetry* (New York: Holt, Rhinehart and Winston, 1960), 1–22.

18   Franco Moretti, "Maps," in *Graphs, Maps, Trees. Abstract Models for Literary History* (New York: Verso, 2005), 35–64, here 57 (emphasis in orig.).

conceived of aesthetic forms as relatively autonomous social forms of *representation*, Levine postulates the autonomy of aesthetic and social forms, which share the same basic operational principle—ordering, patterning, shaping. Social reality is conceptualized as produced by a welter of different forms which interact and supplement and reenforce each other, but also collide with each other and vie for primacy. As a consequence, there are numerous overdeterminations, but also contradictions and fissures in the social fabric.

Following Foucault, Levine maintains that the individuals' agency to select or discard social forms is very limited, as these forms are already in place and determine the individuals' living conditions, biographies, and political choices. What individuals do is work with or around the existing forms: they learn how to check and balance one form with another form, and eventually conceive of new forms.[19] Levine's model does not address such negotiations, improvisations, performances as categories of practice however, but treats them as variations of forms. She does not systematically consider the knowledge or the interests of social actors, nor does she take the institution of the law into account, as adjudicating the validity claims of different social forms. She only envisions collaborations or collisions between forms.

Referring to a remark by Hayden White who wrote in the preface to *The Content of the Form* that "narrative form teaches people to live in unreal, but meaningful relations to the social formations in which they are indentured," Levine argues that "literary forms and social formations are equally real in their capacity to organize materials, and equally *unreal* in being artificial, contingent constraints" (14). The problem addressed by White is not an opposition between real social forms and unreal literary ones, however, but the interest of people and philosophers in the narrative form of historiography.[20] Causality, coherence, the characters and their motivation for action—for White, such features of narrative form in historiography address and reenforce "an imaginary relation" of the writers and readers of history "to their real conditions of

---

19   See Levine, "Three Unresolved Debates," *PMLA* 132, no. 5 (2017): 1239–1243, here 1242.

20   See White's programmatic statement: "Recent theories of discourse, however, dissolve the distinction between realistic and fictional discourses based on the presumption of ontological difference between their respective referents, real and imaginary, in favor of stressing their common aspect as semiological apparatuses that produce meanings by the systematic substitution of signifieds (conceptual contents) for the extradiscursive entities that serve as their referents." Hayden White, "Preface," in *The Content of the Form* (Baltimore: Johns Hopkins University Press, 1987), ix–xi, here x. This passage occurs on the same page as the sentence quoted by Levine.

existence."[21] White's term "imaginary" is indebted to Lacanian psychoanalysis, and means driven by desire.[22] Levine misses several of White's points by
reading his argument as an ideology critique that seeks "to reveal the reality suppressed by literary forms" (14). She in turn stresses the real effects of
all forms in organizing material; why the constraints of form are described
as "unreal" remains unclear. At any event, Levine wishes to do away with the
concept that literary form is secondary to social form, an epiphenomenon.
Literary form has its place in the social world, alongside with forms such as
marriage, bureaucracy, or racism (14). "I do not imagine a special role for the
aesthetic in a left political formalism," she declares in a response to a critical
comment on her work.[23] That is, she regards aesthetic form neither as more
revealing nor as more oppositional than any other form.[24]

To account for the functions a form can fulfill, Levine introduces the term
"affordance" taken from design theory, where it refers to the constraints of
its use, which in turn depend on the material of a form. A bounded whole—a
container, an enclosure, a box, a body, a prison cell, a poem—invariably or-
ganizes inclusion and exclusion, she argues, but the specific function of the
form determines the selection of the material. Prison cells are made from
stone and steel, durable materials in order to keep the inmate in and other
people out. But how does this logic work for poetry? What is the function of
sonnets? The form and material of a sonnet can be described easily enough.
Pointing to the compact form of the sonnet, Levine answers to the question
what a sonnet contains (includes?) by quoting Dante Gabriel Rossetti: "a moment's monument" (6). But what does a sonnet exclude? Alexandrines? Prose?
A plot? Scientific discourse?

To conceive of the form of a poem as a container may not be very illuminating, not least because it reintroduces and literalizes the opposition of
form vs. content. But the salient point for Levine is that once the prison cell
and the poem are recognized as "comparable patterns that operate on a common plane" (16), they can be constructed as reenforcing or disturbing each
other's organizing power (17). At first, this argument appears consequently

---

21   White, "Preface," x.

22   See White, "Narrativity in the Representation of Reality," in *The Content of the Form*, 1–25,
     here 10, 20, 24.

23   Caroline Levine, "Not Against Structure, but in Search of Better Structures: A Response
     to Winfried Fluck," *American Literary History* 31, no. 2 (2019): 255–259, here 259.

24   For a critical counterpoint, see Pecora, "Limits," as discussed above.

materialist, treating language as just another material like concrete or steel. But questions abound. Levine argues that the prison "activates other forms as well," (8) such as the temporal patterns of prison life, educational trajectories, the length of the prison term, legal issues such as a pardon, illegal networking of inmates, drug trafficking. Some of these forms "may disrupt the prison cell's containing power" (8). Levine also mentions the literary form of a story of remorse or redemption: "the arc of a narrative can pry open a cell's enclosing walls" (18). One might also construct more examples. A literary narrative about a successful flight may "disturb" a prison cell's capability of including/excluding by instigating an inmate to escape. Or a modernist poem may work against the prison cell by using line breaks, blank spaces or dashes for example. Or one might think of a poem which foregrounds its linguistic materiality and juxtaposes it to the materiality of the prison cell. But in all these cases, is this a matter of the "interaction" between the form of the poem and the form of a prison cell?

Levine observes how the poetic form fits or works against the poem's *referential content*, for instance the prison cell. What old-school formalists used to describe as the interplay of poetic form and meaning is thus translated into the interaction of forms with different functions and materialities. But in order to establish "a common plane" of a prison cell and a poem, wouldn't one have to consider legal and political discourses as a mediation? As language practices that build and fill prison cells due to their institutionalized forms of defining crimes and sentencing criminals, and are distinct from poetic language practices?

So what is the mutual imposition of forms that occurs in literary texts according to Levine? A literary form can be adapted to a social form and its affordances, effectively reenforcing the social form—or a literary form can work against a social form and its affordances in a way that the literary form with its affordances is foregrounded in its difference from the social form it incorporates. In other words: the two forms either fit each other or exist side by side, with contradictory programs of ordering and shaping. But wouldn't it be more convincing to consider *discourses* which create and maintain social forms as the *material* of literary form, which as any material *resists* form?

3.   Mutual Impositions

Levine replaces the Aristotelian notion of mimesis and the New Historicist terms of negotiation and exchange between text and context by the collaboration or collision of social and literary forms in the literary text. This central tenet of Levine's is a reformulation of arguments put forward by the Russian Formalists.[25] Shklovsky's terms were motivation and defamiliarization: the literary devices of a given text are typically selected to fit its thematic concerns; if they don't fit, the artificiality of the literary form is exposed, and the thematic concerns appear unfamiliar and are experienced in a new way. According to the Russian Formalists, this is the logic of literary evolution, and the reason for the formation of new genres over time.

Levine maintains that it is not only literary texts or art that may produce such a "strange effect" which points towards "unfamiliar opportunities *for action*" (18). I will discuss the notion of "action" below. Referring to the Brazilian legal theorist Roberto Mangabeira Unger and the French philosopher Jacques Rancière, Levine goes on to argue that such effects and opportunities occur any time in everyday life as well, where numerous forms interact with each other, creating an overlay and a dense interwovenness of forms, but also some major or minor collisions and irritations. But such irritations go largely unnoticed, which is why Levine proposes to export the formalist method of close reading to sociology in order to account for such complexity and track such strange effects in everyday life or in institutions.

Let me construct an example to elucidate Levine's analytic perspective as I understand it. Narratives of adventure typically tell stories about masculinity, heroism, risk-taking, about testing one's physical strength, endurance and will-power in the face of adversity. Such stories have been told for ages; aesthetic forms "hang around" (12) and are available for re-use—for instance in nineteenth century colonialism, where the adventure novel imposed its order on colonialism as a political form, and colonialism in turn imposed its order on the adventure story. The adventure novel had affordances that shaped colonialism *as* a narrative of adventure, *as* a test of manhood etc., and colonialism in turn carried its affordances with it into the narrative of adventure by shaping the protagonists according to the hierarchized and racialized binary of colonizer and colonized, and the plot according to a teleological sense of history or evolution.

---

25   I disagree with Bozovitch here (see above, footnote 3).

What this approach will allow the literary critic to observe according to Levine (if the sample is large enough—there are references in *Forms* to Moretti's work based on statistics) is an "experimental" treatment of the forms of colonialism by way of their interaction and occasional collision with the form of the adventure story. The outcome of such mutual impositions will be a series of variations within the genre—many of them recurrent, some of them singular and new.[26] Trying to work around Foucault's argument that any challenge to political forms is enabled by the dominant discourses of knowledge and power and hence remains within the structural parameters established by them, Levine recuperates and extends the theories of Russian formalism. She translates the latter's concept of literary evolution into a process of social evolution as signified by literary texts where the collisions of literary and social forms result in "aleatory and sometimes contradictory effects" (7). Such effects are not themselves productive of social change—for that they would have to be linked to readers/social actors—but indicative of its latent possibility.

As already mentioned, for Levine, the interactions of literary and social forms constitute only one class of manifold interactions between various forms. The specificity of the interactions of literary form and social forms appears to be that both the operational logic of all forms—ordering, patterning, shaping—and the collaboration and competition of different forms can be more readily observed in literary texts than in the dense texture of everyday life for instance, where social forms and their interactions are naturalized and normalized in routinized performances (or rather, as Levine would have it, forms). If force were part of Levine's conceptual design, one might argue that a literary text can be studied in order to observe how the force of a given social form can be supported, impeded, or blocked by the force of another (social or literary) form, and how forms are shaped in this very process. James Dorson makes a similar point: "Levine first defines forms in terms of their affordances, their latent potentialities, and only then does she set them in motion to observe how they collide with other forms. Which is to say that Levine's theory of formal interaction assumes that forms exist prior to

---

26   See Moretti, "Graphs," in *Graphs, Maps, Trees*, 3–33.

their encounters with other forms. (...) Levine's account of form is essentially taxonomic."[27]

To return to my example, Levine's basic argument is familiar from the earlier New Historicist combination of deconstruction and Marxism: literary texts both affirm and challenge the social and political forms they cite and incorporate. What is new is Levine's insistence on an analysis of the inter-action of different *forms* to account for nineteenth-century adventure novels which support colonialism and for those which call colonialism into question. Given her extensive conceptualization of social forms, some of her research questions might be: how does the binary form of gender interact with the binary of colonizer/colonized? How does military hierarchy fare, given the affordances of an adventure story, which tells of individual agency? What is the impact on the form of colonialism when the affordances of the adventure story are modified to include a psychological drama of guilt? With her con-ceptual framework, Levine may also think of the impact on colonialism if a hero is replaced by a heroine, or an English colonial officer by an Irish colonial officer, or if the colonized is given a voice.

In all these cases, the exchange of specific elements of literary form al-ters the interaction of literary and social form. But is this to be regarded as an *aleatory effect*? This appears to be a view indebted to the Russian formal-ist idea of literary evolution. In contrast, New Historicists would have linked such an exchange of elements to social contexts, for example to social move-ments. Levine's remarks on intersectionality show that she wishes to connect her approach with the politics of oppressed groups as well: as social forms of gender, race, and class collide with each other and with the countless small forms that organize everyday life, intersectionality produces opportunities for "unconventional strategies" (17), which can be detected and made public by close readings of everyday life interactions. Some of the "aleatory effects" may expose and delegitimize unjust forms of power. But Levine does not set her political hope only in the analyses of collisions of forms, in the breaking down of binaries, or the dissolution of form into formlessness, since by imposing order forms enable social life. She rather wishes to observe and analyze the complexity of social life in order to identify possible "local rearrangements."[28]

---

27   James Dorson, "Unformed Forms: Genre Theory and the Trouble with Caroline' Levine's *Forms*," in *The Genres of Genre: Forms, Formats and Cultural Formations*, ed. Cécile Heim, Boris Vejdovsky, and Benjamin Pickford (Tübingen: Narr, 2019), 23–41, here 29.

28   Levine, "Not Against Structures," 259.

Yet, the position of the reader/critic is undertheorized by Levine. Jonathan Kramnick and Anahid Nersessian have pointed to her tendency to "add a personal approval or disapproval to the recognition of a form in order to arrive at a political conclusion."[29] In her response to a number of critical essays dedicated to *Forms* which appeared in *PMLA* in 2017, Levine underlines the longevity and the power of social forms and the constraints they put on people's agency, and repeats her argument in *Forms* that the observation of the collision of a form by another form can be used strategically, presumably by creating new social forms that challenge the old ones. She implicitly relies on social actors, on their moral judgments, their political interests, their taking action—but without integrating them and their creativity into her conceptual design.[30] For this would amount to another version of ideology critique (or of cultural poetics): given the "aleatory and sometimes contradictory effects" of the interaction of forms, their accommodation and the confirmation of the social status quo appear to be the rule.

4.   An "Ecology" of Forms

Levine expresses her discomfort with ideology critique as the allegedly dominant mode of current literary criticism, and she is not alone in this. But in contrast to Rita Felski for example, who in re-articulating Susan Sontag's battle cry from the 1960s has called for a new inquiry into the affective response to literary texts, or to Amanda Anderson, for whom reading literature is an ethical practice of relating to characters and ruminating on different modes of thinking, Levine's readings are solely concerned with the interaction of forms.[31] The affective or ethical or cognitive impact of literary texts on readers are her personal, but not her analytic, concern.

---

29   Jonathan Kramnick and Anahid Nersessian, "Form and Explanation," *Critical Inquiry* 43 (2017): 650–669, here 659.

30   See Caroline Levine, "Three Unresolved Debates," *PMLA* 132, no. 5 (2017): 1239–1243, here 1242.

31   For a comparison between Felski's and Levine's approaches see Winfried Fluck, "The Limits of Critique and the Affordances of Form: Literacy Studies after the Hermeneutics of Suspicion," *American Literary History* 31, no. 2 (2019): 229–248. See also Amanda Anderson, Rita Felski, and Toril Moi, *Character: Three Inquiries in Literary Studies* (Chicago: University of Chicago Press, 2019).

A small selection of forms—whole, rhythm, hierarchy, and network—is analyzed in *Forms*, because these can be shown to "move across" different materials and to be operative both in society and in literature. Eva Geulen has pointed out that Levine does not distinguish between "whole" and "hierarchy" on the one hand, as forms that have long been regarded as repressive, and "network" on the other hand, whose form has been described as connective and democratic. Geulen reads this as a sign of the times: to conceive of the breaking up of holistic form in modernist art and literature as liberatory has become pointless in a globalized culture where the combination of heterogeneous elements is the rule in most practices of everyday life, while networks have lost their lure due to the recognition that, at least as far as labor is concerned, this type of organization raises the expected level of individual performance and erases the difference between work and leisure.[32]

That Levine consistently ignores the force operative in literary and other forms I've already pointed out. Wishing to demonstrate the new insights into the make-up of the social world to be gained from her approach, Levine works toward a reconstruction of everyday life by analyzing the interaction of a bounded spatial form (whole), a temporal form (rhythm), various hierarchical forms, and an egalitarian form of connectivity (network) in order to account for them as conjointly building up our contemporary social environment. To illustrate her point, she offers a close reading of the TV series *The Wire*, which she credits with *showing* the complexity of the interaction and overlay of multiple social forms. She takes for granted that the form of a TV series with its numerous aesthetic and commercial affordances (its cast of characters, plot structures, dialogue, management of suspense, camera shots and angles, editing, the predetermined length and sequence of episodes, etc.) reliably renders the interaction of social forms and their affordances—or perhaps compellingly, given the force of such presentations for our understanding of the social. In her effort to read like a sociologist (135) and claim social relevance for her formalist readings, she neglects the detailed description and analysis of the TV series in favor of the description and analysis of the complex and contradictory interactions of the represented social forms. She thus falls back on a mimetic understanding of the TV series.[33] Its aesthetic affor-

---

32   Eva Geulen, "Agonale Theorie: Adorno und die Rückkehr der Form," *Zeitschrift für Ideengeschichte* 13, no. 3 (2019): 5–19, here 6–7.

33   See Hammer, "Fantastic Forms," 1205; see also Fluck, "Limits of Critique," 244.

dances are not taken into account—and the affordances of the TV series as a commodity form are left out altogether.

3. Relate, Resist, Resurface
On Stefano Harney and Fred Moten's *The Undercommons* (2013)

Dustin Breitenwischer

> "I FEEL LIKE A CITIZEN IT'S TIME TO GO
> AND COME BACK A DRIFTER"
> Jean-Michel Basquiat, The Notebooks
> (no date)

This is writing against the backdrop of a manifesto, the transformative spirit of poetry and marronage. It's the pleasure—the desire that lurks underneath—of drawing matters into one's own relations. It's the excitement and anxiety of placing and displacing, of diving right in. It's reading and relating within *The Undercommons: Fugitive Planning & Black Study*, and putting placement and displacement into effect. For every sentence, every sentiment in the book has been an invitation to resist and assist, to refuse and effuse, to withstand and to understand. The following is a concession to movement, to a state of always already being on the move, to "study," as Harney and Moten refer to it.[1] Harney and Moten do not explain. They relate to study as a relation. In my "study" of *The Undercommons* (and the undercommons), a study which is neither an analysis nor an interpretation, movement is a three-fold affair, a three-headed monster that exists in a space-time of radical dislocation. Movement as *relation*, movement as *resistance*, movement as *resurfacing*—force, communication, and journey. This study is itself an invitation to understand "relation" as a form and as a genre of the art of

---

1   I will refrain from issuing and engaging in tentative definitions of what Harney and Moten "mean" when they use certain terms such as *study*, *logistics*, and, ultimately, *the undercommons*. Rather, I will relate to these concepts, play with them, think with and through them.

essayistic intervention. It seeks to relate to *The Undercommons*, it seeks to unfold the book's aesthetics of resistance, and it seeks to think its premise of Blackness in and through the cultural mobility of what I refer to as "resurfacing." Resurfacing as movement is resistance and mobility in relation; it is improbable and inappropriate. To resurface, or, as Harney puts it, "the way we read a text, we come in and out of it at certain moments"—this "sense of dispossession, and possession by the dispossessed," "the riotous production of difference" (109)—is to wonder what happens once we realize that the horizon cannot be found ahead but simultaneously above and below.[2] What if it unfolds in a state of simultaneously touching upon and moving beneath the surface? These are not esoteric or religious questions. These are theological and aesthetic questions, questions emerging from and carefully relating to what Martin Luther King, Jr. refers to as "creative suffering."[3] These are, in short, questions that center on a struggle that is in and of itself always already a relation of struggles—of struggles in the making.

For Harney and Moten, the struggle of the undercommons is the struggle of "Black study," which is not the study of a racially or ethnically defined collective, but the study in and through Blackness as a "social force."[4] It's the study of the "modality of life's

---

2   All parenthetical citations in the text refer to Stefano Harney and Fred Moten, *The Undercommons: Fugitive Planning & Black Study* (New York: Minor Compositions, 2013).

3   Martin Luther King, Jr., "I Have a Dream," in *A Testament of Hope: The Essential Writings and Speeches of Martin Luther King, Jr.*, ed. James Melvin Washington (New York: Harper, 1991), 219. King, Jr. unfolds this idea in his famous "I Have a Dream" speech. It revolves around the Bonhoefferian trope (which Bonhoeffer most strikingly develops in his letters from prison) of a Christian God who does not intervene, but who, after sacrificing his only son, retreats to suffer compassionately with mankind. And it is in and through suffering that new things emerge. King, Jr., in turn, uses the idea of creative suffering as a transhistoric characterization of Black life in the United States. See especially parts II, IV, V in Dietrich Bonhoeffer, *Prisoner for God: Letters and Papers from Prison*, ed. Eberhard Bethge, trans. Reginald H. Fuller (London: Macmillan, 1959). I want to thank my brother for inviting me to think about the relationship between Bonhoeffer and King, despite the fact that I have certainly failed to do justice to the more complex theologian argument.

4   Fred Moten, "T. S. Eliot Memorial Reading," April 25, 2019, Carpenter Center for the Visual Arts, Harvard University, video recording, www.youtube.com/watch?v=Mp-Bjl3i1Fzs. During the Q&A that followed his reading, Fred Moten states that "Blackness is best understood as a social force and not an identity"—a claim, of course, which could never be made by someone in my subject position, but I nonetheless feel that Moten's definition marks an opening, a gracious invitation, in and through which I can relate my particular reading experience with a larger scope of Harney and Moten's writ-

Relate, Resist, Resurface   51

constant escape" (51), "an instrument in the making" (94), "the site where absolute nothingness and the world of things converge" (95).[5] Blackness, for them,
is an "aesthetic sociality" (96), but even though this aesthetic sociality of Blackness may be related to what is commonly referred to as the "Black aesthetic,"
it is, as *The Undercommons* makes abundantly clear, certainly not tantamount
to it.[6] According to Harney and Moten, it is not a politicized means of cultural expression and expressive difference, but a submerged mode of relation
that quite bluntly *occurs*. It is a set of practices and, at the same time, the
scrutinizing relation to their inherent resistance and refusal. It relates in the
tradition of Frantz Fanon, Hortense Spillers, and Moten himself. It is, in a
way, difference that extends below, relates, and resurfaces from (the) within.

Blackness as a social force, as I understand Harney and Moten, expresses
itself in an aesthetic sociality and it ultimately unfolds as a dynamic of poetic relations—in a "poetics of relation," as Édouard Glissant reminds us. And
thus I desire to *relate* most emphatically my reading of Harney and Moten's
book to the vulnerable sensitivity of the social force they seek to evoke. I trust
in the relatability and proportion of communication, commensurability, and
connectivity—I trust that there is "feel" in the non-binary thicket of our ever-
growing poetic relations. And I hear Fred Moten's call for creative resistance
in the concluding interview of *The Undercommons*, that "what it is that is supposed to be repaired is irreparable. It can't be repaired. The only thing we

---

ing experience. I want to thank Laura Bieger for turning my attention to Moten's reading, and I want to thank her even more firmly for sharing an essential insight of her
own research.

5   Anything "of" the undercommons may also be referred to as being, of taking place "in"
the undercommons. Or, to put it differently, when it comes to the undercommons, any
preposition is able to make palpable the dynamics of relationality of the undercommons.

6   Accordingly, Laura Harris in *Experiments in Exile: C. L. R. James, Hélio Oiticica, and the
Aesthetic Sociality of Blackness* (New York: Fordham University Press, 2018) argues that
Blackness has its own aesthetic sociality, which is marked by "dissident forms of congregation and collaboration" (2). These forms are, of course, related and, at the same
time, decidedly resistant to Andreas Reckwitz's definition of aesthetic sociality as a
"form of governmental control when it grows beyond subculture to attain broader legitimacy and attempts systematically to control the production and reception of aesthetic events." See Andreas Reckwitz, *The Invention of Creativity: Modern Society and the
Culture of the New*, trans. Steven Black (Cambridge: Polity, 2017), 209. *The Undercommons*'s aesthetic sociality of Blackness, I argue, may best be understood as the *Un-grund*
of this excess of cultural control.

can do is tear this shit down completely and build something new" (152).[7] The process of tearing down and building anew, the transformative spirit of poetry and marronage—the spirit of study in the undercommons as a relation to "manifesto art," i.e., an exercise in the intricacy of "social theory, political acts, and poetic expression," as Martin Puchner puts it—that I have touched upon in the beginning of this study, is *difference resurfacing.*[8]

All of this has been thought of, has been composed and written in the summer of 2020, during a globally enforced lockdown, at a time of social and individual, of public and personal crisis, a time of social distancing. All of this has been written at a time when individuals and institutions, for the sake of the common good, have endured and might still endure severe government-issued restraints and prohibitions. Distancing, I have learned, brings forth curious modes of relating and associating. It is a false sentiment, almost pitiful, to think that once social life has been reduced to a so-called "bare minimum" you begin to appreciate what's truly important, what's "essential." In reality, you gradually lose the ability to distinguish between what's important and what is not, navigating your affects and intellectual curiosity through a state of collective indifference and anxiety to a point at which you can no longer trust that you are, in fact, dealing with a collective fragility or merely your own. (Who, in fact, are you to yourself in these moments and movements of distance and distancing?)

The lockdown turned out to be a space of relations in which subordinate clauses cease to exist; in which everything becomes a matter of main clauses—maintaining the materiality and purported stability of the minimum, only to overemphasize the minimum as a relation of essential importance. (What is all of this to me? How many people truly understand and care that wearing a face mask not only protects them from others but others from them?) If you were lucky—if you were geopolitically, economically, socially speaking "fortunate" enough—you could look outside the window of your living-room, your study, or your bedroom. You could listen to the birds chirping

---

7   For Harney and Moten, this is not just the task of culture and the community, but a matter of academic credibility—not least in my field of American studies. They write, "[t]he new American studies should do this [i.e. break open the memory of the conquest], too, if it is to be not just a people's history of the same country but a movement against the possibility of a country, or any other; not just property justly distributed on the border but property unknown" (41).

8   Martin Puchner, *Poetry of the Revolution: Marx, Manifestos, and the Avant-Gardes* (Princeton: Princeton University Press, 2005), 2.

in the freshly blossoming trees and realize that you haven't seen or heard a plane in a long time. In Berlin, herons began to nestle on the banks of the Spree because cruise vessels were anchoring indefinitely. In the meantime, delivery trucks would roam the streets because we would still need everything right away, job security in the service industry would decrease with menacing speed because we wouldn't (and we won't) fight for their labor agreements, and universities would hail the digital classroom in the spirit of a "creativity semester" only to put future cuts to the test. The list of "in the meantime" observations is much longer because the list is nothing less than the totality of our social makeup.

I wonder whether the catacombs of the lockdown could ever be shaken by the anxious movement in and of the undercommons. At a time of social distancing, reform movements have begun to repeat themselves in feedback loops of unfounded hope. Greek islands remain filled with the agony of disillusion. The countless ships, boats, and cutters on the horizon of the Mediterranean Sea—the vessels that transport and produce an uncharted mass of bodies—cannot possibly compete with the question of whether the professional soccer leagues can count on the profits from ticket sales. Europe currently dwindles in the afterimages of its cynicism, breathing the stifling air that is stirred up by clapping hands on balconies.

On the opposing shore of the Atlantic, in the summer of 2020, 25-year-old Ahmaud Arbery goes for a run—he is not *on* the run, but goes *for* a run—in Satilla Shores outside of Brunswick, Georgia, when a father and his son, Gregory McMichael and Travis McMichael, track him down in their truck and kill him with two shots from a shotgun. Gregory McMichael is a former Glynn County police officer. A Black man being shot and murdered in public—being *executed*—by two white men who form an armed posse to practice vigilante justice? It is appalling (and appallingly telling) how little you can oversimplify this. There is hardly more to it—because there aren't two sides to this story. There is no right side of history to emerge from. It's just one story that repeats itself in the eternal return of the same. A video documenting the killing has been circulating on the internet, but ultimately, it does not seem to be a matter of images but of the imagination (of "the ghosts of lynching"?[9] Of

---

9   See George Yancy, "Ahmaud Arbery and the Ghosts of Lynchings Past," *New York Times*, May 12, 2020, www.nytimes.com/2020/05/12/opinion/ahmaud-arbery-georgia-lynching.html.

"still living and dying in the slaveholders' republic"?[10]) that won't stop to re-peat itself. All of these killings, all the bodies and bodies and bodies, emerge from age-old narratives and myths of "lockdown" and "social distancing" in the name of race, racism, and violence. They are tantamount to the age-old expe-rience of white supremacy and the resistant study in the undercommons. In her poem "Weather," published in the *New York Times* on June 15, 2020, Claudia Rankine writes the two verses, "Social distancing? Six feet / under for under-lying conditions. Black."[11] And in the police report of the Arbery killing, also published by the *New York Times*, it says,

> I [the police officer typing the report] began speaking with Gregory McMichael who was a witness to the incident. McMichael stated there have been several Break-ins [sic] in the neighborhood and further the suspect was caught on surveillance video. McMichael stated he was in his front yard and saw the suspect from the break-ins "hauling ass" down Satilla Drive toward Buford Drive. McMichael stated he then ran inside his house and called to Travis (McMichael) and said, "Travis the guy is running down the streets let's go". McMichael stated he went to his bedroom and grabbed his .357 Magnum and Travis grabbed his shotgun because they "didn't know if the male was armed or not". McMichael stated, "the other night" they saw the same male and he stuck his hand down his pants which lead [sic] them to believe the male was armed. ... Coroner Rozier pronounced time of death to be 13:46.[12]

And then: 8 minutes and 46 seconds. After I had already handed in the final draft of this essay, a Minneapolis police officer killed George Floyd, and this essay has inadvertently (also) become a reaction to the feeling that, all of a sudden, the world feels differently yet again. The world witnessed yet another lynching. An inescapable need to relate. Study in the undercommons is a matter of relations. It is sickening to feel, to see, and to imagine further how violently Black lives and white silence are intertwined—the contingency that unfolds

---

10   See Ibram X. Kendi, "We're Still Living and Dying in the Slaveholders' Republic," *The Atlantic*, May 4, 2020, www.theatlantic.com/ideas/archive/2020/05/what-freedom-means-trump/611083.

11   Claudia Rankine, "Weather," *New York Times*, June 15, 2020, www.nytimes.com /2020/06/15/books/review/claudia-rankine-weather-poem-coronavirus.html.

12   "Public Release Incident Report for G20-11303," Glynn County Police Department, February 23, 2020, https://int.nyt.com/data/documenthelper/6915-arbery-shooting/b52 fa09cdc974b970b79/optimized/full.pdf.

in the confrontation of the existential and the comfort of a mere privilege. We (that is, in this case, those of us who, in the words of James Baldwin, "think they are white") have constructed and reconstructed and reconstructed a world in which there is a freedom to be silent which is not only greater and looms larger than the freedom of others to exist, but in which the former ultimately impedes the latter. It's the construction and reconstruction of a culture of white supremacy. In his "Anatomy of a Lynching," a contribution to the *Texte zur Kunst* "Notes from Quarantine" columns, Robert Reid-Pharr reminds us, "we exist in lynching culture .... We (Americans, Germans, blacks, whites, indeed the whole of the planet) watch and rewatch George Floyd's being killed because watching black men being killed is what we always do."[13] And so, we watch and listen. "Leave me alone," George Floyd asked repeatedly. "I can't breathe," he unambiguously declared, only to cry for help from his mother moments before he died.

You cannot oversimplify this. You can't. And despite the fact that the officer who killed George Floyd, Derek Chauvin, has been pronounced guilty by now, study in the undercommons is to be responsive. After having read Harney and Moten, I wonder whether it has always been the study of social distancing, the study of a "we" that resists silence, a "we" that is simultaneously exposed and isolated—insulated in the Du-Boisean "veil" of a persistent lockdown. On July 5, 1875, with Reconstruction in full (and arguably fully failing) swing, Frederick Douglass addressed Black Washingtonians on occasion of Independence Day festivities with one of his most explicit speeches on race relations. Amongst other issues, he reflects upon the impact and legacy of the Civil War, and he, ever so wryly, asks, "If war among the whites brought peace and liberty to the blacks, what will peace among the whites bring?" Only to note a moment later, "The signs of the times are not all in our favor."[14] There is a "we" tied up with and within the killings of Ahmaud Arbery and George Floyd, the killings of Breonna Taylor and Rayshard Brooks (and all the events like them that occur on a daily basis); a "we" that moves beyond the juxtapositions of racism, disregard, sympathy, and a general concern for the public good. There is, for that matter, a "we" at stake that transcends the idea of the public, for it unfolds at its core as the momentary

---

13   Robert Reid-Pharr, "Anatomy of a Lynching," *Texte zur Kunst*, June 19, 2020, www.textezurkunst.de/articles/anatomy-lynching.

14   Frederick Douglass, "The Color Question: An Address Delivered in Washington, D.C., On 5 July 1875," *The Frederick Douglass Papers, Series One, Volume 4, 1864-80*, ed. John W. Blassingame and John R. McKivigan (New Haven: Yale University Press, 1991), 417.

breakdown of relatability and social recognition, and, as such, it's not a matter of appropriation and false identification (and certainly not a matter of white guilt that subliminally longs for Black solace). *The Undercommons* acknowledges this breakdown as resistance. The book is an evocation, a provocation, to be more precise, of relations. The book and its authors unfold "Black study" as a relation of the promises and improbabilities, i.e., the "we," of its inherent (undercommons) relatability (the "we" that is, in this case, so much bigger than the aforementioned sum of the people who "think they are white").

One of the prosecutors in the Arbery case who eventually recused himself, George E. Barnhill, wrote in a letter (also published by the *New York Times*) about the motifs of the suspects, "It appears their intent was to stop and hold this criminal suspect until law enforcement arrived."[15] Stop and hold. Ahmaud Arbery went for a run and was violently stopped and held up. He did not run into a hold. In the logic of *The Undercommons*, he already ran *within* the "hold" (the "hold," as Harney and Moten characterize it), within the space that contains, as they argue, Blackness as its "fantasy"—the very space that emerges, as I have quoted earlier, as "the site where absolute nothingness and the world of things converge" (95). Bodies and bodies and bodies, for the hold "repeats and repeats and repeats," as Christina Sharpe puts it.[16] Being in the hold, *The Undercommons* seems to suggest, is comportment to repetition, to the perpetual movement of drawing beneath and resurfacing again and again and again.[17]

All of this has been thought of, has been composed and written at a time of lockdown and social distancing. And lockdown and social distancing are inadvertently tied to privilege. Vice President and Chief Diversity Officer at Johns Hopkins Medicine, Sherita Hill Golden, M.D., M.H.S., a specialist in endocrinology, diabetes, and metabolism, lists five factors why African Americans and people of color in the United States suffer more severely during the coronavirus epidemic: (a) living in crowded housing conditions, (b) working in essential fields, (c) inconsistent access to health care, (d) chronic health conditions, (e)

---

15   George E. Barnhill, "Letter from George E. Barnhill to Captain Tom Jump," *Office of the District Attorney Waycross Judicial Circuit*, April 2, 2020, https://int.nyt.com/data/docum enthelper/6916-george-barnhill-letter-to-glyn/b52fa09cdc974b970b79/optimized/full.p df.

16   Christina Sharpe, "What Exceeds the Hold? An Interview with Christina Sharpe," interview by Selamawit Terrefe, *Rhizomes 29* (2016).

17   See also Christina Sharpe, *In the Wake: On Blackness and Being* (Durham: Duke University Press, 2016), esp. chs. 2 and 3.

stress and immunity.[18] Can one argue that African Americans and people of color in the United States do not suffer excessively from violently established modes of distancing—segregation, isolation, and ghettoization—that exceed, no, that are intentionally excluded from the privilege of social distancing? Exposed to the dangers of dwelling, working, breathing, suffering, enduring: the aesthetic sociality of the undercommons takes shape and form in the hold of racial disparity, it grew out of social distancing and physical lockdown centuries ago, it has unfolded in the aesthetic motion (sickness) of resurfacing ever since, and it continues to echo what *is* with images and ideas of what *has been* and what *can* be. This is, in turn, the potential of the undercommons—its practice of creative placement and displacement.

When I conceptualized this essay, I re-read Harney and Moten's *The Undercommons*, and I started to understand that the two authors engage in and with a notion of aesthetic sociality that is of an utmost fragility and uncertainty; that exceeds the comfortable relativity of compassion and indignation. "The black aesthetic turns on a dialectic of luxuriant withholding—abundance and lack push technique over the edge of refusal," Harney and Moten write, "so that the trouble with beauty, which is the very animation and emanation of art, is always and everywhere troubled again and again. New technique, new beauty" (48). I tried to relate to this idea and thought that the aesthetic sociality of *The Undercommons* (as "Black study")—which I conceive of as 'resurfacing'—must be a matter of "reluctant activism," to use a term coined by Kara Walker.[19] Is it a space-time that either unfolds in the poetics of hyperbole, violence, and manifesto-like rhetoric, or in modes of withdrawal, tranquility, and distancing? I felt that there is an emphasis to this mode of reluctance, a curiously confident and self-resonating gesture: in *The Undercommons*, in its aesthetics alone, the reluctant activism of the (of its) aesthetic sociality of Blackness unfolds and excels in an equiprimordial congruence of urgent vibrancy and unassuming deceleration that is constantly challenged by violence and deprivation. It repeats and repeats and repeats as the Other to the oppressive forces of subjugation and Nietzschean exuberance.

---

18   "Coronavirus in African Americans and Other People of Color," *Johns Hopkins Medicine*, April 20, 2020, www.hopkinsmedicine.org/health/conditions-and-diseases/coronavirus/covid19-racial-disparities.

19   See Colleen Walsh, "Artist Kara Walker: Reluctant Activist," *Radcliffe Magazine* (Winter 2015): 6-7.

There are a couple of sentences in the author's preface of Harriet Jacobs's Incidents in the Life of a Slave Girl *which, to many, may have passed unnoticed, but which have been on my mind for years now. Jacobs writes, "Since I have been in the North, it has been necessary for me to work diligently for my own support. This has not left me much leisure to make up for the loss of early opportunities to improve myself."[20]* Jacobs recognizes, but at the same time rejects, the established conventions of creative expressivity and instead draws on a constant and excitingly productive state of dissatisfaction, discontent, and unrest. In these few sentences, this sentiment, Jacobs resists with impressive reluctance.[21] She relates her writing, herself and her self to the aesthetic sociality, the creative disposition, of Blackness (as Harney and Moten will frame it)—and she exposes the dehumanizing and disenchanting normativity of 'Western' humanism, that "noble study of 'Man' [which] has a quite intelligible history, one based in a set of material realities that are not distinct from the histories of slavery and colonization," as Robert Reid-Pharr reminds us.[22] Jacobs does not so much reinvent herself as a writer and self-liberated subject but resurfaces from a submerged stratum as a "veteran of creative suffering," to once more return to Martin Luther King's aesthetico-theological sentiment. And it is crucial to note here that resurfacing exceeds a moment of *return* in that it excels in a dynamic of *reform*. In this line of thought, in this moment of creative forcefulness, Jacobs has resurfaced from my reading of *The Undercommons*.

So, against the backdrop of lockdown and social distancing, Harney and Moten's book has been, above all, an invitation for me to become and remain invested in this spirit of resistance and resurfacing that seems to constitute the book's approach toward its aesthetic sociality of Blackness. It has been an invitation (and a relation) to reconsider Jacobs in the North and Jacobs in her "loophole of retreat"; to reconsider Ralph Ellison's "invisible man" in the gleaming confines of his basement, and Glenn Ligon's artistic appropriation of the prologue of Ellison's *Invisible Man*. It invited me to reconsider the burning pizza parlor and the final confrontation of Sal and Mookie in Spike Lee's

---

20   Harriet Jacobs, *Incidents in the Life of a Slave Girl* (New York: Norton, 2001), 5.

21   For a more detailed reading of this passage, see Dustin Breitenwischer, "Dis/Claiming the Creative Self: Race, Experience, and the Paratext in Harriet Jacobs's *Incidents in the Life of a Slave Girl* (1861)," in *Rückkehr des Erlebnisses in die Geisteswissenschaften? Philosophische und literaturwissenschaftliche Perspektiven*, ed. Mathis Lessau and Nora Zügel (Würzburg: Ergon, 2019), 205–216.

22   Robert F. Reid-Pharr, *Archives of Flesh: African America, Spain, and Post-Humanist Critique* (New York: NYU Press, 2016), 5.

Do the Right Thing, the intimacy between Branford Marsalis's saxophone and the surreal colors of Lee's images. Everything is too little and too much at the same time, always on the brink of being beyond all bearing and, as such, an experience that Harney and Moten refer to as the "feel." Their book has been an invitation to reconsider Jean-Michel Basquiat's 1983 painting *Death of Michael Stewart* and what art historian Liz Rideal refers to as Basquiat's "permanent grimace of death," and to imagine Basquiat's imagery and reconsider the horrific beauty, the grimy sublimity, of the following verses by avant-garde rap artist Conway the Machine who claims to have "Shot him in the hall / Blew his brains on the Basquiat."[23] It evoked the haunting imagery of Kara Walker's mural *Event Horizon* in the stairway of the New School in New York City where none other than Hannah Arendt taught—Hannah Arendt who writes in "We Refugees," "hell is no longer a religious belief or a fantasy, but something real as houses and stones and trees."[24] *The Undercommons* has been an invitation and a relation to be and become bold and ludicrous, to transcend irony, and exceed the effect of provocative improbability. Against this seemingly endless set of relations, the aesthetic sociality of Blackness in *The Undercommons* seemed to play out—and it seems to exist—beyond the status (and the immovability) of a mere antithesis to the norm. All of this is to say, Harney and Moten invited me to reconsider their book's affectionate ecstasy of evocation—the perpetual resurfacing of relations from the sensitive thicket of an aesthetic sociality expressed in a truly unique form of intellectual writing.

Resurfacing, that perpetual movement in which something or someone surfaces, disappears, and surfaces again, is both a mode of aesthetic sociality and its own process of study. Resurfacing, as I relate it to *The Undercommons*, is not a game of hide and seek, not a means of performativity, but a cultural practice that intricately relates to itself as a mode of being. As the result of creative doing, it simultaneously contextualizes and calibrates the premises and implications of creativity and artistic intervention—the construction and destabilization of

---

23   Liz Rideal, "Essence of Memento Mori," *Basquiat by Himself*, ed. Dieter Buchhart and Anna Karina Hofbauer (Munich: Hirmer, 2019), 22.

24   Hannah Arendt, "We Refugees," *The Jewish Writings*, ed. Jerome Kohn and Ron H. Feldman (New York: Schocken Books, 2007), 265. Unfortunately, Arendt herself was not able to shake off her anti-Black resentment and relate her sensitive recognition of the reality of hell to the reality of the struggle for Black liberation in the 1960s. See, with certain reservations, Kathryn T. Gines, *Hannah Arendt and the Negro Question* (Bloomington: Indiana University Press, 2014).

a physically impairing (white supremacist) social reality. The aesthetic movement, or, rather, the mobility, of resurfacing produces and emerges from the intricacy of evasion and absence—it is, in the dislocating logic of *The Undercommons*, "Black study" against the ever-shifting backdrop of its displacing invisibility, its "undercommon appositionality" (96). When I was reading and re-reading Harney and Moten, I became entangled in their dialogical thinking as a relational poetics that unfolds in socio-aesthetic interplays—a poetics that forces and allows us to complicate the relation to ourselves. Their poetics of the undercommons let us understand that there is a fugitivity and an elegance to relations which has nothing to do with a mere will to connectivity. Rather, it "feels" like a never-ending series of invitations to relate. You follow Harney's and (above all) Moten's poetic gestures, and, all of a sudden, you sense a curious intimacy.

While I contemplated intellectually and emotionally what this invitation to relate might entail, what it enables me to see, and what it refuses me to be—when the study that is *The Undercommons* emerged as a relation to a resistant aesthetic sociality—I stumbled upon Jackson Tisi's short documentary *Leon*, the story of Leon Ford who was shot by a white Pittsburgh police officer during a traffic stop and who was left permanently paralyzed from the waist down.[25] In the shadow of *The Undercommons* (sensing the chambers of the undercommons) unfolded a sociality of immobility, a culture of paralysis. Leon Ford's case had been "a case of mistaken identity," as representatives of the media put it. But is this true? Isn't his case a case of defining and further cementing an identity, of cementing identity as a category of unjust differentiation and cross-differentiation? In Tisi's documentary, we hear Ford saying, "Honestly, I got comfortable in that pain," pausing meaningfully between "comfortable" and "in that pain," then adding, "I'm at war with myself." The aesthetic sociality of *The Undercommons* is a force that relates aesthetic freedom to social and not to individual freedom.[26] In this spirit, the undercommons (and *The Undercommons*) is a resonant space—a state of perpetual and ever-accumulating responses. It's not a flexible network but a fragile community of mutually evoking and resurfacing relations.

'Black study' in The Undercommons *is a social force that impacts the practice, the poiesis, of creative resistance to its created being (its constructedness). The Undercom-*

---

25   *Leon*, directed by Jackson Tisi Leon, 2020, www.vimeo.com/415204754.

26   On the difference between social and individual freedom, see Axel Honneth, *The Idea of Socialism: Towards a Renewal*, trans. Joseph Ganahl (Cambridge: Polity, 2017).

mons unfolds in an aesthetic sociality (in the aesthetic sociality of the under-commons) that seems to be marked by the mobility of a particular "creative social power," to use a term from C. L. R. James's *American Civilization*.[27] In this sense, and in addition to what I have tried to express above, resurfacing is not merely something that occurs, that befalls some/body or some/thing. It is a mode of being, a creative practice, that emerges both of its own accord and in the exploratory action of its agent. The dynamics of resurfacing open up an extremely mobile area—the freedom of its aesthetic sociality—in and through which resistance and difference can be communicated in an oscillating manner. "Knowledge of freedom," Harney and Moten write, "is (in) the invention of escape, stealing away in the confines, in the form, of a break" (51).[28] It is, to play around with another central term from the book, in the "interest"—in the symbolic and literal in-betweenness of resurfacing that transcends and ultimately precludes the violence of subjugation and subjectivity.[29] And yet, it is decidedly not a stable position, but a state in between locating and dislocating—an apposition that is as much opposition as it is composition. To be "in the interest" is to be emphatically unclear and dangerously impure, constantly on the brink of resurfacing, of being that which has resurfaced and may not disappear again (i.e., the looming menace to white privilege and supremacy). To be "in the interest" is the refusal—not merely the disinterest, but the creative social power—to be "in the interest of" some/thing or some/body:

> And so it is we remain in the hold, in the break, as if entering again and again the broken world, to trace the visionary company and join it. This contrapuntal island, where we are marooned in search of marronage, where we linger in stateless emergency, in our lysed cell and held dislocation, our blown standpoint and lyred chapel, in (the) study of our sea-born variance, sent by its pre-history into arrivance without arrival, as a poetics of lore, of abnormal articulation (94).

Interest is that "being in-between" which enables direct confrontation and a comportment beyond oneself and beside oneself while it is marked by an

---

27   C.L.R. James, *American Civilization*, 1950 (London: Bloomsbury, 2016).

28   On the aesthetics of the "break," see Fred Moten, *In the Break: The Aesthetics of the Black Radical Tradition* (Minneapolis: University of Minnesota Press, 2003).

29   Harney and Moten refer to "interest" both in the sense of (curious) interestedness and financial interest. In the interest of my argument, I have decided to focus on the former.

extraordinary sense of vulnerability and fugitiveness. Accordingly, the beautifully mysterious "poetics of lore"—a poetics of Benjaminian character, of storytelling and translation—draw on the collaborative spirit, the in-betweenness, of deviance, of poetry as criticism of division and purity. The ever-shifting relations in *The Undercommons* (and the undercommons) do not allow for positions in the center. There is no center. No relation that steadily holds. And there is no transparency in interest. At which point I keep wondering whether I have come to touch upon the perpetually resurfacing presence (and, to be clear, *not* the essence) of the aesthetic sociality of *The Undercommons*.

Resurfacing is without teleology. It is marked by an aesthetic sociality of redirection that resists the luxury of critical control. It's Fred Moten asking, "How can I begin after all those beautiful beginnings?"[30]

---

30   Moten, "T. S. Eliot Memorial Reading."

The Late Great Age of Literature

4. The McGurl Era?
Literary History, Peak College, and *The Program Era* (2009)

Kathryn S. Roberts

Who wrote this sentence?

> All of our efforts in the world are risky extensions of ourselves, and subject to the mortified recoil of shame, but our efforts at art, like our efforts at love, seem even more so.

No, it's not a self-help book, nor the autobiography of a philandering artist who has read too much Marshall McLuhan. It comes from *The Program Era: Postwar Fiction and the Rise of Creative Writing*, Mark McGurl's celebrated literary history, now more than a decade old (335).[1] This book shaped my professional-intellectual development and sense of scholarly possibility, as an American scholar of American culture, more than any other.

Re-reading it, I was struck not by the argument (now familiar) or the lively case studies (now like favorite tracks on a rediscovered album), but by the voice. It's the voice of a great lecturer: masterful, funny, self-deprecating. *The Program Era* is dense with major and minor literary characters, historical details, systems theory, and literary-sociological coinages like "technomodernism" and "high-cultural pluralism"—which McGurl calls "scholarly barbarisms" (34). If the exemplary format of literary modernism was the poetry anthology, and that of the creative writing program the short story collection, then the not-so-secret scaffolding of McGurl's version of literary history is the survey course syllabus. *The Program Era* is both the best Postwar

---

1   All parenthetical citations in the text refer to Mark McGurl, *The Program Era: Postwar Fiction and the Rise of Creative Writing* (Cambridge, MA: Harvard University Press, 2009).

American Lit course you've ever taken and a tutorial on how to do cultural scholarship in the twenty-first century.

And yet "the McGurl Era," if such a thing existed in the tiny corner of the cultural universe called literary studies, may turn out to have been comically short. With Humanities enrollments in decline, the big Literature survey course might not long survive the era McGurl memorializes. And with tenure-track jobs for English PhDs dwindling—the number halved since the 2008 financial crisis and showing no sign of recovery twelve years later—"big" literary histories may too be a thing of the past.[2]

McGurl's penultimate chapter makes two linked claims about literature: first, that the literary world system described by Pascale Casanova in *The World Republic of Letters*—the system by which writers aspiring to the status of world literature route their careers through cosmopolitan Paris—"may just now be collapsing all around us" (because of technology, or demography, or globalization, or Mandarin). Second, that said era was "a *historical* construction in the cruel colloquial sense" (328). What McGurl wrote about literature may be even truer about literary studies. That scholarly practice is embedded in a historically and nationally specific idea of tertiary education, or as it is known in the United States, "college." This essay reads *The Program Era* in a McGurlian fashion, appreciating it as the virtuosic product of "historical" (in the cruel colloquial sense) institutional conditions that made it possible, and with which the book is itself reflexively engaged.

Systematic Excellence

The Program Era argues that the coupling of university and literature, exemplified by the explosion of creative writing programs after the 1960s, is "the most important event in postwar American literary history" (ix). The university provided salaried employment for writers (as teachers) and trained unprecedented numbers of undergraduates as expert readers, thus shaping

---

2   "Big book" is McGurl's term for his own effort and Hugh Kenner's 1971 history of modernism, *The Pound Era*, to which his title nods (368). On recent job statistics, see Jonathan Kramnick, "What We Hire in Now: English by the Grim Numbers," *The Chronicle of Higher Education*, December 9, 2018, https://www.chronicle.com/article/What-We-Hire-in-Now-English/245255.

production and reception simultaneously. The book fuses a rigorous historical materialism with convincing claims about literary form. Raymond Carver and Joyce Carol Oates, for instance, have little in common beyond their class backgrounds and their dependence on universities, but in Chapter Four ("The Hidden Injuries of Craft: Mass Higher Education and Lower-Middle-Class Modernism"), Carver's minimalism and Oates's maximalism emerge as opposite responses to their progress through higher education, and the dialectic of pride and shame that governed it.

Carver's style, McGurl writes, is a feat of affective control through obsessive revision: "If the modern world is a world of risk, ... then minimalism is an aesthetic of risk management, a way of being beautifully careful" (294). The stories are thus a double of their own characters, who exhibit "wariness and waiting and protective self-concealment" (275). By contrast, Oates's almost monstrous overproduction—long books in every genre—is a performance of virtuosity that talks about shame all the time, "but hardly ever shows it" (300). Thus the mantras of creative writing—"Write what you know" and "Show don't tell"—get translated into art by two lower-middle-class white writers. Their critical reception, meanwhile, illustrates the "unity" behind stylistic opposites. Critics accuse Oates of "slopping words across the page like a washerwoman flinging soiled water across the cobblestones," Carver of "a 'poverty of imagination'" (297). Writers and critics are locked in a barely-conscious version of "symbolic class warfare," whose rules of engagement are set by the canons, rituals, hierarchies, and opportunities of the postwar university.

Thinking through the Program, McGurl reveals deep continuities among seemingly disparate traditions: Carver's minimalism, Philip Roth's postmodern ethnic fiction, Toni Morrison's transformation of modernist style through a confrontation with Black history. The writers on *The Program Era* syllabus are diverse in terms of race, class, gender, style, and politics, but most of them are acclaimed, and that's the point: the university wins when it "offers hospitality to the excellence of individual self-expression" (408). If writers are critical of that system, then that, too, is valuable. By incorporating the artistic or bohemian or revolutionary outsider into the system itself, the university not only appears less "square," in the language of the sixties counterculture, but also performs the kind of conspicuous waste (here McGurl borrows from Thorstein Veblen) associated with high social status (407). Inside the university, writers are examples of unalienated white-collar labor, or maybe they just give art therapy to stressed-out students. For the outside world, they produce "unconscious allegories of institutional quality, aesthetically pure because luxuriously useless" (408).

We could call *The Program Era* a *conscious* allegory of institutional quality, interpretively brilliant because academically luxurious. Appealing to both our love and our snobbery, it reflexively models an aesthetic appreciation of the system that produces great books like *The Program Era*. That book ends where it begins, with love and sarcasm, earnestness and irony, the mixed feelings of an institutional being: part of the system but unable or unwilling to leave.

Fair Harvard

The Program Era is itself the product of "college," the peculiar form of higher education that developed in the United States over the course of the twentieth century. In everyday speech, Americans make no distinction between college and university: "she went to Michigan" and "he goes to Oberlin" may convey whole biographies to those in the know, but the two statements don't differ in kind.[3] To understand where McGurl's book fits in the history of American college, it is worth dwelling on college's origins and legacies.

The story begins with Harvard, founded in 1637 by the elders of the Massachusetts Bay Colony to train ministers and maintain orthodoxy. Harvard aped the great English universities—Newtowne was quickly rechristened Cambridge.[4] Despite the embrace of Enlightenment science in the eighteenth century, most colleges remained religiously oriented until the Civil War. Then knowledge production increasingly specialized into discrete fields of study, while the overall system diversified, aided by "land grants" for public universities in 1862 and 1890.

Some of this history is in *The Program Era*. McGurl explains how the Arts played a key ideological role in the university's post-Civil War secularization, helping to "smooth over" the passage to modernity by "sublimating the traditional moral-religious emphases of antebellum liberal arts training in the

---

3   Andrew Delbanco, *College, What It Was, Is, and Should Be* (Princeton: Princeton University Press, 2015), 2.

4   Roger L. Geiger, *The History of American Higher Education: Learning and Culture from the Founding to World War II* (Princeton: Princeton University Press, 2015), 1–2.

secular values-discourse of humanistic aesthetics" (39–40).[5] But because the book's focus is the vast system of higher education as a whole, inter-institutional differences tend to fade. For example, McGurl doesn't explain the outsized place of Harvard and other "Ivy League" schools in the cultural imaginary. They set the pattern for American college at large, from curriculum, to admissions and financial aid, to the pageantry of graduation, athletics, and reunions; and they are over-represented in the halls of government, business, and media.[6]

Harvard, where Mark McGurl was an undergraduate and where I was once a PhD student and temporary lecturer, has a weirdly specific institutional vocabulary. "The College" is the geographic, historical, and affective heart of the university. First-year undergraduates live in "the Yard," the oldest part of the school. Commencement ceremonies—a ritual performance of membership in the Harvard alumni community—happen there too. Harvard's endowment is more than 40 billion dollars, and yet its appetite for alumni donations remains voracious. This is how private universities, and increasingly, public ones, fund themselves: rich alumni who cherish the memories of their college days. That's why the Ivy League invented American football: to keep alumni vicariously engaged through feats of undergraduate strength, agility, and controlled violence. Today, football games at Penn State or Michigan or Alabama attract hundreds of thousands of fans; in American speech, state and "flagship" university are often synonymous. Colleges offer a compressed version of shared local or regional history in which even non-alumni can participate.

The Ivy League is the font of both modern liberal arts education and a studied irreverence that shapes mass culture. From Harvard came the film *Animal House* (1978), in which misfit fraternity brothers get revenge on the cool frat and the authoritarian dean. *Animal House* was the first film by *National Lampoon*, the comedy magazine started by alumni from Harvard's *Lampoon* (founded 1876). When George Pierce Baker, founder of university creative writing, started giving graduate classes in playmaking in 1905, he was only incorporating into the official curriculum what Harvard students had been do-

---

5   Here McGurl is summarizing the argument of Jon H. Roberts and James Turner in *The Sacred and Secular University* (Princeton: Princeton University Press, 2000).

6   Delbanco, *College*, 6.

ing for decades.[7] In *Animal House*, even the most delinquent frat-boy becomes a senator.

Harvard can stand in for one side of the story of American college; the other is best represented by the University of California system, in which McGurl taught while writing *The Program Era*. The architect of that system was chancellor Clark Kerr, who from 1958 to 1967 oversaw the expansion of the UC into a three-tiered structure of research universities, more numerous "state" universities, and transfer-oriented community colleges. This "multiversity," subsequently imitated by many states, was designed to reach diverse constituencies from its strategically located educational nodes.[8] Kerr was a professor of industrial relations, and his vision was to make universities serve the needs of the postwar economy.

Kerr's project depended on massive investment from federal and state governments. Mid-century social welfare programs—the Serviceman's Readjustment Act ("G.I. Bill") of 1944 and the Education Act of 1965—made it possible for unprecedented numbers of young Americans to pay for more school. The number of bachelor's degrees soared, from 186,500 in 1940 to over a million in 1989-1990.[9] The education boom gave poorer Americans access to college, and the economic boom meant there were jobs for them—some jobs in those expanding universities. The cultural impact of twenty-five years of mass higher education was vast, creating new scripts for middle-class lives, with "college" part of the story. When the withdrawal of government funds made college ever more expensive after the 1970s, those expectations made people more willing to take on debt.

After 1945, college, formerly the playground of the ruling class, became so central to the making and reading of American literature that it was oddly invisible. *The Program Era* finally placed that institution in the foreground, showing how the protocols of the creative writing workshop set the rules for good fiction. Writing programs fed the longing for creativity, self-expression, and craft in an economy dominated by corporate employment and fantasies of individual fulfillment. American writers did well in this system: never before

---

7   For example, the Hasty Pudding Social Club, which tours nationally every year, started writing their own theatricals in 1882.

8   Clark Kerr, *The Uses of the University* (Cambridge, MA: Harvard University Press, 1972), 136, quoted in McGurl, *Program Era*, 41.

9   Thomas D. Snyder, ed., "120 Years of American Education: A Statistical Portrait," *National Center for Education Statistics* (January 1993), 83.

had they achieved such popular success and cultural consequence. College in *The Program Era* is a hegemonic institution whose normal functioning goes largely unquestioned. Reading it now, this picture is full of pathos.

Peak College

The term "Peak Oil" refers to the moment of maximum global oil production, after which production will permanently—because oil is a finite resource—decline.[10] The date of this peak may be uncertain, but governments are sure that its "economic, social, and political costs will be unprecedented."[11] The oil shocks of the 1970s that contributed to the current reign of permanent war and neoliberal austerity will look quaint by comparison. Unlike oil, higher education is, at least in theory, a renewable social resource, but the term "peak college" captures certain affective parallels between oil and American Higher Ed in our time: the sense that their heyday has passed, that their future is ominous, and that what was once considered liquid gold might in fact be destructive.

There is evidence for the decline of college-assisted human capital extraction in the United States. Overall, college attainment rates have held pretty steady since the 1970s. According to 2018 data from the Organization for Economic Co-operation and Development (OECD), 49.4 percent of American 25- to 34-year-olds have BAs, a modest increase from the 42.6 percent of their parents' generation (born between 1954 and 1963).[12] The real change has been elsewhere. American Baby Boomers lead their international peers: only Canada, Japan, and Finland had higher rates of tertiary education. By the time Millennials got to college, the United States had lost much of its competitive advantage, trailing the United Kingdom, Ireland, even Lithuania.

Beyond the bad numbers, the American romance of college is ending. As the first generation with outstanding student loans retires, or dies, no serious politician can deny the emergency around student debt in the United

---

10   R. L. Hirsch, Roger Bezdek, and Robert Wendling, "Peaking of World Oil Production: Impacts, Mitigation, & Risk Management," Science Applications International Corporation, US Department of Energy, National Energy Technology Laboratory, February 2005, 11.

11   Hirsch, Bezdek and Wendling, "Peaking," 4.

12   OECD, Population with tertiary education (indicator), 2020, https://data.oecd.org/edu att/population-with-tertiary-education.htm.

States. In the wake of the 2016 presidential election, the liberal commentariat pondered the sorting of "college-educated" and "non-college-educated" voters into the Democratic and Republican parties. In the 2020 Democratic Party presidential primary, college remained a political issue, from charges that some candidates were unable to win a constituency beyond white, college-educated voters, to Bernie Sanders's promises of "Free College" and student debt relief.

This decline of faith in college has generated a string of laments and prescriptions about universities from within English Departments. Andrew Delbanco gives the Ivy League version of the lament in *College: What it Was, Is, and Should Be* (2015). Delbanco, a Herman Melville scholar, studied at Harvard and has been teaching at Columbia since 1985. His book calls for the renewal of "democratic education": "At its core, a college should be a place where young people find help for navigating the territory between adolescence and adulthood. It should provide guidance, but not coercion, for students trying to cross that treacherous terrain on their way toward self-knowledge. It should help them develop certain qualities of mind and heart requisite for reflective citizenship."[13] These are noble ideas, but Delbanco is describing not democracy, but meritocracy: the rule of the smart and the putatively just.

Christopher Newfield, who teaches at UC Santa Barbara, offers a more expansive account of the crisis in his trilogy on the corporatization of higher education. Newfield calls on government and his fellow citizens to understand universities once again as a public good, and to fund them accordingly. His colleague Joshua Clover, a poet and critical theorist over at UC Davis, points out that the crisis is not solely one of values, but of political economy. With the exception of a mini-boom in the late 1990s (when McGurl was finishing graduate school), the best year of economic growth after 1973 has been worse than the worst year of growth in the postwar period.[14] The response from both Republican and Democratic administrations has been austerity, with devastating effects on the UC system. Despite California being richer than many countries, the state has cut investment in higher education more than fifty

---

13   Delbanco, *College*, 7; 3.

14   Robert Brenner cited in Joshua Clover, "Who Can Save the University?," *Public Books* (blog), June 12, 2017, https://www.publicbooks.org/who-can-save-the-university/.

percent since the 1980s, resulting in massive tuition hikes and plummeting completion rates.[15]

Universities, according to Clover, followed the same formula as other organizations in this period, reducing labor costs through automation and other "efficiencies," including paying workers less for the same work, and "accelerating throughput, the velocity with which goods fly through the production process."[16] This has meant making classes bigger, putting more courses online, expanding the duties of teachers, hiring adjuncts, attacking unions, and "simplifying" degree requirements. The problem is that it doesn't really work. Student "throughput" suffers in an austerity regime. The bigger and more impersonal the class, the less likely students are to pass it. And cutting classes means that students can't accumulate the prerequisites they need to complete their degree. Even if they manage to get a degree, students today leave public universities and community colleges with inadequate skills and mountains of debt.

Delbanco's book is from 2015, and Newfield's latest is from 2016. When the *Program Era* appeared in 2009, the full ravages of the financial crisis had not yet made their way through universities. But in English Departments, undergraduate enrollment numbers had been falling for a long time, and the discipline was in an identity crisis.[17] In the same year *The Program Era* was published, the fall cover story of *The American Scholar* was a jeremiad by former university president and modernism scholar William M. Chace. Though he acknowledged the economic and demographic causes of falling enrollments, Chace blamed his colleagues for failing "to champion, with passion, the books they teach and to make a strong case to undergraduates that the knowledge of those books and the tradition in which they exist is a human good in and of itself."[18]

---

15   Christopher Newfield, *The Great Mistake: How We Wrecked Public Universities and How We Can Fix Them* (Baltimore: Johns Hopkins University Press, 2016), 12–13.

16   Clover, "Who Can Save the University?"

17   Bachelor's degree completions in English dropped 20.4% from 2012 and 2016. In terms of "market share," English has been in decline since 1993. See "A Changing Major: The Report of the 2016–17 ADE Ad Hoc Committee on the English Major," *Association of Departments of English* (July 2018), 49.

18   William M. Chace, "The Decline of the English Department," *The American Scholar*, September 1, 2009, https://theamericanscholar.org/the-decline-of-the-english-depart ment/.

A few years earlier, the French sociologist Bruno Latour asked, in *Critical Inquiry*, "Why Has Critique Run out of Steam?" It seemed to Latour that the English Department had been *too* successful: arcane knowledge once confined to the academy—deconstruction, discourse analysis, ideology critique—had diffused into both common speech and state agencies. In this era of "instant revisionism," Jean Baudrillard could write that the Twin Towers collapsed of their own weight, and both Fox News and the Internet rabble would agree.[19] As an alternative to the iconoclasm of critique, Latour called for "a multifarious inquiry launched with the tools of anthropology, philosophy, metaphysics, history, sociology to detect how many participants are gathered in a thing to make it exist and to maintain its existence."[20] Chace and Latour are very different scholars, but their visions are complementary: one is nostalgic for the days before "theory," the other welcomes a post-theory future. Chace even verges into scientism, imagining teachers and students in a revived discipline, "partly aesthetic and partly detective-like ... like young scientists teaming together with older scientists at the same workbench."[21]

In other words, the future must be both interdisciplinary and collective in spirit. It can be theoretically sophisticated, but it should have a care for the stuff people love. This is a pretty good description of *The Program Era*. One might expect an account of postwar fiction set in the American university to shatter our illusions of creative autonomy and individual excellence. But McGurl interrogated these values only in the interest of "restoring some balance in favor of the claims of the collective life we live through institutions" (21). *The Program Era* was a light at the end of the English Department's gloomy tunnel. By illuminating the university's role in building up a newly diverse canon beloved by student readers, it restored our appreciation of the university as laudable humanistic enterprise and added new fuel to the tank of literary historical method.

Or that's what I believed when I read it in the second year of my PhD. *The Program Era* appealed to me, a trainee in professional literary studies, because it married two powerful and sometimes conflicting traditions in the field: the careful analysis of how canonical literary works hang together formally (call

---

19   Bruno Latour, "Why Has Critique Run out of Steam? From Matters of Fact to Matters of Concern," *Critical Inquiry* 30, no. 2 (2004): 228.

20   Latour, "Critique," 246.

21   Chace, "The Decline."

it "close reading") and historical materialism, the analysis of how transformations in the mode of production drive cultural change. This marriage is accomplished through what McGurl terms "an unfamiliar, because non-individualistic, mode of aesthetic appreciation," the object of which is not a single novel, but rather "the system as a whole" (xi). The idea that unromantic bureaucracies like the postwar university could be beautiful, and worthy of loving examination, was comforting in a time of cascading institutional crises.

McGurl's method isn't exactly new. He credits his understanding of the "totality" to Fredric Jameson, the Marxist literary scholar and author of *The Political Unconscious* (1981)—undergraduate Mark wrote his BA thesis on Jameson and J.M. Coetzee back in 1989. At Johns Hopkins, McGurl studied with Walter Benn Michaels, a founder of the New Historicism. Michaels's other graduate students, in those same years, were writing about how the welfare state, the Democratic Party, and the free market shaped American literature.[22] By the 2000s, this combination of politico-economic rigor and interpretive virtuosity was the dominant mode in the field. But in *The Program Era*, self-reflexivity reached new heights: McGurl was writing about the institution where most of his readers sat. Rather than an Ivory Tower, the university was a white-collar workplace. Fiction writers and scholars, while *excellent*, were still ordinary Americans, human beings more like us than unlike us.

McGurl told a story about the university as an integrative engine of aesthetic excellence. That is, the postwar university epitomized a relatively organic relationship between economy and culture: "insofar as American culture is a corporate culture, the rhetoric of excellence could be understood as a deep expression of that national culture" (407). In 2009, the book could still end on a note of "strategic triumphalism" (409), claiming that the ideology of excellence "seems for now to be holding educational institutions together fairly well" (407). But the conditions that made *The Program Era* possible—that is, the tail end of the Program Era itself—are increasingly rare in American universities. When I was a graduate student, the university police smashed the tent city in Harvard Yard, bringing the local Occupy movement to a violent end. A few years later, the graduate students unionized, and in 2019 they held

---

22 Michael Szalay, *New Deal Modernism: American Literature and the Invention of the Welfare State* (Durham: Duke University Press, 2000) and *Hip Figures: A Literary History of the Democratic Party* (Stanford: Stanford University Press, 2012); Michael Clune, *American Literature and the Free Market* (Cambridge: Cambridge University Press, 2010).

their first strike. A week before I wrote this sentence, UC Santa Cruz fired 54 graduate student strikers.[23] If *The Program Era* were written today, it would inevitably sound different.[24]

Like the late modernist novels it elucidates, *The Program Era* is mimetic as well as descriptive. The book is, in its own vocabulary, an example of *autopoiesis*: the system telling its own story in terms that help sustain it. It thus partakes of the limitations it describes. What were the canons, rituals, hierarchies, and opportunities of the system in which *The Program Era* was nurtured? The culture of academic training was highly competitive and stratified. PhDs from the top programs filled the top two tiers of jobs, resulting in a kind of trickle-down excellence: public university professors had expectations for themselves and their students that were sometimes at cross-purposes to the priorities of state governments. In the "up or out" tenure-track model, assistant professors had to produce at least one monograph with a top university press, or they were consigned to the academic scrapheap. Meanwhile, more and more of the teaching was done by adjuncts, majority female, paid sub-minimum wages.

This all seems obvious now, and it produces a certain dissonance in the reading experience. "Museless pedants," McGurl calls literary scholars as a class, including himself and the reader (27), but the self-deprecation no longer welcomes a young scholar into that class; it only pronounces a class divide. He writes brilliantly about shame and art—about how our worldly efforts at art and love are subject to "the mortified recoil of shame" (335); about shame as the ultimate social emotion, a form of negative feedback from the system, self-reflexivity gone toxic (285)—but what about shame and precarity?

The Platform Era

If *The Program Era* reads differently now, it nonetheless gives us some powerful conceptual tools for understanding the cultural system after Peak College.

---

23   Vivian Ho, "UC Santa Cruz Fires 54 Graduate Students Participating in Months-Long Strike," *The Guardian*, February 29, 2020, https://www.theguardian.com/us-news/2020/feb/28/university-of-california-student-strike-fired.

24   For a less sanguine analysis of literary institutionality, see Mark McGurl, "The Institution of Nothing: David Foster Wallace in the Program," *Boundary 2* 41, no. 3 (2014): 27–54.

Consider the private monopolies of hyper-mediated sociability that flourish in the wake of governmental dis-investment from public goods like the university system. Many of those monopolies' "platforms," through which users' data and attention are sold to advertisers, were created in the dorm rooms of Peak College. It is part of the mythology of our time. In addition to the famous Mark Zuckerberg example, Reddit was made by roommates at the University of Virginia in 2005, and Snapchat was the brainchild of Stanford students. But the baby billionaires of Silicon Valley—many of whom never deigned to graduate—are mere symptoms of a systematic interconnectedness of college and cultural marketplace today.

Web 2.0—associated with slick new interfaces for social media and online commerce—has democratized cultural production on a scale that dwarfs the ambitions of mid-century mass higher education. Not to be outdone, universities become content producers, selling Massive Open Online Courses ("MOOCs") to online masses craving knowledge or sophisticated entertainment. To be sure, universities have always done mass culture. In 1909, Harvard's President Charles William Eliot said that anybody could obtain a liberal education by reading for 15-minutes a day from works that would fit on a five-foot shelf. The publisher Collier and Son saw a business opportunity, and *Harvard Classics*, or "Dr. Eliot's Five Foot Shelf," was born. The Book-of-the-Month Club also has an Ivy-league pedigree.[25] Critics and scholars have called these ivory tower incursions into mass-culture "the middlebrow," and MOOCs, among other things, belong in this tradition.

The Program Era's charming, general-public-facing narrator might also belong in this tradition. Harvard University Press is an aggressive seeker of scholarly manuscripts with potential mass-market appeal, and Harvard's faculty often writes for the reading class. Elite universities' orientation toward the public sphere is best described as "uplifting," uplift being the gently entertaining cultural complement to technocratic social control. It is not surprising that the 2020 Democratic Party presidential primary included a Harvard College graduate who reads Norwegian and a Harvard Law School professor with "a plan" and a selfie line, both of whom present themselves as Heartland authentics who can fix a broken Washington.

Middlebrow politics is partly a response to mass politics. McGurl would have us think dialectically about this opposition: "independent" media turn

---

25   Joan Shelley Rubin, *The Making of Middlebrow Culture* (Chapel Hill: University of North Carolina Press, 1992), 98 and passim.

out to be no less dependent on the protocols of the university than are the efforts of middlebrow professors. Harvard shaped both Mayor Pete Buttigieg and *Current Affairs*, the independent left magazine that dismissed Buttigieg as a pseudo-progressive, McKinsey-generated SIMs character, "optimizing [the] candidate attribute matrix for maximal cross-national vote share."[26] Countless podcasts, including that of *Current Affairs*, take the form of a "hangout," not only because that format can be made cheaply and fast by aspiring podrepreneurs, but also because it resembles beer-soaked conversations you're supposed to have had late at night in your college dorm room. The Program Era produced *Animal House*; Peak College has *Chapo Trap House*, in which five millennial socialists drink, vape, and talk shit about liberals from Brooklyn. This informal parasociality around politics appeals to a generation that is debt-burdened, underemployed, depressed, and longing for community.

The Program Era helps us trace the way "college" continues to shape the cultural system today, from platforms to podcasts. But the social form it centers—the creative writing workshop—might be less important now than the ones it doesn't mention: the picket line where graduate students stand with cafeteria workers, the union, the late-night dorm room confab. What once seemed a prescient elegy-in-advance for the system that made me what I am, now seems ideologically dated and limited in scope. I say this not with triumph, but with melancholy.

To put it bluntly, no pedant in my generation can afford to be museless. My fellow Americanists of the Harvard English Department, who wrote McGurl-inspired dissertations—well-wrought literary histories of glossy magazines or writers' colonies or the National Endowment for the Arts—now work in other fields: journalism, university administration, consulting. Of those who stayed in academia, not one is on the tenure track, and while teaching academic writing or hopping between Visiting Assistant Professorships, they write reviews for magazines, or start podcasts, or compose viral tweets and Instagram performance art. As American universities become ever more indistinguishable from globalization's mediascapes and exploitive labor practices, studying them as an autonomous space of literary production seems quaint, if not quietist.

---

26   Nathan J. Robinson, "All About Pete," *Current Affairs*, March 29, 2019, https://www.curr entaffairs.org/2019/03/all-about-pete.

Solidarity for Miles

Institutions of higher education may have a different function and a different potential now. The resurgence of labor organizing among public school teachers and graduate students suggests that schools are not only sites of mass education and literary conditioning, but also, as Raymond Williams wrote of the city and factory, sites of political "massing."[27] After generations of organizing efforts, my cohort of graduate students managed to unionize a string of private universities. Some of them see universities not as systems through which subjects negotiate their individual performances of excellence, but rather as a workplace where teachers, nurses, custodians, and food service workers are under the same roof, and might be brought to a level of proletarian consciousness once associated with steel mills and auto plants.[28]

There are no picket lines in *The Program Era*, and the subject of groups brings out some of its most clinical language. Philip Roth's self-reflexive autofiction is revealed to be "a trans-individual enterprise" (54). "Collective struggle," though named at the end of the introduction, appears only in the weak sense of the simultaneous, mass adaptation of individual organisms to the system. From Olympian heights, the literary systems theorist watches the ants' progress, which can be "experienced as beautiful" (74). Aesthetic appreciation of the system as a whole tends to render the system static. The forms of solidarity that could potentially disrupt the system—mutual recognition of class interests, commitment to comrades, defining an "us" that can fight against a "them"—are absent.

Whether consciously or unconsciously, *The Program Era* anticipates this criticism. McGurl knows there are limitations to his focus on individual and system, to the exclusion of the stuff in between. The book ends by contemplating problems of scale in cultural scholarship through a reading of the novel *Mr. Spaceman* (2000) by Florida State University's chair of creative writing Robert Olen Butler. An alien named Desi transports a bus-full of diverse individuals to the dock of his spaceship, brings them into a trance, and has them narrate the deep, meaningful stuff of their lives: the "traumatic events that made them *who they are*" (386–387). The spaceship's quasi-therapeutic workshop is a mirror of the creative writing classroom in the pluralist American university,

---

27   Raymond Williams, *Culture and Society, 1780-1950* (Edinburgh: Penguin, 1961), 287.
28   See for example Gabe Winant, "Who Works for the Workers?," *n+1*, August 3, 2016, https://nplusonemag.com/issue-26/essays/who-works-for-the-workers/.

"with its familiar protocols of diversity and the proportional representation of identities" (388). Institutional allegory at its most obvious.

Less obvious, and most interesting to me, is the hovering sense that McGurl wonders if *he* is Desi/Butler: "Butler's Desi is a dream dreamed by a man of the system, and indeed could be said to personify himself *as* that system" (393). Does the author of *The Program Era*, who dives into the semi-conscious longings of a full syllabus of writers, fear himself to be a hairless grey-green alien with big eyes and brain and a disappearing body (393)? The problem with Desi is that his universalism is provincial. He may be "a personification of the global information economy," but for all his cosmic distance, "Desi sees only America" (395). To escape this provincialism, McGurl turns to Octavia Butler, whose popular space fiction defies the parochial pluralism of the program and reaches a "*transplanetary* perspective": an anti-nostalgic, posthuman vision of species survival that requires openness to true otherness; that is, hybrid breeding with alien slugs (397).

Having zoomed out past the solar system, and past the "high" literary to genre fiction, McGurl ends on a note of humility.

> It might finally be even simpler than that. To perform in the world is to say "I am," and to say "I am" is the most essential motive of every human perfor-mance, no matter how mundane. As an exercise of the imagination, creative writing supplies a special effect of personal agency in that performance, a way of saying not only "I am" but "I am whoever I want to be," which unfortu-nately I am not. (398)

Who would the narrator of *The Program Era* be, if he could be anybody? A queer, dyslexic black woman, who self-identified as a hermit, had a brilliant career as a science-fiction writer, and died of a stroke at 58? Perhaps not, but his more recent work on posthumanism, digital humanities, and Amazon indi-cates a persistent preoccupation with questions of scale. The subject of *The Program Era* is both all of modernity and a small corner of postwar literary history, from the perspective of a museless pedant in the English Depart-ment. The book knows this about itself, so my effort to tether it back to its own temporally- and spatially-limited conditions of possibility has been less critique than tribute, a lesson well-learned about the collective life we live together through institutions: that life will change.

5. Reading and Writing (at) the Site of the Social
Or, David Alworth's *Site Reading* (2015) as a
Pandemic-Proof Model of Cultural Critique

Laura Bieger

David Alworth's *Site Reading: Fiction, Art, Social Form* opens with an epigraph
from Henri Lefebvre's *The Production of Space*, one of the most influential books
of cultural criticism of the past century. Positing that space, in being produced
from an intricate and ever-shifting web of social relations, is not static but
dynamic, not a stage on which history plays out but an active participant in
shaping its course, Lefebvre's book helped an entire generation of scholars to
formulate concerns about space and place, turning the concept of space into
a trailblazing notion for such diverse paradigms as cultural geography, environmental criticism, literary ecology, and media archeology. Impulses from
these fields have profoundly shaped the practice of cultural criticism in the
past decades. With its seemingly modest aim of challenging the view of the
literary concept of setting as "a static backdrop for narrative action," *Site Reading* actualizes this tradition for the twenty-first century in substantial and far-
reaching ways (2).[1] Before I say more about how it does so, I want to quote
Alworth quoting Lefebvre in his book's epigraph to set the stage for what is
indeed one of the more ambitious projects in literary criticism of recent years:

> There is a question implicit in the foregoing analyses and interpretations.
> It is this: what is the mode of existence of social relations? No sooner had
> the social sciences established themselves than they gave up any interest in
> the description of "substances" inherited from philosophy: "subject" and "ob-
> ject," society "in itself," or the individual or group considered in isolation. In-
> stead, like the other sciences, they took *relationships* as their object of study.

---

1 All parenthetical citations in the text refer to David Alworth, *Site Reading: Fiction, Art,
   Social Form* (Princeton: Princeton University Press, 2016).

The question is, though, where does a relationship reside when it is not being actualized in a highly determined situation?

Making use of literary fiction to read such "highly determined situations" as sites at and through which we can see the social take shape is the project of Alworth's book. *Site* is Alworth's spatial term of choice, for it "implies both human activity and sociality" (19). Linking the term to Lefebvre's investment in the concrete and material relations that converge at specific sites (and thus constitute them), Alworth argues that "sites figure in novels as determinants of sociality—as dynamic networks of *actants* in Bruno Latour's sense, exercising a kind of agency with and through their human and non-human constituents" (2).

For Alworth, drawing on Latour, sites are *actants* (or actors, two terms that Latour uses interchangeably) in two different ways: they are "determinants of sociality that invite sustained attention from novelists," and they are "material environments that give rise to constellations of cultural artifacts" (20). In this dual capacity, "sites mediate sociality," and one of the points that Alworth drives home over the course of reading his "test sites" (11)—supermarkets, dumps, roads, ruins, asylums, bunkers—is that literary fiction theorizes social experience "by transposing real sites into narrative settings and thereby rendering them operative, as figures in and of collective life" (2). If Latour helps us to see that such mediations are active participants in collective life, Alworth zeroes in on the formative role that literature plays in giving them agency. The focus of this book is clearly on literature, but one of its great virtues is that it approaches these mediations as intermedial phenomena. Each test site links literary and visual art: the supermarket put on display by Andy Warhol at a New York gallery in the early 1960s to the supermarkets imagined by Allen Ginsberg and Don DeLillo; the dumps that give form to William Burroughs's *Naked Lunch* to the dumps that inspired performance artist Mierle Laderman Ukeles; the cars featured in Jack Kerouac's *On the Road* and Joan Didion's *Play As It Lays* to the cars turned into sculptures by concept artist John Chamberlain; the ruins explored in Thomas Pynchon's *V.* to the ruins engaged by earth artist Robert Smithson; the asylums written about by Ralph Ellison and Erving Goffman to photographic approximations by Gordon Parks and Jeff Wall of Ellison's "invisible man's" famous hibernation space (read by Alworth as an asylum); the bunker that gives shelter to the father and son in Cormac McCarthy's *The Road* to the family shelters depicted by photo artist Richard Ross. This is not the place to rehearse Alworth's nuanced transmedial and transdisciplinary readings of these sites. Suffice it to say that the critical advantage of dealing with constellations of cultural artifacts rather than individual (or even clusters of) literary works is twofold: it indicates how the material environment of the site can serve as a synchronic and diachronic mediator in a full-fledged cultural history of social form (which *Site Reading* does not attempt to write), and it helps us, via its transmedial perspective, to gain a firmer grasp on literature's special capacities to mediate the social and theorize the experiences associated with it.

This project demands the new methodology—*site reading*—which the book develops by conducting "an experiment in literary criticism whose hypothesis is that writing a novel is a way of knowing about collective life" (21). This experiment has two closely related goals: it aims to trace *what* novels know about collective life as a way of showing *how* they know about it. And this means that the book engages in a genuinely reflexive form of knowledge production, one that is firmly committed to second-order observation of all human and nonhuman actors gathered at and through a specific site. The form of this experiment—its critical *style*—bears striking resemblances with novelistic writing, most notably through its firm commitment to careful (implying truthful) observation of all social actors assembled in a given setting, which brings to mind the "show, don't tell" formula of a Henry Jamesian kind of realist fiction.[2] Rather than being a mere pleasantry, this style is indeed a driving force behind the critical agenda of Alworth's book. Consider, for instance, the narrative drive of these opening lines:

> With the close of the door, the room gets quiet. The scene is familiar enough: a college English class, where the topic of the hour is narrative setting. The assigned reading might be Wendell Berry or William Faulkner, but it also could be Jane Austen or James Joyce, Geoffrey Chaucer or Cormac McCarthy. After all, what literary narrative (aside from the most experimental) omits setting? When the instructor starts to speak, the mode of sociality here, what Erving Goffman would call the "interaction order" at this site, begins to shift: the students peer up from their iPhones, turning away (hopefully for the hour) from Twitter, Facebook, and Instagram, to begin addressing the complex questions raised by literary form. (1)

The narrative drive animating this passage is essential to setting up the literary experiment that Alworth is after. Note how "the room" takes the place of

---

2   See Walter Besant and Henry James, *The Art of Fiction* (Boston: Algonquin Press, 1900).

the subject in the first sentence, and how the beginning of class is described as an instance of reassembling the human and nonhuman actors gathered in it. True to the book's central claim that setting is a dynamic network of actors with the capacity of "exercising a kind of agency with and through [its] human and nonhuman constituents" (2), the classroom is imagined as "a social site where a whole range of nonhuman entities (books and other cultural artifacts, laptops and tablets and projection equipment, a fully operational heating or cooling unit) are central to the pedagogical enterprise" (4). Note further how the passage transforms the site of the classroom into a literary setting in ways that lend force to the projected method by way of poetic enactment. This commitment to novelistic narration is hardly unique to Alworth's book. And if Mark McGurl has made the case that "show, don't tell" and "write what you know" are among the mantras of the creative writing programs that have vastly transformed the modes of literary production in the United States in the postwar years, passages like the above make me wonder about the extent to which they have disseminated into literary criticism with the effect of *novelizing* it in a Bakhtinian sense.[3] While this is not the place to explore this question further, there can be no doubt that *Site Reading*'s novelistic borrowings sustain its methodological ambitions.

These ambitions are anchored in the claim that unearthing what novels know about collective life not only demands a new way of reading but also a new literary sociology, one that breaks with the conventional wisdom of "locating the deep roots and meanings of literary form in the social forces that underlie it" to clear the stage for "a newly productive encounter between sociology and literary studies" (2). Latour is such a useful guide for thinking anew about literature's relationship with the social because, for him, "there is no such thing as society or the social, traditionally understood: no such thing as a special domain of reality (distinct from, say, the material or the natural), governed by abstract laws, structures, and functions" (3). And if we are willing to follow Latour's proposal that the "social is just the act and fact

---

3   See Mark McGurl, *The Program Era: Postwar Fiction and the Rise of Creative Writing* (Cambridge, MA: Harvard University Press, 2009), 21–28. It is fair to say that McGurl's book, in successfully marrying the pleasures of reading with the bliss of scholarly insight (in ways that Kathryn Roberts, in her contribution to this volume, reads as middlebrow), paved the way for this novelistic mode of criticism. For Mikhail Bakhtin's idea of novelization as a driving force of literary production and creativity, see his essay "The Novel and the Epic," in *The Dialogical Imagination: Four Essays*, ed. Michael Holquist (Austin: The University of Texas Press, 2010), 361–78.

of association, the coming together of phenomena to create multiple assemblages, affinities, and networks," literary form can no longer be seen as a surface effect—a symptom—of social forces.[4] It comes into view as the result of a process—or *practice*—of assembling and networking that intersects and interacts with other social practices. While the notion of practice is not central to Alworth's new methodology, I think that it could be, and perhaps even should have been, because it is an extremely helpful tool to make sense of the distributed form of agency that this method is invested in. Practices are forms of action that are collective rather than individual, and a claim recently made about them is that they are the very stuff out of which the social world is made.[5] Thinking about literature in terms of a collective action distributed among shifting constellations of human and nonhuman actors opens up possibilities to further refine Alworth's goal of dynamizing received views of literary properties, including those of setting as a stable container for narrative action, character as an entity that is clearly distinguishable from the setting in which it emerges and acts, form as a solidification of social forces—and, one might add, a stable and singular text as the site in which such solidification occurs.[6]

---

4   Rita Felski, "Context Stinks!," *New Literary History* 42, no. 2 (2011): 578; qtd. in Alworth, *Site Reading*, 3. Felski was among the first literary scholars to turn to Latour in order to rethink literature's relation to the social. See also Rita Felski, "Latour and Literary Studies," *PMLA* 130, no. 3 (2015): 737–742; *The Limits of Critique* (Chicago: Chicago University Press, 2015), discussed in this volume by Ramírez; and, most recently, *Hooked: Art and Attachment* (Chicago: Chicago University Press, 2020).

5   For an introduction to what is often referred to as the "practice turn" in critical theory, see Theodore R. Schatzki, "Introduction: Practice Theory," in *The Practice Turn in Contemporary Theory*, ed. Theodore R. Schatzki, Karin Knorr Cetina, and Eike von Savigny (London and New York: Routledge, 2001), 1–14. Not all practice theories include nonhuman actors. For two that do, see Karin Knorr Cetina, "Objectual Practice" in *The Practice Turn*, ed. Schatzki, Knorr Cetina, von Savigny, 175–88; Andrew Pickering, "Practice and Posthumanism: Social Theory and a History of Agency," in *The Practice Turn*, ed. Schatzki, Knorr Cetina, and von Savigny, 163–74. On literature as social practice, see Laura Bieger, "Jean-Paul Sartre, Richard Wright, and the Relational Aesthetics of Literary Engagement," in *The Return of the Aesthetic in American Studies*, ed. Johannes Voelz, Rieke Jordan, Stefan Kuhl, *REAL Yearbook of Research in English and American Literature* 35 (2020): 169–88. For more scholarship on the praxeological dimension of literature, see the body of work produced by the Cluster of Excellence 2020 "Temporal Communities: Doing Literature in a Global Perspective" at Freie Universität Berlin.

6   For a philosophical reflection on the praxeological understanding of art, see Georg W. Bertram, *Art as Human Practice: An Aesthetics* (London: Bloomsbury, 2019).

So yes, a praxeological understanding of art in general and of literature in particular helps to gain a firmer grasp of the role that cultural artifacts play in generating and distributing agency at and through concrete and ever-shifting constellations of actors. A main reason for this is that the relations between these actors do not merely exist; they are forged and maintained through practices, with literature being one of these practices. From this point of view, literature's form-giving capacity (and thus its capacity to mediate sociality and theorize social experience) is both shaped by and gives shape to the practices with which it intersects and interacts. One of the practices with which literature has had a long tradition of intersecting and interacting is sociology. When literature interacts with the sociological practice that does not treat the social "as a preconstituted domain" (as generations of sociologists drawing on Émile Durkheim have done) but as something that is "literally figured out" in the sense of being "given a kind of figuration in the sociological monograph, not unlike that which is proffered by narrative prose fiction" (28) (as assumed by Latour and actor-network theory), *the existence of the social comes into view as the result of a quintessentially descriptive, narrative effort*—an effort in which "the sociologist and the novelist [are potential] collaborators" (35).[7] So, here is my attempt to redescribe the methodological project of Alworth's book in praxeological terms: based on the hypothesis that literature has a truly versatile relation to the social (as well as the sociological), the ambition of *Site Reading* is to develop a model that does justice to scholarly reading as a social practice that actively participates (to a significant degree through its critical style) in the continuous act of fabricating the social by tracing (and thus making comprehensible via reflexive, second-order observation) the ways in which "literary texts assemble an impression of social form" (4).

Moreover, and crucially, in practicing such a reading, the form-giving act of assembling that constitutes a literary text comes into view as an especially powerful mediator of sociality—because it exposes how the act of fictional world-making involves raising such pertinent questions as the following: what counts as a social being? What are the limits of the social, that is, where does the social begin and where does it end? How is a self conditioned by the site it inhabits by way of the relations that it maintains to the human

---

7   For a lucid discussion of Latour's literariness, see Sianne Ngai, "Network Aesthetics: Juliana Spahr's *The Transformations* and Bruno Latour's *Reassembling the Social*," in *American Literature's Aesthetic Dimensions*, ed. Cindy Weinstein and Christopher Looby (New York: Columbia University Press, 2012), 369–92.

and nonhuman actors gathered at this site? Even though Alworth's model does not reflect on the role of the reader, it does seem compatible with the idea that literary texts are sites that, in engaging readers with these kinds of questions in the act of reading them, assemble constellations of human and nonhuman actors across the boundary that both separates and connects the world of the text and the world of the reader at and through the site of the text. In a riff that blends Alworth and Wolfgang Iser, one could even say that, in crisscrossing this boundary, the act of reading can perform such magic tricks as turning "a strange social being"—be it a fictional character, a narrator, or a reader—into "a keen social analyst" (8).[8]

As I am writing this text, the new coronavirus has altered my web of relationships in ways that have turned *me* into a strange social being—one that avoids touching her face, religiously washes her hands, uses her elbows to open doors and push elevator buttons, wears a mask over her mouth and nose when entering public spaces, has recently celebrated a hug-free birthday, and finds solace when reading that someone else "just realized that [she has] not touched another living being, nor … been touched, for more than 4 weeks," and that this peculiar state makes her wonder "whether we will later on have split humanity into those who were touched and those who were not."[9] While this split is not exactly a positive outlook, the strange social being I have become finds solace in it because strangeness is eased by social analysis (in this case even one that, despite its bleakness, offers a sense of belonging). In any case, I have no doubt that this yearning for a vision of the shape that sociality will take once the crisis is over has turned the strange social being that I have become into a tireless analyst of how the new protocols are affecting my interactions with myself, with friends and neighbors, with the clerks at the grocery store and with the groceries (and everything else) brought home from an outside world ravaged by an invisible enemy. If I was uncertain how far I was willing to follow Latour's claim that the social does not exist outside of the continuous act of assembling it, the coronavirus pandemic seems to

---

8   For the idea of reading as a performative act of crossing the boundary between the world of the text and the world of the reader, see Wolfgang Iser, *Prospecting: From Reader Response to Literary Anthropology* (Baltimore: Johns Hopkins University Press, 1989).

9   The lines stem from a Facebook post by art curator Ruth Noack, quoted by Masha Gessen in her op-ed "The Political Consequences of Loneliness and Isolation During the Pandemic," *The New Yorker*, May 5, 2020, https://www.newyorker.com/news/our-col umnists/the-political-consequences-of-loneliness-and-isolation-during-the-pandemic.

prove it right. Society and the social have never felt so ephemeral to me. The world as we know it has disappeared almost overnight as a result of a tear in the fabric of our collective lives that prompted a perfectly haphazard instance of reassembling social actors, some of them human, many of them not.

When the editors of this volume invited us to write about books that may "help us articulate and navigate crucial concerns that are still beyond the horizon," they certainly did not have this situation in mind, just as I did not imagine anything like it when proposing to write about Alworth's book. But the guidance it happens to offer for dealing with some of the most pressing questions raised by the current pandemic gives me an even clearer sense of the pertinence of its vision. How long can we stand social distancing, and how long should we tolerate limitations to our fundamental rights? How do we measure the value of work, of culture, of one life over another? How shall we live, and how can we live together? How do we reassess the place of the human species in a world in which the modern phantasy of progress has come to a halt? And while neither the editors nor I have envisioned a situation in which questions like these would be ubiquitous, some novelists have. In *The End of October*, a novel inspired by Cormac McCarthy's *The Road*, Lawrence Wright imagines a virus that, in the language of the jacket copy, "brings the world to its knees."[10] Part detective fiction, part crash course in virology, part social critique, the novel, which had been written before anyone knew about COVID-19, and published as country after country was shutting down from it, is so poised with the promise of knowing about collective life under the conditions of a global pandemic that critics and readers have hailed it like an oracle. In *Station Eleven*, a New York Times bestseller first published in 2014 and about to be released as a mini-series by the streaming service HBO Max, Emily St. John Mandel imagines an even deadlier virus that kills most of the world's population to explore the sociality reassembled in the lifespan of the generation coming of age in the ruins of late modern civilization.[11]

Two of Alworth's test sites—roads and ruins—are featured prominently in this novel, and in its post-apocalyptic world they blend into each other in intriguing ways. Just as in Alworth's readings of roads in Kerouac and Didion, the site of the road is emblematic of a vision of human progress distilled in automobility, prompting us to reimagine sociality based on "a redemptive relay between human and nonhuman" (90). But in *Station Eleven* redemption

---

10   Lawrence Wright, *The End of October* (New York: Knopf, 2020).

11   Emily St. John Mandel, *Station Eleven* (New York: Knopf, 2014).

takes the desolate shape of a caravan of cars pulled by humans and stripped of everything that would add unnecessary weight to their efforts of hauling them across roads gradually turning into ruins. The novel's most prominent ruin, an airport, is imagined as the shattered emblem of a vision of human progress distilled in aeromobility. Yet even in its dilapidating state the airport gives shelter to so many people that it brings to mind Alworth's point that the ruins protecting Malta's tormented population against Nazi air raids in Pynchon's *V.* exemplify "how sites sustain sociality, shoring up an entire society against its ruins" (120). So yes, in *Station Eleven*, both the site of the road and the site of the ruin are inscribed with failed visions of mobility and progress. Yet failure is not the only thing that welds them together. The novel imagines these two sites as conjointly assembling artistic practices and artifacts in ways that suggest a resilience and a recovery of a cultural dimension of social life that had nearly collapsed in the face of the threat of extinction. The members of the human species pulling the caravan of dismembered automobiles across the ravaged landscape in the Great Lakes area belong to a theater company that moves from settlement to settlement in this frontier-like setting to perform Shakespeare plays. One of them, a woman in her thirties, whom we first meet as a little girl at a *King Lear* performance at the Elgin Theatre in Toronto on the eve of the deadly pandemic (and whose character thus indicates that the social continues across the divide), is interviewed by a reporter for a newspaper published at the settlement that flourishes in the ruins of the airport. If the theater performances are animated by an air of timelessness that stems from the universality with which Shakespeare's plays deal with human fallibility, the launching of a newspaper is marked by a sense of a new beginning, a rebooting of modern sociality replete with civic media and a reading public that bears the potential of political agency.

I am drawing out these contours of a site reading of *Station Eleven* to show how astutely Alworth's method directs us toward what novels know about collective life when we turn our attention to how their settings "assemble an impression of social form" (4), and how keenly attuned this method is to articulating and navigating concerns with the limits of the social, which the coronavirus pandemic has indefinitely set on the agenda of cultural criticism. Yet I also have reservations about this method, especially regarding its claim to site specificity. How much sense does the term make to redescribe the importance and agency of the literary concept of setting in which the critical practice of site reading is anchored? As a term, "site specificity" was coined in the visual arts to lend force to the avant-garde spirit of "challeng[ing] the modernist orthodoxy of the art object as autonomous, autotelic, and thus indifferent to its site of display" (22). It is important to bear in mind that this challenge unfolded along a distinctive spatial trajectory, driven by an anti-institutionalism that was at first acted out by artistic movements such as minimalism and concept art within the confines of galleries and museums, then taken outside of these institutional spaces by movements such as earth art and performance art. Yes, works from all of these movements are typically made of materials such as cardboard, strip lights, chalk lines, pieces of junk, rocks, soil, human bodies and excrement that challenge received ideas about the objecthood of art in ways that highlight the web of actors and relations assembled through them. But only earth artists made artworks out of the very materials found at and bound to a given site.[12]

Alworth is keenly aware of this, and he brings in Miwon Kwon's extended model of site specificity to sustain the claim that his "investigation of social form" depends on concrete sites at which these practices are performed in ways that make it site specific, describing this investigation (with Kwon) as "an attempt not merely 'to integrate more directly into the realm of the social' but to theorize sociality itself through artistic practice" (22). Social relations are always situated, for sure. But are the artistic practices under scrutiny here defined by being *in situ* or *in socius*? [13] Is the investigation conducted through reading the artifacts assembled by Alworth around the idea of the site more invested in understanding the situatedness or the relationality of the social? Alworth explains that using site rather than terms such as place, space, or environment with a wider currency in literary studies serves "to underscore the sociological ambition of [his] book" (19). But does this choice not obscure rather than clarify the specific materiality of setting, which is distinctly different from the materiality of any site that is not a text? Sites have locations—places, if you will. Following Doreen Massey's understanding of place as "formed out of the particular set of social relations which interact at a particular location," all places are sites in Alworth's sense of "impl[ying] both

---

12   I have given extended thought to the site specificity of earth (or land) art and its trans- and intermedial dimensions in my essay "Putting Machines into Gardens: Walter De Maria's *Lightning Field*, Robert Smithson's *Spiral Jetty* and the Pastoral Imagination," in *Rereading the Machine in the Garden*, ed. Eric Erbacher, Nicole Maruo-Schröder, Florian Sedlmeier (Frankfurt am Main: Campus, 2014), 121–47.

13   I borrow this distinction from Nicolas Bourriaud, who coined the term relational art to describe a turn from the site to the social in some of the art of the 1990s. See Nicolas Bourriaud, *Relational Aesthetics* (Dijon : Les presses de réel, 2002).

human activity and sociality" (19).[14] And yet, the reverse is also true: all sites are places in Massey's sense of being "formed in part out of the specificity of the interactions which occur at that location (nowhere else does this precise mixture occur) and in part out of the fact that the meeting of those social relations at that location (their partly happenstance juxtaposition) will in turn produce new social effects."[15]

Setting bears a distinctive relation to sites understood in this way, for sure—one that deserves a profound and systematic rethinking along the lines that Alworth proposes. Even so, any question about the materiality of a site transformed into a literary setting is also and irrevocably a question about the *media-specific materiality* at work in this transformation. Setting is a genuinely discursive phenomenon, which also means that to understand fully the relation between site and setting, we need to ask: what is the materiality of the medium in and through which discursive site specificity does its mediating work? *Site Reading* comes closest to engaging these questions when talking about "site *specification*, the process by which imaginative literature defines and delimits locale" (10–11, emphasis mine). To me, this is a decidedly more compelling term, for it directs us toward the media-specific activities through which literary texts theorize sociality. Yet while Alworth gives substantial thought to how the novel, in being a narrative medium with a long-standing tradition of self-reflection and social analysis, has the capacity to put forth complex sociological imaginaries, the materiality of the novel as the medium that lends agency to the discursive site specificity of setting, and the book as the place where this agency resides are conceptual blind spots in *Site Reading*'s proposed methodology. Indeed, it seems to me that conflating the materiality of the site with that of the setting is responsible for this. I should add, however, that Alworth's work following this book has begun to fill this gap by focusing on book jackets and covers as specific and utterly neglected sites in understanding literature's relation to the social world, and on cover art as a transmedial form of "giving a reading."[16]

If my doubts about the adequacy or usefulness of the term site specificity to redescribe the concept of setting as a way of rethinking literature's rela-

---

14   Doreen Massey, *Space, Place, and Gender* (Cambridge UK: Polity Press, 1994), 168.

15   Ibid.

16   See David Alworth, "Paratextual Art," in *ELH* 85, no. 4 (Winter 2018): 1123–48, here 1130; and David Alworth and Peter Mendelsund, *The Look of the Book: Jackets, Covers, and Art at the Edges of Literature* (New York: Penguin Random House, 2020).

tion to the social may seem meticulous, my other, related contention could not be more general. What is the price for subsuming the cultural under the social in the ways it has been done here? For Alworth, drawing on Latour, culture means the "cultural network that emanates from [a site]," and consequently, studying culture means tracing this network (20). From this point of view, reading becomes an almost mechanical act of assembling. The sensory, aesthetic dimension—be it grounded in the interpretative and imaginative work of filling gaps between letters on a page or actors in a network, or in the tactile engagement with the materiality of the site and/or the medium at and through which this work occurs—is bracketed. Conceiving reading in terms of assembling aligns Alworth's book—at least in theory (its reading practice being pleasantly steeped in interpretation)—with current efforts to replace hermeneutics (which is always and inherently aesthetic) with description (which, even though it is a narrative technique that involves literary principles such as selection and combination, resonates with empirical facticity). If these efforts have caused a tectonic shift in literary criticism in the past decades that comes in tow with a style that, like Latourian sociology, courts a literary aesthetics to reinvigorate a critical practice, one of the ironies of this development is that the aesthetic dimension of literature receives no critical attention whatsoever.

I am not addressing this issue to dismiss the centrality that Alworth assigns to the social with Latour's help. In fact, I believe that the pathways opened up by his proposal for a "sociology *of* literature [that] seeks to discover the sociology *in* literature" (27) are crucial for the task of the cultural critic to reclaim the value of literature (and literary studies) for dealing with "the immensely difficult task of comprehending something as complex as *society*" (13)—a task that is especially taxing in times like ours, when not only the social but also the cultural artifact/social actor of the literary text, the constellation of actors and artifacts within which this text competes for attention, and the modes of engaging with it (on screen or on paper, in audio or audiovisual form) are in rapid flux. I am addressing this issue because I think it leads to an impoverished understanding of culture. And I find this problematic because I believe that we cannot fully grasp literature's special capacities to mediate the social and theorize the experiences associated with it—the very thing that Alworth is interested in and that makes his book so relevant today—without factoring in the aesthetic dimension of literature as a vector of critical engagement.

I further believe that the notion of practice offers a promising way of doing this. In his praxeological aesthetics, Georg Bertram defines art as an interactive, intersubjective practice that revolves around making collective judgments about its own meaning and value. Understood in this way, art is "not simply a specific kind of practice, but rather a specific kind of *reflective* practice, a specific formation of practices by means of which we take a stance towards ourselves in the midst of practicing our culture."[17] And while there are many different reflective practices (talking about speech, religion, therapeutic conversations, or philosophy), art is the practice we use to reflect upon what it means to be human—which means in a most general sense that "we have to define what we are always anew."[18] (I should also add that, for Bertram, what it means to be human is not a matter of defining the ontological status or essence of humankind but of defining the relations with and within the world that give shape and expression to human subjectivity.) In this constantly evolving process of *becoming rather than being human*, art (as a collective, reflective practice) gives occasion to take a stance on ourselves and grasp our "taking a stance" as "a practical occurrence."[19]

I am concluding on this note because I think that we are experiencing a moment in which we do have to define anew what it means to be human. The COVID-19 pandemic has made it painfully clear that social inequality—in splitting humanity into those who are more or less vulnerable to the pandemic because of inhabiting a position (or place) of relative social privilege—has become a vital threat to our survival as a species. In this situation, becoming human hinges, perhaps more than ever, on a commitment of those privileged enough to afford it to suture that split, both locally and globally. As cultural critics, it is our privilege and responsibility to articulate and acknowledge the indispensable role that culture can play in this collective endeavor.[20] One promising way of doing this is to connect Bertram's praxeological aesthetics with Alworth's view of literary art as an especially potent mediator and theorizer of sociality. The critical practice of site reading would thus become a

---

17   Bertram, *Art as Human Practice*, 3.
18   Bertram, 3.
19   Bertram, 3.
20   Together with my co-editors Joshua Shannon and Jason Weems, I am presently exploring the changing figurations of human being that undergird the practice and history of American Art in the volume *Humans* of the series Terra Foundation Essays (forthcoming with the University of Chicago Press in the fall of 2021).

driving force in confronting the question of the social with the question of the human: by way of reconfiguring human beings as quintessentially networked, collective, and dependent on nonhuman agents. And if climate change were not enough to expose the degree to which the limits of the social are determined by the corrosive effects of social inequality on the one hand and the possibilities of a peaceful coexistence of human and nonhuman actors on the other, perhaps the present pandemic could be. In any case, *Site Reading* offers a powerful vision of how the intersecting and interacting practices of literary art and cultural criticism can do their share in figuring out a just and sustainable form of sociality for times to come.

Humans and Other Species

If humans could talk, what would they say? Would they speak about the light on a wet pavement after the rain? Would they give names to their neighbors? Would they set little word traps to catch each other unawares?

6. Cloud-Reading with John Durham Peters's *The Marvelous Clouds* (2015)

Sarah Wasserman

As a child, I prayed to two gods. The first one, known to me through my mother's Catholicism, looked in my imagination like, well, God. I pictured a burly father figure with clouds of white hair and an ample beard: a new-age Ernest Hemingway, Zeus from D'Aulaires's *Book of Greek Myths*, Karl Marx. The god I learned about at temple with my father, though, always appeared in my imagination like a fastidious scientist: he wore wire-rimmed glasses and a white lab coat, like a young Louis Pasteur or perhaps like (the excellently named) August von Wassermann, whose moustache is nearly as remarkable as his research that led to the development of a diagnostic test for syphilis (Fig. 1).

I cringe now to recall how stereotype and convention conditioned my imagination, but I'm also struck by the fact that my "Jewish god" seemed to draw his authority from the scientific knowledge symbolized by his lab coat. There's nothing *right* about these two images of God, the paternal and the professorial (and perhaps nothing wrong), but while dwelling in the pages of John Durham Peters's dazzling 2015 book, *The Marvelous Clouds*, I found my old Jewish chemist-god waltzing across my mind's eye. Why had he returned? And what does any of this have to do with Peters's erudite study that takes readers, as the subtitle promises, "toward a philosophy of elemental media?"

Fig. 1: Portrait of August von Wasserman.

Credit: Wellcome Collection. Attribution 4.0 International (CC BY 4.0)

In the concluding chapter of *Marvelous Clouds*, "The Sabbath of Meaning," Peters confesses that his "efforts at crossing disciplinary borders" have caused him "plenty of fear and trembling" (378).[1] After deftly guiding readers through seas full of dolphins, skies full of stars, landscapes dotted by fire, and a panoply of objects including stone tablets, paper scrolls, clocks, calendars, and mobile phones, Peters admits that the project's central goal—to "invite media studies to be friendlier to the natural sciences as well as to theology and philosophy"—still causes him some discomfort (378). The challenges and potential pitfalls of crossing so many disciplinary boundaries are real, not least because within a European context, the humanities and the natural sciences have been separated from one another, and both from religious studies, since the fifteenth century. Diderot's famous *Système Figuré des Connaissances Humaines* ("Map of the System of Human Knowledge," see Fig. 2) from the 1750s—frequently cited as foundational to the division and organization of academic disciplines—in fact resonates with the tentacular reach of Peters's mind. For Diderot, the category "Science of Man" (*science de l'homme*) includes the fields we today call media studies: the "Art of Remembering" (*art de retenir*) and the "Art of Communicating" (*art de communiquer*). All of this falls under the same general heading of "Reason" (*raison*) with, surprisingly enough, "The Science of God" (*science de dieu*). By thinking expansively about media as civilization-ordering devices, Peters reminds us that human experience and meaning don't respect disciplinary divides or historical periodization; the species seeks and creates meaning in stars as well as Snapchats. I guess that's why my lab-coated YHWH has reappeared: he is my personal cipher for the confluence of religion, science, and the humanities, a childhood mascot for the methodological aims Peters's book brings back together.

---

1   All parenthetical citations in the text refer to John Durham Peters, *The Marvelous Clouds: Towards a Philosophy of Elemental Media* (Chicago: University of Chicago Press, 2015).

Fig. 2: Diderot's Map of the System of Human Knowledge.

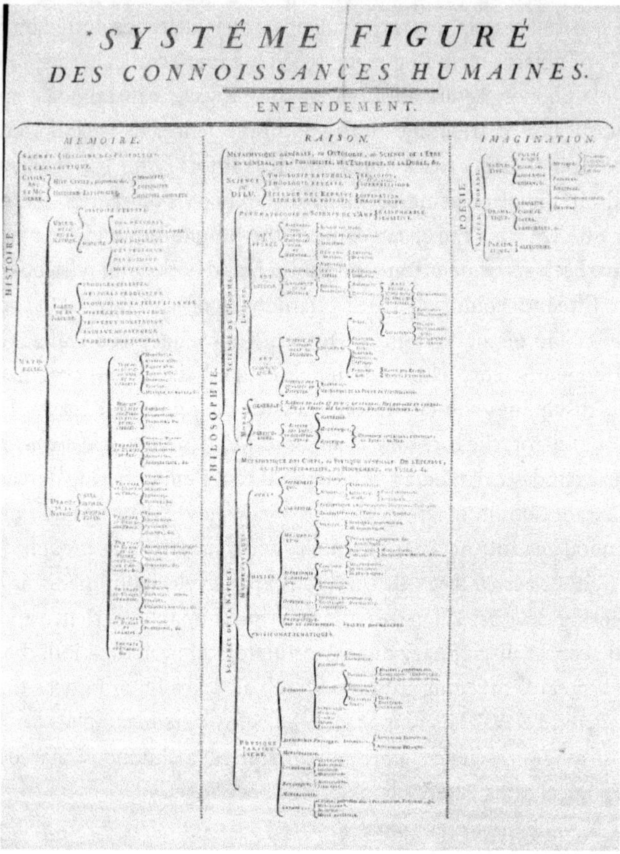

SYSTÉME FIGURÉ
DES CONNOISSANCES HUMAINES.

ENTENDEMENT.

MEMOIRE.   RAISON.   IMAGINATION.

Source: Wikimedia Commons, https://commons.wikimedia.org/wiki/
File:ENC_SYSTEME_FIGURE.jpeg

It's also perhaps because I can't help but recall one of the Hebrew equiv-
alents for cloud, *Anan*, which is marvelous indeed. The term is explained in
Rabbinical literature as naming a phenomenon that renders people "pleasant
toward one another through prosperity," presumably because clouds bring

rain to nourish crops.[2] This is an apt metaphor for Peters's book, given his efforts to make disparate methods and thinkers "pleasant toward one another." The scholars who inhabit the landscape of cultural criticism should welcome such *Anan*. Broadly intellectual, Peters's approach is technology-literate but also environmentally-attuned and literary in its sensibilities. By bringing a hermeneutic spirit as well as historical depth into the sometimes-arid terrain of communications or technology-driven media studies, *The Marvelous Clouds* ... makes it rain. This is what Peters would call "a real howler." In the current moment, when literary studies and media studies continue to overlap, Peters's book draws upon both without collapsing the core of each discipline. He cites familiar, foundational media scholars and, like Marshall McLuhan and Friedrich Kittler, explores the way that every medium extends and changes the human sensorium. But in *The Marvelous Clouds*, Peters is not narrowly bound to media as technological devices or systems; in this way he takes a running leap from the springboard of McLuhan and Kittler, vaulting into our present internet age carrying all the tools of the past along with him. Peters draws particular inspiration from an unlikely historical source, one that is usually seen as antithetical to media studies: American transcendentalism. Herman Melville, Emily Dickinson, Henry David Thoreau, and Ralph Waldo Emerson serve as models who knew "the splendor and strangeness of being a humanoid in this particular cosmos" (43). Like them, Peters seeks to be a student of "anthropozoic comminglings" (43).

Given the book's environmental concerns, the transcendentalists are logical muses. *The Marvelous Clouds* tracks the convergence of nature and culture: it argues that our environment (the sea, the sky) has always been made of media and that technological media saturate the atmosphere so that they become environmental—an argument more urgent than ever given the current reality of climate change. Media, for Peters, are ontological as well as semiotic. They are not only *about* the world, they *are* the world. The sea, for instance, is not a natural entity that ebbs and flows outside all human influence; for Peters, "the ocean is the medium of all media, the fountain from which all life on earth emerged" (54). The sea's cetaceans teach us how environment shapes mind and body. While whales and dolphins and vampire squids flourish at sea, humans can survive at sea only by ship, what Peters describes as "the archetype of artifice become nature, craft become environment" (102). In addition to a

---

2   *Jewish Encyclopedia*, s.v. "cloud," accessed June 29, 2020, http://www.jewishencyclopedia.com/articles/4424-cloud.

chapter on the sea and seafaring, the book covers fire and technologies of domestication; the sky and astronomical and meteorological practices of timekeeping and forecasting; the earth and techniques of writing and storage; as well as operations of memory, searching, and navigating information overload. If, as these chapters suggest, media comprise the entire infrastructure underwriting human existence, then media studies must encompass theology along with science and technology, the science of God and the science of man.

Beyond its disciplinary-smashing ambitions, it's easy to imagine why *The Marvelous Clouds* might interest literary scholars. The emphasis Peters puts on writing (the noun, not the verb) offers compelling fodder for book historians and anyone interested in what is happening to books as they become increasingly digital things. Spoiler alert: "Defining a book is as difficult as defining a language, and Google revives a way to think about both: they are networks" (323). More than just broadening the typical things that literary critics want to do with network analysis—trace relays between publishers and readers, or visualize contacts between characters in plays—Peters's book has important implications for how professional readers of literature read. Here, the mists of *Anan* helpfully roll in. Peters attends to each medium, be it sundial or no-smoking sign, with historical and material specificity. But the metaphysical nature of his claim that "expression and existence merge" (15) means that alongside such precise analysis lies the overarching sense that similarity and contiguity are as powerful as difference. If we see media as elemental, we can better recognize productive relays and slippages between device and environment, object and subject, past and present. Peters's goal is not so much a "flat ontology" à la Latour than, well, as Bob Ross might put it: a happy little cloud (Fig. 3). Through this silly metaphor I mean to capture something of what I find so compelling about Peters's model of the world. Peters isn't just espousing a friendly hippie sense that the planet would fare better if humans better understood their interdependence with plants, animals, and the elements, but is acting as a generous guru of technique, inviting us to tune in and see how it's done. Peters's protocols for reading are broad and close and deep: on container technologies, for instance, he ranges from the Ancient Greeks to twentieth-century urban studies, from the *Genizot* where unused Hebrew religious texts are stored to agricultural monocultures that have changed human food habits. With precision and immense breadth and openness to the histories and traditions of media studies, Peters foregoes a

shallow digital field and instead tills a landscape as plentiful as the ones Bob
Ross paints.

Fig. 3: Bob Ross at his easel

Source: "Bob Ross Mystic Mountain (High Quality) Season 20
Episode," Dailymotion Video, https://www.dailymotion.com/video/
x3d66l2

What's more, Peters's insistence on co-existence—of creatures, histories,
and disciplines—works against the note of discord that has been sounding in
recent conversations about literary method. In the first two decades of this
century, a dizzying array of supposedly new methods have come to define
literary studies. Big data, surface reading, postcritique, new materialisms,
new formalism, and the digital humanities name just a few of the methodological imperatives that scholars have developed to innovate literary studies
and push disciplinary boundaries. Recent debates about what interpretation
can and should look like in the twenty-first century have led some scholars
to suggest that literary and cultural critics are embroiled in "method wars."
Rita Felski has argued that method debates have taken center stage following the era of high theory and the subsequent entrenchment of historicism.[3]
This concept of a method war depends in large part upon a sense that these
methods are new—that the attention to "non-literary" objects, the curation

---

3   Rita Felski, "Interpretation and Its Rivals: Introduction," *New Literary History* 45, no. 2
     (Spring 2014): v–xi.

of digital archives, and the expansion of algorithmic analysis represents a meaningful shift from earlier modes of study. My own sense (and here I'll be presumptuous enough to say that I think Peters would agree) is that this adversarial angle obscures many continuities, both between recent and older methods and across seemingly different methodologies. You say surface; I say symptom. You say big data; I say new formalism. Or as Peters might put it: all of it can be accommodated within the current ecumenical state of cultural studies.

The polemical crackle and pop of recent methodological conversations in literary studies has, as Julie Orlemanski notes, been largely in excess of any substantial difference in practice.[4] Even as scholars trumpet correction, revision, novelty, and plucky push-back against methodological hegemons, they in fact offer very modest changes in how literary studies actually gets done. In an article about the many lessons queer theory has to teach us about "method melodramas," David Kurnick deftly argues that method manifestos "offer not new ways to interpret texts but new ways to feel about ourselves when we do."[5] This seems right to me insofar as the "new" offerings of literary method often focus on critics' attitudes rather than whether or not they should continue to read closely, historicize, and contextualize: be generous, not suspicious; be modest, not heroic; be attentive, not adversarial. The growing infatuation on the part of literary critics with media studies may be motivated, at least in part, by fatigue with all of these injunctions. Certainly the burgeoning attention to materiality and the ubiquity of digitality have compelled scholars of literature to look to media studies. But seen from the shores of literary studies, media studies offers a relatively peaceful reprieve from methodological infighting. This is not to say that there are no disagreements in media studies—about which objects to study or how to study them—but less ink has been spilled of late pitting one method against another. *The Marvelous Clouds* says to readers, "more, not less." Peters's approach is expansive and inclusive, but his commitment to precision even in trans-temporal, trans-cultural study means that he does more than simply glop about in the "honey of the media concept [that] is being smeared all over the place" (10). Rather he tells us that we'd best think bee, beekeeper, and honey all together.

---

4   Julie Orlemanski, "What Our Notions are Made Of" (Lecture, Annual MLA Conference, Chicago, IL, January 13, 2019).

5   David Kurnick, "A Few Lies: Queer Theory and Our Method Melodramas," *ELH* 87, no. 2 (Summer 2020): 349–374, here 351.

What does this actually look like in practice? And what could it look like in practice for scholars examining poems or novels? Let me consider one example that suggests what Peters's method has to do with the Jewish god I ushered on stage above. In a chapter entitled "Lights in the Firmament: Sky Media (*Chronos*)," Peters surveys the various media that have filled the sky and examines "our current celestial predicament" by "sketch[ing] its long prelude in cyclical and linear sky media such as clocks, calendars, and their celestial sources, and punctual or fractal sky media such as towers, bells, weather, and clouds" (167). Calendars, Peters notes, play a central role in religious ritual for Christians as well as Muslims, Buddhists as well as Jews. In a single paragraph, Peters moves from the Qumram sectaries of the Dead Sea Scrolls (who resisted the Greek lunisolar calendar) to the prophets of Y2K doom, drawing a long line through this history in which "every calendar invites resistance" (193). Peters is most interested in this section in the Jewish calendar that uses both the sun and the phases of the moon and also has a curious history of being governed by central authority. (The diaspora calendar used to be co-ordinated by flares and messengers from the Sanhedrin in Jabneh.) The sky sets our calendars, which determine our rituals and our religions. Or is it the other way around, the sky determining rituals and religions, which then shape the calendar? In Peters's account and in true dialectic fashion, it is both: media are elemental precisely because they are the moon and the month, the stars and the Sabbath. The convergence of theological and hermeneutic traditions in such analysis makes Peters's approach to media helpful for literary scholars; it also makes theology and science helpful to one another. Planetary rotation and belief in the gods matter equally in this story of time-keeping; a meaningful understanding of calendars requires engagement with both.

This example illustrates how *The Marvelous Clouds* reminds readers of the exciting and historically provocative ways in which literary and cultural texts are always embedded in media systems—what we read, be it calendar or novel, always comes to us through and as media. The example also points to a kind of reading that might today feel somewhat alien to literary scholars for the way that it moves across many levels and traditions of thought. When Peters reads the Jewish calendar, we are left to wonder: is this surface reading, since he is just telling us what the calendar looks like and what it does? Is it depth, since he uncovers hidden meanings that an average reader wouldn't perceive? Is it comparative, insofar as he places the Jewish calendar in context among many other calendars? Or is it theological, as he teases out the mythic significance that the calendar holds for the human species? Of course we can pose the grumpier version of the question: who told John he's allowed to read in all these ways at once? Surely he has to choose one, plant a methodological flag, delineate a single approach for the rest of us mere mortals to use in our own research! Such questions not only reveal the limits of the method wars, they also bring to mind a much older tradition of reading that I can't help but see at work in *The Marvelous Clouds*.

In the late thirteenth century, the term *Pardes* first appeared in the writings of Spanish rabbi and Kabbalist Moses de León (known in Hebrew as Moshe ben Shem-Tov).[6] Pardes, frequently written as PaRDeS, refers to a set of layered approaches to biblical exegesis in rabbinic Judaism. The term is an acronym formed from the initials of four ways to interpret the text in Torah study (Fig. 4). As readers proceed through each of the four methods in the order indicated by the acronym, they perform a more intense level of interpretation, revealing the meaning of the text at hand as if they are peeling back the layers of an onion.[7] First up, *P'shat* is the plain, simple meaning of the text. Much like surface reading, *P'shat* looks at the literal meaning of scripture, seeking the customary meanings of the words used in their original historical and cultural setting.[8] Next, *Remez*, which means "hint," is something like reading for depth and uncovering the implied meaning of a text. For example, while *P'shat* would read Proverbs 20:10, "Different weights, and different measures, both of them are alike an abomination to the Lord," as a statement about merchants using the same scale to weigh goods for all of his customers, *Remez* understands this line to be about the importance of fairness and honesty in life more generally.[9] *D'rash*, the next level of reading, means

---

6   *Jewish Encyclopedia*, s.v. "Leon, Moses (Ben Shem-Tob) De," accessed June 29, 2020, http://www.jewishencyclopedia.com/articles/9767-leon-moses-ben-shem-tob-de.

7   In *The Political Unconscious*, Fredric Jameson discusses the medieval system of biblical exegesis that proceeds along four levels similar to those of Pardes. The four levels include literal reading, allegorical reading, moral reading, and anagogical reading (uncovering the political message or "collective meaning of history" from the text). Jameson notes that this medieval system served a practical function in late antiquity, "its ideological mission as a strategy for assimilating the Old Testament to the New, for rewriting the Jewish textual and cultural heritage in a form usable for Gentiles." Jameson, *The Political Unconscious: Narrative as a Socially Symbolic Act* (New York: Routledge, 1983), 14–16.

8   *Jewish Encyclopedia*, s.v. "Peshat," accessed June 29, 2020, http://www.jewishencyclopedia.com/articles/12060-peshat.

9   See "The Rules of *Pardes*" at http://www.yashanet.com/studies/revstudy/Pardes.htm, accessed June 29, 2020.

"concept," but points toward something like a comparative reading. It usually entails the exposition of the *P'shat* and the *Remez*, and often involves combining unrelated verses in allegorical ways.[10] Finally, *Sod* (also written as *Sud*), "secret" or "hidden," is the divine meaning that is given through revelation.[11] *Sod* holds that the Torah contains divine secrets that can only be laid bare by patient readers open and attuned to the mystical sense given by the Kabbalah. In some traditions, *Sod* involves "returning" the letters of a word to a material state and giving them new form—such as numeric values—in order to reveal a hidden meaning.[12]

Fig. 4: Guide to Pardes

PARDES: Orchard, Garden

Hebrew	Letter	Meaning
פְּשָׁט	(p)	*P'shat*: simple, literal
רֶמֶז	(r)	*Remez:* hint, suggestion
דְּרַשׁ	(d)	*D'rash*: insight
סוֹד	(s)	*Sod:* mystery

Chart by author. For more, see https://www.hebrew4christians.com/Articles/Seventy_Faces/seventy_faces.html

---

10 *Jewish Encyclopedia, s.v.* "Biblical Exegesis," accessed June 29, 2020, http://www.jewishencyclopedia.com/articles/3263-bible-exegesis#anchor29.

11 Given Peters's interest in American transcendentalism, it's a happy coincidence that Emily Dickinson's poem "I never lost as much but twice," in which the poet arrives at God's door to ask for the return of her two deceased friends, includes a reference to (secular) sod: "I never lost as much but twice / And that was in the sod. / Twice have I stood a beggar / Before the door of God." Dickinson, *The Complete Poems of Emily Dickinson* (Boston: Little, Brown, 1924), 201.

12 Chaim Potok's 1967 novel *The Chosen* features vivid scenes of a Rabbi's son, Reuven Malter, and his friend Daniel Saunders, learning *Sod* from Reuven's father.

Admittedly, Pardes makes of texts some pretty weird onions. But this four-fold way of reading has always informed the secular hermeneutics of new historicism, new formalism, new materialism or the new whateverism that is popular by the time this essay is published. Kabbalah and related traditions of biblical hermeneutics have long given literary theory and interpretation its root structure; why not media studies too? Walter Benjamin, a favorite and foundational thinker for media scholars, was deeply interested in the Kab-balah. Benjamin's correspondence with Gershom Sholem, the German-born Israeli philosopher who is widely regarded as the founder of the modern, aca-demic study of the Kabbalah, attests to this interest. As Susan Buck-Morss details in *The Dialectics of Seeing*, Kabbalist thought provided for Benjamin "an alternative to the philosophical antinomies of not only Baroque Christian the-ology, but also subjective idealism, its secular, Enlightenment form. Specifi-cally, Kabbalism avoided the split between spirit and matter ... and it rejected the notion that redemption was an antimaterial, otherworldly concern."[13] It's not difficult to think of Benjamin's readings—of German tragic drama and Baudelaire, but also of train stations, World's Fairs and Mickey Mouse—as Kabbalistic. Benjamin's attempt to locate the past flashing up in the wish im-ages of the present feels often like a mystical mode of cognition, one that reveals the previously concealed truths within nature and shows how they are meaningful in a Messianic Age (for Benjamin, and in Marxist terms, a just, classless society).[14] The Kabbalah, as Buck-Morss argues, offered Benjamin a "metaphysical base for revolutionary pedagogy vital to Marxian politics, but it is expressed in the fully secular, historically specific discourse of women's fashions and street traffic."[15]

---

13   Susan Buck-Morss, *The Dialectics of Seeing: Walter Benjamin and the Arcades Project* (Cambridge, MA: MIT Press, 1991), 230.

14   On this point, Scholem writes: "A totally different concept of redemption determines the attitude to Messianism in Judaism and Christianity ... Judaism, in all its forms and manifestations, has always maintained a concept of redemption as an event which takes place publicly, on the stage of history and within the community .... In contrast, Christianity conceives of redemption as an event in the spiritual and unseen realm, an event which is reflected in the soul, in the private world of each individual, and which effects and inner transformation which need not correspond to anything outside." Gershom Scholem, *The Messianic Idea in Judaism, and Other Essays in Jewish Spirituality* (New York: Schocken Books, 1971), 1.

15   Buck-Morss, *Dialectics of Seeing*, 232.

Before I fall too far from the clouds into the rabbit hole of Benjamin's Messianism, I want to simply stress that, strange as Pardes may sound, there is often (if not always) a bit of mysticism in a reading that compels or moves us. When a scholar shows us the deep well of meaning that inheres in a poem or a map or a mirror or a search engine, we thrill at the knowledge they share but also, perhaps, at the sense that such knowledge might be the key to another way of being. This is precisely what Stephen Best, Heather Love, and Sharon Marcus have critiqued in their work on surface reading and thick description. To them, such mysticism can seem to be the preserve of an empowered (white, male) elder rather than a democratically available, albeit disenchanted reading process.[16] But I think it's possible to see Pardes not as a way to claim such power or assert the self-aggrandizing mastery Rita Felski describes as a hallmark of literary critics doing close reading; it can instead entail humility in the face of a text that contains multitudes. Pardes serves as a model for reading in more ways than one, for remembering that until we contextualize, compare, *and* read closely, we have yet to really understand a text. And even when we've done all that, the text will exceed our analysis, evading capture like a cloud that changes shape just as soon as we've seen in it a dragon or a knight. Peters's approach evokes Pardes insofar as it historicizes widely and interprets deeply while still creating room for a little bit of magic to float to the top. That's yet another reason why *The Marvelous Clouds* is a book for our current critical moment. As media and literary scholars alike work to understand networks of media and meaning in new, often seemingly empirical ways, they (re)-discover a kind of magical object: a novel, an image, even a device that continues to move us even after it has been run through an algorithm or pressed into a spreadsheet. The *D'rash* of Peters's readings, cutting across large swaths of culture and time, puts our newest devices in a long arc of media that dismantles whatever Silicon Valley hegemony might be lingering in media studies; his *Sod* reminds us that media (and readings of media) still have the power to enchant us, even when they have been rigorously analyzed.[17]

---

16   See Stephen Best and Sharon Marcus, "Surface Reading: An Introduction," *Representations* 108, no. 1 (2009): 1–21; Sharon Marcus, Heather Love, and Stephen Best, "Building a Better Description," *Representations* 135, no. 1 (2016): 1–21; and Heather Love, "Close but not Deep: Literary Ethics and the Descriptive Turn," *New Literary History* 41, no. 2 (2010): 371–391.

17   An unlikely but memorable example of such "enchanted" media comes at the beginning of Thomas Pynchon's 1965 novel, *The Crying of Lot 49*. A can of hairspray menaces

It may sound as though I'm enamored of Peters's work because its magi-cal mystery tour of media allows for a benevolent humanism, one blind to the urgent political concerns of the day. Peters is explicit that his argument has implications for the environment, but thinking about Pardes reminds me that criticism can be additive, harmonizing, a humble but meaningful exercise in imagining a better world. This is what Edward Said says is the task of literary scholarship in his essay, "Secular Criticism" (an *ur*-text of debates on method worth revisiting). There, Said writes that "criticism must think of itself as life-enhancing and constitutively opposed to every form of tyranny, domination, and abuse; its social goals are noncoercive knowledge produced in the inter-ests of human freedom."[18] The generous alchemy of *The Marvelous Clouds*, its desire to take different forms of knowing seriously and to explain how they congeal in our oldest media and our newest, *feels* "life-enhancing." Instead of method wars, Peters ushers in method peace. This is not an unprincipled stand, a wishy-washy everything goes approach; instead it's a way of asking whether everything possible—all the contexts and cultures, including those outside our own purview—has been taken into account. It's no coincidence that Pardes means orchard in Hebrew. The English word PaRaDiSe comes from the same Persian root *Pardis*, an ancient word for an enclosed garden.[19] This root reminds us that enclosure isn't only unfreedom—it is also structure that facilitates flourishing, an apt metaphor for the productive delimitation of fields and expertise. Combined with the drift and lift of clouds—*Anan*—we have the potential to produce meaningful knowledge while also seeing our enclosures with more perspective, and more wonder. Peters's clouds are mar-velous because they show us media studies as plenitude, not poverty. Literary scholars should take note.

This is just one more way in which Peters's book is timely for scholars in the humanities. As neoliberal rationalization and austerity measures are

---

the protagonist, Oedipa Maas, when she knocks it over in a hotel bathroom: "The can hit the floor, something broke, and with a great outsurge of pressure the stuff com-menced atomizing, propelling the can swiftly around the bathroom. … The can knew where it was going, she sensed, or something fast enough, *God or a digital machine*, might have computed in advance the complex web of its travel." Thomas Pynchon, *The Crying of Lot 49* (London: Vintage, 2000), 24 (emphasis added).

18   Edward Said, "Introduction: Secular Criticism," in *The World, The Text, and the Critic* (Cam-bridge, MA: Harvard University Press, 1983), 29.

19   *OED* Online, s.v. "paradise, n.," accessed June 26, 2020.

forced upon universities by a global pandemic, the humanities are compressed into smaller and more enclosed spaces. While actively resisting such downsizing, we can also consider the conceptual effects of contraction and disciplinary proximity. It gives us an opportunity to learn from each other's ways of reading the world, demanding that we become less parochial and also giving us common ground from which to fight cuts and reductions. Peters's work suggests it might be time to look for inspiration toward theology, the form of study foundational to the modern university that has been most banished from the sciences and the humanities alike. Theology and its methods help Peters describe integrative aesthetics and encounter the integrated world as finite and vulnerable in ways that inspire secular critics. And truth be told, when it comes to religion, Peters knows Judaism better than I do. Though it's a part of my identity and my experience in the world, it turns out that having two different gods often results in having none at all. Whatever beliefs I once held have long faded, along with both my bearded god and the mustachioed one. But when Peters discusses the Jewish calendar, Jewish scrolls, the *Shofar*, or Hebrew scripture, he validates my sneaking suspicion that one reason I study literature has to do with my religious background. Funny how in Peters's hands, the Jewish hermeneutics I dismissed as too odd and too religious when I was a teenager have renewed appeal. You don't need to believe in god or in Pardes or even in media studies to believe the lesson of *The Marvelous Clouds*: that "the world does not need to be re-enchanted; it is already wondrous" (381).

7. Infinite Fungus
Capitalism, Nature Writing, and Anna Lowenhaupt Tsing's *The Mushroom at the End of the World* (2015)

Christoph Ribbat

1. Map and Microterritory

Almost at the end of the journey, you find the gem. It is hidden away in the underground. After roaming the forests of Oregon and Finland and China and Japan and after investigating all sorts of late twenty-first-century capitalist practices (foraging, collecting, exporting, consuming, destroying the planet), you spot it in the endnote section. A writer more hungry for attention than Anna Lowenhaupt Tsing would have moved it out into the open. In this study it's buried on page 297, in note 1 to chapter 5, in the final sentence of a paragraph explaining how mushroom pickers in the Oregon woods are supplied with maps by the Forest Service. These maps indicate where fungi should and shouldn't be picked. Nobody pays much attention to the maps. People pick wherever the picking is good. But apparently these maps lead second lives. Certain mushroom pickers use them "as toilet paper, which is scarce in the campgrounds." (297).[1] Fascinating ideas pop up here regarding the map and the territory, representation and the real, epistemology and personal hygiene. It's a joyful struggle to wrap your head around what all that might mean.

Maybe that bit's too odd and minuscule to really matter. Then again, to reflect on things from a decidedly weird microperspective is the whole point of Anna Lowenhaupt Tsing's *The Mushroom at the End of the World: On the Possibility of Life in Capitalist Ruins*. Most definitely the book counts as a "lens history." Swarms of books claim that the widest range of ideas will take flight if you

---

1 All parenthetical citations in the text refer to Anna Lowenhaupt Tsing, *The Mushroom at the End of the World: On the Possibility of Life in Capitalist Ruins* (Princeton: Princeton University Press, 2017).

only look intently at this superfine detail that some hyperactive historian, ethnographer, or cultural studies person considers multi-layered enough to command your attention. There's the one on the zipper and the one on the paper clip and all the other ones on the saxophone and the banana and the toothpick and ostrich feathers and sand.[2] Tsing's work self-identifies as a study of the matsutake mushroom and of that particular mushroom only. There's nothing on chanterelles here and nothing on porcini, not even nicely sautéed ones. For better or worse, there's also nothing about fungi growing on and in people's bodies. Instead, Tsing presents an in-depth, intercontinental exploration of the way people relate to matsutake and how matsutake relate to us as people and to the fragile planet we live on for the time being. She gives us an ethnographic study of men, women, and highly specific objects, a study of international commodity chains, and a riff on Ursula K. Le Guin's reflections on storytelling as foraging. To call up Bill Brown's reflections on "thing theory," it is more than a study of how matsutake "organize our private and public affection."[3] Against a global backdrop, she explores work, business, and power.

Hence, while its focus may seem narrow, the study's key ideas root in openness and largesse. The matsutake mushroom impresses the ethnographer as a truly cooperative creature. She explains how trees and matsutake support each other. The mushrooms live off the tree roots. In turn they make it possible for the trees to live in otherwise barren soil. And so far, this kind of inter-species solidarity has been working only in the wild. According to *The Mushroom at the End of the World*, Japanese investors have wasted "millions of yen ... making matsutake cultivation possible." But these subversively altruistic fungi don't thrive in a plantation system. They are utterly wild. They need "the dynamic multispecies diversity of the forest" (40).

Why spend all this money on industrial matsutake production? In Japan, many feel fondly about these mushrooms. They smell like "village life," matsutake lovers say. Their scent recalls "pinewoods" and "chasing dragonflies" and, more generally, the past (in case the past seems attractive). To one of

---

2   On "lens histories" as "mundane studies" see Cullen Murphy, "Out of the Ordinary: 'Mundane Studies' Comes of Age," *The Atlantic*, October 2001, https://www.theatlanti c.com/magazine/archive/2001/10/out-of-the-ordinary/302310/.

3   Bill Brown, "Thing Theory," in *Things*, ed. Bill Brown (Chicago: University of Chicago Press, 2004), 1–16.

Anna Tsing's interviewees, matsutake smell like the paper dividers of a traditional Japanese home, simply because someone in that person's life used
to wrap each new batch of fungi found in the forest with the paper annually
taken down in that house. With all this nostalgic mindfulness floating around
Japan, it comes as no surprise that haiku also praise these fungi. Take Akemi
Tachibana's nineteenth-century poem: "The sound of a temple bell is heard in
the cedar forest at dusk, / The autumn aroma drifts on the road below" (qtd.
in Tsing 7). Consider twentieth-century poet Ko Nagata: "The moving cloud
fades away, and I smell the aroma of the mushroom" (qtd. in Tsing 7).

   And yet, in matsutake country, there's only so much room for tasteful lyricism. Tsing compares her protagonists to "rats, raccoons and cockroaches."
Stubborn survivors, they prosper in the "environmental messes humans have
made" (3–4). A matsutake mushroom was the first living thing to emerge from
the area struck by the Hiroshima nuclear bomb. To notice and praise them
seems less like a nostalgic ritual and more like a semi-optimistic microprac-
tice in the environmental crisis we all find ourselves in. As Tsing posits: "In
a global state of precarity, we don't have choices other than looking for life
in this ruin" (6). We might as well emulate trees and fungi, living together
"without harmony or conquest," existing in "disturbance-based ecologies" (5).
By and large, however, *The Mushroom at the End of the World* sidesteps overly
utopian concepts of humankind finally living like mushrooms. Her study explores capitalism—no matter how wondrous the matsutake's smell.

2.   Capitalism in the Woods

People pick matsutake in the forests of Oregon. Native Americans pick.
Latinos pick, White people pick, Asian refugees pick: Mien, Hmong, Cham,
Khmer. A Khmer picker tells Tsing that he speaks four languages: English,
Lao, Khmer, and Ebonics. These are truly cosmopolitan woods. There are
noodle tents in the forest campsites, karaoke tents, gambling and barbecue.[4]
The Mushroom at the End of the World zooms in on the Asian pickers, their

---

4   Not everyone loves foraging the way most foodies do. George Packer, in *The Unwinding:
     An Inner History of the New America* (New York: Farrar, 2013), 184–189, calls California
     restaurateur Alice Waters "Radish Queen," because the contemporary obsession with
     regional, organic, and wholesome food that is not trucked in from God knows where
     has turned into a class marker, suggesting a sort of delusional version of social change.
     The radish, the carrot, the berry: they're adored as if they had utopian potential in

stories, their perspectives. In a particularly moving segment, the study sketches what time spent in these woods means to Cambodian refugees. On the one hand, it returns them to forests and thus to traumatic experiences in the wartime jungles of Southeast Asia. On the other hand, they now roam "in the safety of American imperial freedom," as one Cambodian matsutake expert explains (88). Thus, Oregon turn into a more peaceful version of the Asian jungle. It morphs into a space of freedom. "Mushroom picking," Tsing explains, "layers together Laos and Oregon" (91).

Then again, as one of the Lao pickers says about these woods, "Buddha is not here" (76). The pickers aren't foraging matsutake to take them home, gaze at the clouds, wait for the temple bell to ring and then write haiku. They pick mushrooms in order to survive. At the end of the picking day, they take them to a market: situated in a few tents by the side of an Oregonian highway. In these tents, buyers buy matsutake from the pickers. It's safe to say that these buyers aren't haiku specialists either. They don't buy fungi for inspiration. They are middlemen for the bustling Japanese matsutake market.

The Mushroom at the End of the World doesn't categorize pickers as helpless victims and buyers as evil mycological Scrooges. In these tents by the roadside a highly dynamic, flexible ritual unfolds. People negotiate prices. Things get intense. Very few rules are in place. To Tsing, pickers, buyers and field agents are engaged in dramatic choreographies. Sure, all these interactions revolve around money and mushrooms. But the ethnographer sees "freedom" as the most important exchange going on in these forests: a kind of "mushroom fever," an emotionalized practice inspiring pickers and buyers to liberate themselves. To the amateur reader of her work, this very much looks like a version of Geertz' Balinese cockfight, a superspecific, highly intense, and yet quite universal site of symbolism and competition. Unlike the rituals interpreted in Geertz' study of cocks, these negotiations aren't "based on the deep psychological identification of men with their" fungi.[5]

Tsing cites an economist who sees the mushroom microeconomies in these Oregon tents as a prototypically pure market where all things are equal and it's all about buying and selling: capitalism in its most egalitarian form. Mushroom aren't "alienated commodities" in this remote place. Though it's

---

themselves. And thus, it would seem at first glance, this particular fungus might have the same sort of potential.

5   Clifford Geertz, "Deep Play: Notes on the Balinese Cockfight," in *The Interpretation of Cultures*, ed. Clifford Geertz (New York: Hachette, 2017), 435–474.

no easy task at all, matsutake picking doesn't count as "work." As one of the interviewees explains, to work means to obey your boss. Pickers don't have bosses. And the negotiating practices in the buyers' tents can go either way. On good days, the pickers will be in charge and the buyers will have to do whatever it takes to satisfy them (80–82).

A niche is a niche, though, and apparently capitalism is no wholesome outing in the woods. Nothing accumulates in these tents. There are matsutake and there's money, but there's no capital. The lives of the pickers are completely precarious, utterly dependent on fungi pushing their way up toward the light in the few months of the picking season (and on the coincidence of reaching the right spots before other pickers will). In places like Vancouver and Tokyo matsutake trading may enable individuals and corporations to amass capital. The exhilarating scenes in the forest, however (pickers haggling for higher prices and buyers shouting into their cell phones), function less like an allegory of an utterly free market (everyone competing on the same level) and more like a homogeneous community that includes pickers and buyers both. They may seem to collide in these negotiations. And yet, in the greater scheme of things they are all engaged in a kind of outdoor theater production subsidized by Japanese companies and matsutake consumers as affluent as they are nostalgic. Transnational corporations put up with the strange display of what one matsutake importer calls "American psychology"— quasi-anarchic trade in the woods—because, as Tsing puts it, they can "translate the exotic products of American freedom into Japanese inventory—and, through inventory, accumulation" (83).

Thus, woods, mushrooms, pickers, haggling, noodle tents, and sylvan karaoke bars come together to form a link in the global supply chain and there's not much freedom and not much exhilaration in what happens to the matsutake once trucks have taken them away, out of Oregon, in crates cooled by ice gel. Gig workers handle the mushroom in warehouses. These are people "without benefits" (127), far from the freedom of the forest, standing all night underneath bright lights to group fungi by size and age. The objects found by people who don't have bosses turn into "an acceptable export commodity" in these warehouses—and only when they have finally reached Japanese shores does their aroma prompt any sort of association with the past and its poetry (128). That's another matsutake haiku, composed by Anna Tsing, twenty-first-century author: "[T]he concentration of wealth is possible because value produced in unplanned patches is appropriated for capital" (5).

3.   Nature Writing and Fish Fingers

People praise *The Mushroom at the End of the World* for its literary appeal. As they should. One blurb finds "the flowing prose of a well-crafted novel" in these pages. Another credits Anna Tsing with "weav[ing] an adventurous tale." The writer herself insists on the formal experiments and attractions of her study. She points at the "riot of short chapters" she presents and how they might remind us of "the flushes of mushrooms that come up after the rain." These fungus-like chapters, she states, "build an open-ended assemblage, not a logical machine." She wants her readers to "experience" the type of "mushroom fever" she herself has felt in so many different places, with so many different actors involved (viii).

Like matsutake mushrooms, though, such writing will end up as a commodity at some point. It brings pleasure. People will want to consume it. The market in this case is the one for "nature writing," one of the hottest nonfiction genres on our hot planet. And smelly fungi and remarkable prose really do have a lot in common. People (mushroom pickers / nature writers) roam the woods. They look for things. Rare things. They find things, if they're lucky. They hold on to things. They see intermediaries (buyers in tents / literary agents) and then they sell matsutake to Japan or manuscripts to publishing houses. In the same way that matsutake grow in forests marked by destruction, the current fascination with nature writing emerges from a gripping sense of ecological crisis.

Take Robert Macfarlane, the most popular nature writer of our time, and his massive 2019 book *Underland*. Like Anna Tsing's study, this book makes a major effort to understand stuff usually hidden underground. Macfarlane explores the hidden spaces underneath Yorkshire and Paris, the Slovenian Highlands and Greenland: "We know so little of the worlds beneath our feet," Macfarlane writes.[6] Amazed by what he knows and we don't, he delivers his account from these worlds. There are many spectacular things in *Underland* and fungi are high up on the list. Macfarlane asks us to consider the biggest fungus in the world. Coincidentally it makes its home in Oregon. We humans call this thing the "honey fungus." It covers an area of four square miles. "The blue whale is to this honey fungus as an ant is to us," Macfarlane says.[7] But

---

6   Robert Macfarlane, *Underland: A Deep Time Journey* (London: Hamish Hamilton, 2019), 11.

7   Macfarlane, *Underland*, 102.

it's not just size, it's the otherness of fungi that seems to unsettle him: the way they connect, the way they cooperate with trees. As the embodiments of cooperative existence, they "thwart our usual sense of what is whole and singular, of what defines an organism, and of what descent and inheritance means."[8] Deleuze and Guattari's rhizomes seem to grow somewhere close, their "fuzzy aggregates, in other words, multiplicities of the rhizome type," but these men don't count as nature writers, nor as true fungus experts.[9]

Like matsutake pickers, nature writers do a lot of walking. In one chapter of *Underland*, Macfarlane hikes through Epping forest. A mycologist tags along and shows an even higher awareness of this terrain than the renowned author/peregrinator preparing his next tome. Macfarlane cites Anna Tsing in this segment: her essay "Arts of Inclusion, or How to Love a Mushroom" and her appeal to look down more in the woods, in order to get a sense of the "city … under your feet."[10] Then Macfarlane and his attendant mycologist lie down and gaze up (even though Tsing had told them to look the other way). Gazing at the treetops, the writer finds it "hard not to imagine these arboreal relations in terms of tenderness, generosity, and even love: the respectful distance of their shy crowns, the kissing branches that have pleached with one another." He then remembers "something Louis de Bernières has written."[11] And the scholar of fungi explains a few things to him about what's going on down below.

In contrast to such implausible meditations, *The Mushroom at the End of the World* never once aims for the monumental. Anna Lowenhaupt Tsing doesn't have time for super-giant creatures nor for grandiose literary inspiration suddenly springing up in the woods. You never sense that its author roamed the world (even though she has). Anna Tsing's approach resembles the much more modest subgenre of nature writing that Kathleen Jamie has defined as prose produced by people "who can't spend a year crawling in bushes" because they need to come home at night "to make the kids fish fingers."[12]

---

8   Ibid.

9   Gilles Deleuze and Felix Guattari, *A Thousand Plateaus: Capitalism and Schizophrenia*, 2nd ed. (London: Continuum, 1987), 558.

10   Anna Lowenhaupt Tsing, "Arts of Inclusion, or How to Love a Mushroom," *Manoa* 22, no. 2 (2010): 191–203.

11   Macfarlane, *Underland*, 99.

12   Helen Macdonald et al., "Country Files: Nature Writers on Books that Inspired Them," *The Guardian*, April 30, 2016, https://www.theguardian.com/books/2016/apr/30/country -files-nature-writers-books-inspired-them.

Then again (and even though Henry David Thoreau did spend a fairly long time in bushes), *The Mushroom at the End of the World* acutely resembles the largest specimen of big-ego nature writing: the text that is to Robert Macfarlane as the honey fungus is to the whale (or vice versa, it's hard to keep track). Anna Lowenhaupt Tsing's study will definitely echo Thoreau's work if your favorite passage in *Walden* is the scene in which one hundred laborers move toward and onto frozen Walden Pond, "harvesting" ice.[13]) Lawrence Buell imagines Thoreau not as the "androcentric" writer of the "Imperial self," but as a "more complexly gendered" thinker, one actor in "an extensive, variegated literature of environmental prose."[14] Following Buell, we could read *The Mushroom at the End of the World* as a twenty-first-century *Walden*: exploring both what's beneath the surface and what is the surface itself and how it's being transformed.

Like Thoreau in his pastoral retreat right by the railroad tracks, Anna Tsing explores disturbed worlds. Matsutake grow in sites utterly changed by volcanoes, sand dunes, glaciers, or by human destruction (50). Her nature writing emerges from two kinds of landscape most conducive to matsutake growth. First, there are forests created by humans to produce timber: industrial forests. Then there are peasant woods, where trees are constantly cut back, chopped, where landscapes become "denuded" (171). In these territories, industrial or peasant, pines thrive. And where pines thrive, matsutake may not be too far. "Together turning rock into food," the study observes, "matsutake-pine alliances stake out places with little organic soil" (171). From this fungus/tree coalition, the study unfolds larger concepts of cooperation. It explores assemblages, pine/mushroom/soil/human. Polyphonic music serves as a guiding metaphor for Tsing. She suggests combining ethnography and natural history. "Human-disturbed landscapes are ideal spaces for humanist and naturalist noticing" (160). Disturbance, not the yearning for harmony, drives her book forward. In response to disturbance, "ways of life come together," and thus, "patch-based assemblages are formed" (163).

That sounds like a concept much different from gazing at tree branches kissing in Epping forest. It certainly leads to a different kind of nature writing, a kind of "noticing" less dramatic than the excited accounts of continually

---

13   Henry David Thoreau, *Walden*, ed. Stephen Fender (Oxford: Oxford University Press, 1999), 265.

14   Lawrence Buell, *The Environmental Imagination: Thoreau, Nature Writing, and the Formation of American Culture* (Cambridge, MA: Harvard University Press, 1996), 26.

amazed explorers. To Tsing, for instance, a "soggy box of Zhong Nan Hai Super Chinese cigarettes" is not just a piece of trash in the forest (247). It will help the picker in the Oregon woods find the right kind of picking grounds. They will notice that a previous noticer, a Zhong Nan Hai-smoking Southeast Asian mushroom expert, has passed through these woods before them. Hopefully, though, he will have stopped and bent down in slightly different places. Matsutake reappear close to where matsutake have appeared. So trash helps. To truly notice, to find mushrooms and to write nature, it is important to "slow down": to be "[c]alm but fevered, impassioned, but still." Find the bump on the ground, even if it's not really a bump. More the idea of a bump. Or a crack. A minuscule one. Look for "lumps and cracks" indicating "a living thing slowly, slowly pushing" (242). You see huckleberries around? Not a good sign: too much humidity. Recent tracks of heavy machinery: bad signs. But animal tracks and excrements: these should make you optimistic. Anna Tsing calls this kind of data interpretation "a form of forest knowledge and appreciation without the completeness of classification." What happens instead, this particular nature writer argues, is that beings, like these particular mushrooms, are "experienced as subjects rather than objects." (243).

4.   Research & Recipes

Yes, there is an organization named "Matsutake Worlds Research Group." Reading this book, you will learn more about this collective. And ever the collaborative scholar, Anna Tsing tells us about her fellow researchers and about what else may be coming our way after *The Mushroom at the End of the World*: Michael Hathaway's work on mushroom picking and selling in Yunnan, China, for instance, or Shiho Satsuka's studies of the construction of Japanese matsutake knowledge. But she also sheds light on the limits of international cooperative research in the field. Reporting from the first international matsutake studies conference, she acknowledges that much of the event seems to have been shaped by silences and misunderstandings. Apparently, only one conference segment really worked out. Before the papers were given and the audience settled into the rhythm of not getting each other's points, the scholars from China, Japan, North Korea, and the United States spent two days together doing fieldwork. As Anna Tsing puts it: "we watched each other watching the forest" (224).

To cooperate nonetheless and to profit, like pine and matsutake, from collaboration in crisis—that is a central idea of *The Mushroom at the End of the World*. Countless parallels grow from fungi to people and back again. It's one of the study's magical feats that these parallels hardly ever seem forced. Anna Tsing teaches on two continents and she sees two tendencies at play in Europe and the United States. In the Old World, scholarship has turned into a numbers game. Authorities assess research with statistical precision. In the United States, she finds that scholars are forced to define themselves as brands, as entrepreneurs, as actors in a star system. Against these two tendencies, she pits "the pleasures of the woodland" (286). She hopes that experts won't transform this territory into a "garden." She plans "to keep it open and available for an array of species" (286). Scholars, in her dictionary, function as gatherers, not as hunters. They tell stories "simultaneously true and fabulous" (viii). It is, she argues, the only way we can "account for the fact that anything is alive in the mess we have made" (viii).

In this spirit, you finish the book with some sort of hunch that it has turned you into a better and/or happier person and that there's a slight chance of survival in "capitalist ruins." But if you're an anti-metaphorical modernist or just a plain old homemaker looking for useful hints on how and why he should cook these things that the members of the Matsutake Worlds Research Group have devoted their working lives to, then Anna Tsing doesn't really pamper you. Sure, it's fascinating to see how someone takes that wonderful fungus, rips it from its universe and turns it from a communal product into a "privately owned mushroom" (271). And it's inspiring to think about how the most interesting fungus of all emerges from "an underground common" (274) only to turn into a "fully alienated creature of exchange" (272). But how does the matsutake mushroom smell, how does it taste? Does it go well with fries? What kind of pasta would work? The book reserves some, but relatively little energy to these questions. Tsing cites a mycologist who finds a note of "dirty socks" in the fungus' aroma (51). To the cuisinier, that is not much more than a slightly underwhelming start.

Here then, foraged from *The Mushroom at the End of the World*, some truly useful information. These idiosyncratic mushrooms do not respond well to metal. So don't chop them with a knife. Take them apart with your fingers. Grab a frying pan. Heat the pan. Don't use oil. It will change the smell. In no case should you use butter. That would ruin everything. Dry grill them. You may want to reconsider your approach if you've found your own personal batch of matsutake close to a type of tree called "white fir," affectionately nicknamed "piss fir" for its distinct smell. The tree will have passed on its scent to its fungal friend and the result of this marvelously symbiotic anticapitalist relationship will have traveled all the way to your kitchen and will definitely move on to your taste buds. Change course, in that case: you might have to pickle and smoke these particular objects (or subjects). But if piss firs haven't grown nearby, grill these creatures of exchange. Then use a few drops of lime juice.

Structures of Feminist Feeling
and Storytelling

We tell ourselves stories in order to live
We tell ourselves stories in order to give
We tell ourselves stories in order to grieve
We tell ourselves stories in order to believe
We tell ourselves stories in order to achieve
We tell ourselves stories in order to deceive
We tell ourselves stories in order to retrieve
So, dear Reader, let me tell you a story:

8. Sorting through Feminist Cabinets with Clare Hemmings's *Why Stories Matter* (2011)

Maria Sulimma

The cover of Clare Hemmings's *Why Stories Matter: The Political Grammar of Feminist Theory* (2011) shows the minimalist art installment *Cabinet VIII* (2007) by artist Rachel Whiteread, an open cabinet filled with fortyish square boxes paper-wrapped in discreet colors. For the purpose of their 2008 auction, Sotheby's lauded Whitehead's use of "negative spaces" as well as an overall impression of the "post-minimal austerity of a white cabinet."[1] The neat, organized cabinet is less an allegorical illustration of the compelling book it graces than it may serve as the starting point for its theoretical undertaking. Feminist thinker Hemmings sets out to unwrap packages, to disturb their deliberate arrangement, and to take stock of what it is that we pack and store when we speak of feminist history and theory. There is an aesthetic at play on the book's cover which minimalist celebrity Marie Kondo would be delighted by, but, fortunately, Hemmings is not one to push aside a feminist past that does not "spark joy" in favor of a more adequate retelling, a clinical clean slate. Her goal is less to develop an alternate Western feminist intellectual history than to experiment "with how we might tell stories differently rather than telling different stories" (16).[2]

This essay on her work hence amounts to a kind of "culture cubed" rather than squared. After all, hers is a book *about* feminist theory which takes writing in feminist theory as its material, but is also a book *of* feminist theory

1   "(Auction) Red: Rachel Whiteread, Cabin VII," Sotheby's, accessed March 31, 2020, www.sothebys.com/en/auctions/ecatalogue/2008/auction-red-n08421/lot.10.html.
2   All parenthetical citations in the text refer to Clare Hemmings, *Why Stories Matter: The Political Grammar of Feminist Theory* (Durham: Duke University Press, 2011).

nonetheless, an important and innovative contribution to this vibrant inter-disciplinary field. Hemmings is interested in feminist knowledge production, feminist theory-writing, and feminist academic cultures and frames such practices as feminist storytelling. "Story" is her term for the accounts feminists give of what happened in the past forty years of Western feminist theory; with "narrative," Hemmings describes the repetitive patterning of stories in content, context, and format across time (rather than referring to them as Foucauldian "discourses" or more generally "history"); and lastly, "(political) grammar" is her term for the narrative techniques these stories employ. This vocabulary is, of course, part of the inventory of literary studies and narratology. It is this disciplinary rooting that the following contribution suggests as a way to further appreciate Hemmings's intervention in our current moment, in which feminism after being repeatedly pronounced dead is commercially and socially ever-present.

To sort through a cabinet, to reorganize, to take stock or inventory—these are basic principles of housekeeping, traditionally coded as feminine and (often invisible) domestic labor. As metaphors, those activities allow me to describe and interact with Hemmings's work. Just like the kind of meta-theoretical analysis of her study, such housework is reproductive and keeps a household, or in this case feminist theory, alive, although it may not seem relevant at first. The book cover also evokes a bathroom medicine cabinet and thus recalls an illness or disease to be remedied by Hemmings's work. However, her reader cannot hope for a quick fix, a few easy guidelines that would help us be better feminist storytellers and feminist theorists. Rather what Hemmings suggests, is much harder and more substantial: she urges readers to sit with discomforts and uncertainty, to embrace ambiguity, and to decenter Western feminist theory. Such interventions and transformations are neither absolute nor definitive: "This works as a kind of serious joke ... intended to open up rather than close down other possibilities in the present. I believe that keeping meaning open in this way is a primary feminist responsibility."[3] Rather than mending holes by including what was previously erased, for Hemmings, openness and unfinishedness of meaning and meaning-making should be a collective goal of feminist theory.

---

3   Clare Hemmings, "What is a Feminist Theorist Responsible for? Response to Rachel Torr," *Feminist Theory* 8, no. 1 (2007): 69–76, here 75.

The Politics of De-Authorization and Recitation

In the first half of the book, Hemmings dedicates a chapter to each of the dominant stories of feminist theory: they are stories of progress, loss, or return. Her dazzlingly massive corpus consists of the issues of sixteen major peer-reviewed journals in feminist studies and gender studies as well as social and cultural theory published between 1998 and 2007. Hemmings offers close readings of the narrative strategies/grammar of these stories and cites only the year and journal of a publication, not its author(s), title, or topic. By following this tactic of de-authorization, she draws attention to feminist storytelling as a collective practice resonant with institutional logics. Because processes of peer-reviewing involve academic communities—aside from the individual author(s), active agents in knowledge production include editors, reviewers, boards, and responders—journals lend themselves to Hemmings's notion that feminist storytelling is created through collective repetition.

Despite their different subjects, the different affective attachments they inspire, and their different prognoses for feminist futures or rather the future of feminism, the feminist stories that Hemmings finds interact and share several commonalities. They firstly all rely on a decade-by-decade approach to feminism's history (the 1970s, the 1980s, the 19990s, the present/the 2000s).[4] Secondly, they all diagnose the current death, demise, or antagonism of feminism in the present. They use the "cultural turn" of the 1990s as a signpost (albeit evaluated differently by each story). Thirdly and lastly, they are "presumed" in that they rely on seeming common sense knowledge which the writer/theorist and reader should be able to agree upon. Here, Hemmings's findings immediately stand out, because these stories do not correspond to the prominent waves-metaphor so often used to speak about Western feminism's different stages. The stories cannot be conceived of as temporal phases but comprise three overlapping ways that feminist theory has found to speak about itself, about its past, and about what would need to happen in its future.

---

4   This chronology leaves individual decades "overburdened yet curiously flattened despite each story's unique truth claims" (5). For example, it contains the contributions of feminists of color as well as lesbian feminists solely in the 1980s—with few exceptions reframed as postcolonial or queer theory in the 1990s. Such a characterization not only erases these writers' earlier and current work but "fetishizes" their contributions as pillars of anti-essentialism or activism celebrated or mourned in the present (162).

Stories of progress emphasize improvement or maturity; they celebrate how far feminism has come since "the 1970s" and what has been won in the intellectual debates of the decades since. Among the achievements, such stories prize intersectionality and diversity. They pride themselves on moving away from inadequate, earlier essentialist and universalized categories like "woman." In these accounts, the past is "cast as irredeemably anachronistic in order that the present can represent the theoretical cutting edge" (38). A story of progress highlights an evolutionary move of feminist theory from simplicity to complexity, and from singularity to multiplicity, as well as opportunities the future offers for feminism to expand further.

As a mirror image of the optimistic subject of progress stories, the subject of stories of loss mourns the present as having moved away from past feminist activism. Such stories nostalgically view "the 1970s" as a time of rich feminist collaboration, a time of robust social movements and vibrant activism. They find that the poststructuralist influence of the 1990s has replaced activism with a depoliticized and overly theoretical career-feminism located primarily in the universities. Because the feminist theorist/storyteller relating these stories is herself likely an academic, the stories have to establish her as different from her career-driven peers. Interestingly, this differentiation occurs on the basis of disciplinary belonging. Those stories blame poststructuralist "theory play" for the decline of activism in the feminist academy: "(disciplinary) social science rigour and certainty is contrasted to [and pitted against] (interdisciplinary) humanities fluidity and openness" (85). In this thinking, poststructuralism becomes a catch-all to describe postmodernist, poststructuralist, or deconstructivist critique, methods, and theories. For stories of loss, queer theory is a significant part of an "elitist" cultural turn and incompatible with the kind of social science feminism these stories hope to reinstall in the present.

Western feminist stories of return seek to reconcile the other two strands of storytelling. In their conciliatory approach, they admit losses but also seek to continue a celebratory, positive stance to regain what has been lost. Thus, the subject position of a return narrative can be taken up by theorists previously signed up for progress or loss narratives, if they renounce what is presented as an already "unwanted critical and political burden": poststructuralism (106). As a compromise, they find poststructuralism to have offered relevant insights, like the abandonment of essentialism, but, in a nod to loss stories, argue it may now be time for more sturdy social-science approaches in light of continued gendered inequality worldwide.

Both the method with which Hemmings traces the manifestations of the three different stories as well as one of her proposed practices to intervene in their formations—to tell them differently—depend on citation. She calls these two different citation tactics de-authorization and recitation. By emphasizing citation, Hemmings follows in proven feminist practices of taking stock: counting names in indexes of publications, syllabi, conference programs ("congrats, you have an all-male panel!"), or faculty lists to make arguments for the inclusion of women.[5]

As explained above, by withholding author names, de-authorization avoids the singling out of individual authors as embodiments of larger trends. This allows Hemmings to respectfully accentuate academic practices without pointing fingers. I was reminded of Michael Z. Newman and Elana Levine's *Legitimating Television: Media Convergence and Cultural Status* (2011). Newman and Levine highlight gender- and class-based value judgments in US-American television studies, yet do so by discussing the work of individual colleagues whom they find complicit in those legitimating discourses. By focusing on specific academics, their examples run the risk of drawing attention away from the institutional dynamics so rightfully criticized. De-authorization may in this case serve as a productive kind of plagiarism.

Some of *Stories*'s reviewers found this "unique,"[6] but others felt it was bordering on the "unethical or ungenerous."[7] Hemmings expresses understanding for such concerns since "feminist theorists' contributions are too often sidelined in social theory already" (236). Her risky maneuver (and that of her publisher Duke University Press, since this book is as much the result of a collective practice as the articles it analyzes) serves as an important lesson in the dangers of peer-reviewed academic writing. Hemmings highlights how academic writing is shaped by "technologies of the presumed" and "politics of the rehearsed": "these resonances across and between narratives situate us as feminist subjects in ways we are not fully in control of" (19, 20, 134).

---

5   In the words of Sara Ahmed, "I am referring to all those who travel under the sign women. No feminism worthy of its name would use the sexist idea 'women born women' to create the edges of feminist community, to render trans women into 'not women,' or 'not born women,' or into men."*Living a Feminist Life* (Durham: Duke University Press, 2017), 14.

6   Ilya Parkins, "Affecting Feminist Subjects, Rewriting Feminist Theory," review of *Why Stories Matter*, by Clare Hemmings, *Cultural Theory* 2, no. 2 (2011): 30–34, here 31.

7   Deborah M. Withers, review of *Why Stories Matter*, by Clare Hemmings, *European Journal of Women's Studies* 19, no. 2 (2012): 253–256, here 254.

Her proposed method to tell stories differently also utilizes the "surprising—if a little cheeky—experiment" of "recitation."[8] Recitation is inspired by practices of feminist and postcolonial rewriting of literary "classics" and canonized works because in both instances "the potent absences or half-presences in the original text become central in their rewriting" (181). Birgit Spengler argues that such rewritten fictions "direct their readers to a mode of reception that will acknowledge the text's deliberate association with a literary predecessor and take it into account."[9] Not to be mistaken with mere substitution, recitation becomes a method to reorganize and repack the feminist cabinet in a reflexive and reflecting manner. In her demonstration, Hemmings recites Judith Butler by replacing their intellectual alignment with Michel Foucault with the rarely acknowledged influence of Monique Wittig. Through the seemingly simple act of replacing Foucault's name with that of Wittig, Hemmings changes the meaning of select quotations and reinterprets the stories they contribute to. Her intervention disrupts Western feminist stories that hold feminism and postmodernism apart, draws out the influence of lesbian materialism in Butler's work, and troubles the division between feminist theory and queer theory. In response to a critique for focusing on an academic "star,"[10] Hemmings argues that is precisely Butler's exceptional role in Western feminist storytelling, as either the heroine or villain equated with poststructuralism and/or queer theory, that lends itself to telling stories differently (176).

For this "repetition with a twist" to work, Hemmings centralizes her attachments: "I am, once again, not a neutral observer of these histories and citation practices, but someone who has vested interest in challenging them, and these investments are brought to the text rather than only being produced in the moment of reading" (178). Some reviewers found recitation to be a limited practice specifically because it requires prior textual attachments as well as an awareness of the way those attachments are erased in stories. "What if," Deborah Withers wonders, "the readers of a text have no experience

---

8   Michelle Meagher, review of *Why Stories Matter*, by Clare Hemmings, *Women's Studies* 41, no. 5 (2012): 601–604, here 603.

9   Birgit Spengler, *Literary Spinoffs: Rewriting the Classics—Re-Imagining the Community* (Frankfurt: Campus, 2015), 13.

10   Rachel Torr, "What's Wrong with Aspiring to Find Out What Has Really Happened in Academic Feminism's Recent Past? Response to Clare Hemmings' 'Telling Feminist Stories,'" *Feminist Theory* 8, no. 1 (2007): 59–67.

of dissonance that forces them to rewrite or reconsider the dominant critical narratives in the first place? The answer, one suspects, is simply that the dominant modes of critical storytelling remain intact."[11] Carla Lam similarly concludes that "whether one agrees they [recited stories] would, ipso facto, be better epistemologies and ontologies ultimately depends on one's affective attachments."[12] Such criticisms miss how Hemmings's newly recited story neither seeks to replace a previous story nor claims to be a "correct" version that definitively settles the score.

Instead, the impulse that *Stories* offers feminist theory (or feminist scholarship generally) is to embrace the partiality of storytelling without aspiring to represent wholeness. It aims to generate productive discomforts and ambiguity. It urges scholars to not only reflect on one's own textual attachments but to begin theory-building from precisely these attachments whichever form they take. Hypothetically, if a reader felt she could not notice erasures in feminist stories, her textual insecurity may serve as a productive point to recite (in Hemmings's sense) their accessibility. Hemmings does not propose a method that would be available only to the most confident and well-read feminist theorists but conversely one that may make feminist theory more accessible. It increases the things we can do with theory and the ways in which we can engage with the writing of others. It is central that this call to redesign and rethink feminist theory comes from someone so expertly versed in the landscape of Western feminist theory. It recalls a related intervention in literary theory by Rita Felski, another eloquent theorist who suggests a reevaluation of the craft she so impressively masters, the revision of a field she is well established in.[13]

(Un)Folding Feminisms

One of Hemmings's favorite words to describe the interventions she proposes is striking in this regard. Frequently she describes how her approach "folds"

---

11   Withers, review, 255.
12   Carla Lam, "Know(ing) the Difference: Onto-epistemology and the Story of Feminism," review of *Why Stories Matter*, by Clare Hemmings, *Hypatia* 30, no. 2 (May 2015): 486–493, here 489.
13   On Felski, see the contribution by Jesse Ramírez in this volume.

... textual and political absences in the stories we already participate in ... back into narrative in order to reconfigure the political grammars of Western feminism. (27)
... the hauntings of Western feminist stories that matter to me ... back into the textual heart of narratives of progress, loss, and return. (165)
... what haunts these stories back into them, making visible what is, importantly, *already there*. (180)

Gilles Deleuze has written extensively about the fold as a philosophical-theoretical concept to think about a world compressed and shaped in multiple visible and invisible pockets. The borders between folds, their differences and sameness, interested Deleuze who finds folding to create a labyrinth-like structure hidden away and always only partially revealed:

Always a fold within the fold, like a cavern within the cavern. The unit of matter, the smallest element of the labyrinth, is the fold, not the point, which is never a part, but only an extremity of the line. That is why the parts of matter are masses or aggregates, as corollary to the compressive elastic force. The unfold is thus not the opposite of the fold, but follows one fold until the next.[14]

There is much here that can be applied to Hemmings's reworking of familiar stories through practices of folding. Hemmings folds "hauntings" into stories, ghostly presences or vectors that hover, that seek entrance, and that the attentive storyteller becomes aware of. The recited story is just another version of feminist storytelling—never the last call but only a more detailed loop in the labyrinth of folds. Deleuze, like Hemmings, prioritizes the process of (un)folding as a productive yet endless activity. However, to recite Hemmings through Deleuze would create the kind of "heterocitation" that Hemmings is rightfully weary of, so instead let's consider more commonplace, everyday uses of folding as they are more coherent with the housework of cabinet inventory I am interested in.

The OED defines the act of folding as follows: "To arrange (a piece of cloth, a surface, etc.), so that one portion lies reversed over or alongside another; to double or bend over upon itself. ... Often contextually implying repeated action of this kind. to fold up: to close or bring into a more compact form by

---

14   Gilles Deleuze, "The Fold," *Yale French Studies* 80, Baroque Topographies: Literature/History/Philosophy (1991): 227–247, here 231.

repeated folding."[15] Many things can be folded: clothing, books, furniture, or appliances are unfolded to be used and folded to be stored for various reasons, among them utility, convenience, preparedness, or aesthetics. The much-quoted advice that "If they don't give you a seat at the table, bring a folding chair," attributed to Shirley Chisholm, the first African American woman elected to the US Congress and first presidential candidate of color, reminds us that the preparedness and utility of the folded appliance have feminist potentials for independence and self-reliance. To unfold is to allow for greater complexity and more consumption of space. Bodies or body parts fold and unfold during exercise demonstrating flexibility and endurance. When Hemmings folds absences back into narratives, she makes these feminist stories less palatable, less convenient, possibly less aesthetically pleasing, and also less flexible to be utilized for non-feminist purposes.

In a podcast interview, Hemmings expressed the hope that her work "opens up for the reader and the writer a possibility of multiplicity in what has happened in feminist thinking that makes it much harder to coopt multiplicity because cooptation tends to require a very seamless narrative that can be taken over by a different political discourse."[16] While *Stories* is an important lesson about feminist knowledge production, it also makes an urgent case for why feminist stories "matter" in regard to their amenability for non-feminist, and even antifeminist, or postfeminist purposes. Feminist stories lend themselves to "a broad range of accounts of gendered meaning in a contemporary global sphere" (156). Commercial dynamics are part of these institutionalized gendered meanings, as well, even though the extreme commercialization and commodification of feminism were not as pronounced yet when Hemmings published her book.

Rescuing Feminism from its Desire for Heroines

In *Stories*, Hemmings finds the trope of the death or demise of feminism to accommodate a kind of quest for the feminist subject; her desire to rescue feminism serves as the driving force of her storytelling. In recent years, however,

---

15   *OED Online*, s.v. "fold, v.1," accessed March 31, 2020, https://www.oed.com/view/Entry/7 2479?rskey=Sejlcw&result= 5&isAdvanced=false#eid.

16   "Interview with Clare Hemmings," interview by Yasmin Gunaratnam, *Case Stories*, 2013, audio, 6:05-6:28, http://www.case-stories.org/clare-hemmingsnew-page.

feminism(s) in popular culture have changed from paradoxical postfeminist iterations in *Sex and the City* (HBO, 1998-2004) or *Bridget Jones's Diary* (2001) toward the more celebratory stance and increasingly commercialized appropriation of feminist images and rhetoric within "marketplace feminism."[17] These days, pop stars like Beyoncé refer to themselves as feminist—most prominently at the 2014 MTV Video Music Awards. Designer Christian Dior sells a $710 T-shirt telling us that "We Should All Be Feminists" with budget versions available from H&M and Forever21; "political" femvertising seeks to "empower" female self-acceptance. We have moved far from times in which popular culture did not present feminism as fashionable, young, and aspirational, but as passé: the unspeakable f-word that only clichéd figures like "feminist killjoys," angry "feminazis," "hysterical" or lesbian man-haters would use.[18] The problem with the seemingly "evolved," recent messages, as Sarah Banet-Weiser puts it, is that the politically sounding statements reduce feminism to the surface and the individual. As a result, even when "spectacular, media-friendly expressions such as celebrity feminism and corporate feminism achieve more visibility ... it often stops there, as if *seeing* or purchasing feminism is the same thing as changing patriarchal structures."[19] Popular feminisms amount to mere proclamations of identity ("this is what a feminist looks like"), as if proclamations are enough to change systemic inequalities.

It would be easy to spin new feminist stories out of this trajectory: a feminist story of progress, of popular culture bringing students into our seminar rooms eager to learn feminist scholarship; a feminist story of loss, of a postfeminist marketplace that profits off of and depoliticizes feminist work; and a feminist story of return, because both previous versions sound true. Hemmings's work demonstrates how claims to feminism as an accessory for self-expression and self-fashioning are not opposed to feminist theory-building. Just like in the commercial co-optation of feminism, in feminist storytelling, there is an extended emphasis on the storyteller as the subject of her stories. Even if her quest or mission may have changed (feminism does not require much redemption these days), its stories are imagined as stories of femi-

---

17   Andi Zeisler, *We Were Feminists Once: From Riot Grrrl to Covergirl, the Buying and the Selling of a Political Movement* (New York: Public Affairs, 2016), xiii.

18   On "feminist killjoys," see Sara Ahmed, *Living a Feminist Life*, 37–42.

19   Sarah Banet-Weiser, *Empowered: Popular Feminism and Popular Misogyny* (Durham: Duke University Press, 2018), 4.

nist subjectivity that easily lend themselves to the commercial exploitation through consumer culture.

Feminist storytelling is driven by "a desire to be the heroine not the anti-heroine of feminist theory" (80), a heroine absolved of all doubts about her story which are instead cast onto the enemy it proposes to blame for the demise of feminism. "The right to be the heroine," Hemmings writes "is one of the main prizes fought over within Western feminist narratives," in contests or battles over being the "real feminist theorist" (191, 80). Narratologist Gérard Genette described the narrator who appears as the protagonist of her own story as "autodiegetic."[20] Western feminist storytelling (or most writing in and about theory) tends to privilege modes of autodiegetic writing and asks readers to share in this perspective on the storyworld. Whether readers identify with one particular feminist story over another depends on their ability to identify with the feminist subject produced by the story: her successes, frustrations, realizations, and hopes for the future. "Unsurprisingly, we usually prefer the tales that present us in a favorable light over those that do not" (80). This "favorable light" involves shedding all "taints" of privilege and casting ourselves as the underdog a reader should root for. Again, Hemmings's self-reflexive consideration of her involvement in the stories demonstrates their "affective pull": "These narrative appeals draw me in and spin me round, sometimes spit me out" (136; 63).

To give an example of the ways that casting oneself as an underdog occurs in the cultural repertoire of the moment, there appeared to be a ubiquitous desire to shed the taint of privilege(s) in the year 2020. Cultural critic Lauren Michele Jackson calls this tendency "a kind of verbal tic of the pandemic, an oral asterisk assuring others of our consideration and responsibility—very unlike *those* heedless people over there."[21] Like other intellectuals of color, Jackson describes experiencing an inconsiderate kind of "unchecked privilege-checking" engaged by everyone from celebrities to "acquaintances and estranged friends, family members and hookups," all of whom "came out of the woodwork, confessing a privilege that they hoped to be comforted for. One began to realize that for some people there must be ecstasy in saying,

---

20   Gérard Genette, *Narrative Discourse: An Essay in Method* (Ithaca: Cornell University Press, 1980), 244–45.

21   Lauren Michele Jackson, "Kim Kardashian and the Year of Unchecked Privilege-Checking," *The New Yorker*, December 23, 2020, www.newyorker.com/culture/2020-in-review/kim-kardashian-and-the-year-of-unchecked-privilege-checking.

over and over, for whomever would receive it, 'I am ... ,' 'I am ... ,' 'I have ...,' 'I have ...' ... It did not occur to many people in 2020 that unbosoming can be worse than silence."[22] That is because the person casting themselves in this autodiegetic mode is completely unaware or inconsiderate of the pain, discomfort, or plain inconvenience that their "confessions" and desire for absolution cause in the person they are speaking to—and whose absolution for their privilege they seek. Jackson's analysis demonstrates the popularity of wokeness in the current moment, and how it is used in such "confessions" to enact exactly what Hemmings criticizes as a problematic kind of storytelling with the goal of ridding oneself of guilt and presenting oneself as morally good, a worthy protagonist of the story.

But although these iterations might be new, reflective of a different moment in history, their baseline position is not. The literary and cultural figure of the female storyteller is well established; it ranges from fairy tale narrators—Scheherazade of the Middle Eastern folk tale collection *One Thousand and One Nights* who saves her life through cliffhangers in her captivating stories—to the female trickster figures explored by Lori Landay.[23] These cultural archetypes have long been attractive to feminist audiences and may be unconsciously mobilized in the stories feminist theory tells about itself and the types of engagements its stories offer. Storytelling has always been relevant to pedagogy and (political) education, and it seems little surprising that theory and other genres of academic writing also utilize its tropes.

The Death of the Feminist Author?

But if this subject status is also a problem, how does Hemmings propose we proceed? Does the feminist theorist have to (symbolically) die in her writing, thus replaying the much-proclaimed death of the author? The feminist theorist-cum-subject may not have to die but she will have to move to the sidelines to tell stories that do not exclusively depend on her subject status and quests to rescue feminism.[24] Hemmings here takes her cue from Gayatri Spivak who

---

22   Jackson, "Kim Kardashian." (first four ellipses in original)

23   Lori Landay, *Madcaps, Screwballs, and Con Women: The Female Trickster in American Culture* (Philadelphia: University of Pennsylvania Press, 1998).

24   On the role of first-person narrative in sociology and cultural studies, see the essay by Alexander Starre in this volume.

challenges Western feminism's insistence on itself as a subject in a relationship with a postcolonial subaltern to which only it can extend subject status. The solution is neither to propose a new feminist subject nor to do away with subjectivity altogether but to move from autodiegetic storytelling to storytelling from a homodiegetic narrative position, in which the theorist is not at the center but a minor character. Hemmings suggests that the transformation of the relation between the feminist subject and object allows for "other histories and *intersubjective* relationships that are less routine or overdetermined" (196).

Following from Hemmings's observations on older types of feminist storytelling, we need to be careful to not merely rephrase our stories and present ourselves as the new feminist heroes out to save feminism from either capitalist commodification or teenage Instagrammers posing in feminist H&M t-shirts with copies of Butler's *Gender Trouble* (1990).[25] The neoliberal capitalist market did not merely grab our passion and our work—feminist stories—and we cannot be the innocent victims on a revenge quest to redeem feminism. The responsibility to "save" feminism, be it from its demise through the "wrong" feminist subjects or postfeminist capitalist forces, is too much for an individual subject to shoulder: such constructions overstate "the difference a feminist subject position will necessarily make to how narratives work, and … [allow] a feminist eye to be deflected from the politics at work in her own invested construction," Hemmings concludes. Ultimately this produces "epistemological and political dead ends" (136–137).

The realization that "she may not be the subject of history at all" will spark different textual engagements and affects for the writers and readers of feminist history and theory (214). To tell narratives differently, the Western feminist storyteller will have to give up her position as the exclusive subject, regardless of how uncomfortable and even horrific the new dimensions of her familiar stories will become. In media and film studies, work on shock, horror and the abject, as well as in postcolonial responses to this scholarship, Hemmings finds productive concepts to express these consequences and describe her desire for a feminist future with "some unpredictability" (226). Both of Hemmings's methods to make feminist theory less amenable to co-optation—de-authorization, recitation, and the encouragement of uncomfortable

---

25   Granted, young Instagrammers (and especially female-identifying ones) get dunked on enough as it is. Yet, this adds to my point, that such social media users and their self-fashioning cannot serve as an enemy for feminist theory and feminist activism.

alternative textual affects—serve to disorient readers. Hemmings imagines feminist storytelling and feminist theory as uncertain and undecided. Hers is a plea to allow oneself to become unsettled, to unlearn the landscape of feminist theory, to give up the safety and security that certainty offers.

Through Hemmings's interest in affect and feminist knowledge production, her work intersects with that of fellow feminist thinkers like Lauren Berlant and Sara Ahmed.[26] To recite Hemmings with Berlant, Western feminist stories stem from their narrator's desire for a kind of "feminist good life" in which the demise of feminism is prevented, the feminist heroine becomes united with the reader of her text, and their shared feminist efforts are recognized. Each of these stories sets up its own antagonists as obstacles for why this feminist good life has not manifested yet and constitutes a future to aspire toward. Hemmings in a way suggests that we need to reflect upon the desire for this good life as a fiction that does political work in the present.

Similarly, in *Living a Feminist Life* (2017), Ahmed argues for an understanding of feminist theory as "homework," an encompassing activity not reduced to the academy or the classroom, but a continuous work of building: "we need to resist positioning feminist theory as simply or only a tool, in the sense of something that can be used in theory, only then to be put down or put away. It should not be possible to do feminist theory without being a feminist, which requires an active and ongoing commitment to live one's life in a feminist way."[27] Like Hemmings, Ahmed encourages feminists to embrace the multiplicity of one's engagements and experiences shaped by feminism and shaping feminism: "What's my feminist story? Like you, I have many."[28] Hence, the cabinet that we may sort through with Hemmings will become even messier: this is a feminist politics of ambivalence that is interested in "the entanglement of the space of the present encounter (imagined or real) as the space of [home]work, rather than the space that must be cleaned up in order for judgments to occur" (226). Our awareness of the amenability of feminist stories is something we have to assume to be part of these stories, something we cannot neatly tease out and separate.

---

26   See contributions by Frank Kelleter and Samuel Zipp in this volume. Ahmed's work is an ideal candidate for future installments of this publication.

27   Sara Ahmed, *Living a Feminist Life*, 14.

28   Sara Ahmed, 30.

Ambivalent Futures

Hemmings's follow-up book to *Stories* was eagerly awaited by feminist readers such as myself, curious to find out how she would do feminist theory after the interventions of her earlier work. *Considering Emma Goldman* (2018) continues Hemmings's interests in displaced subjectivity, the uncertainty of feminist theory and history, recitation, and affective attachments. In this book, it is not solely the desire to be the feminist subject but also the desire for the feminist icon (which resonates with the celebrity feminist or the feminist spokesperson) that sparks her interest. Hemmings walks this tightrope with patience for herself and the feminist stories she tells about/with Goldman as well as her own complicated relationship with the controversial figure. Again, Hemmings folds ambivalence back into the stories she explores, for example with regard to Goldman's racism, instead of following the desire to neatly repackage Goldman for a feminist present. Not to make one's limitations and affects something to be overcome, but instead to turn them into the foundation of theory-writing: this is what Hemmings encourages by example. Her feminist politics of ambivalence are demonstrated in her affective engagements with Goldman: "She speaks back in the ways that those represented have a habit of doing: in her resistance that I feel in my belly, in the ways words or images will not bend to my interpretation, in the fervency of her own writing that seeps into mine, so that at times I feel more like a fraudulent medium than a queer feminist theorist."[29]

In her response to a critic of her earlier writing, Hemmings has similarly described how she struggles not to rely on established academic mechanisms. Defending an alternate story of feminist theory is hard when also dealing with criticisms of her work that rely on the grand narratives that her books precisely critiques. To defend herself in this manner would result in an unproductive deadlock for her: "And so we face one another, in irritation and in mockery, under- and over-reading both, imagining each other. Was that what I wanted?"[30] As both of the above quotations demonstrate, the critical persona Hemmings takes up in her work is no confident heroine but characterized by self-reflexivity, aware of her desires in writing theory, and interested in where these desires stem from rather than giving in to their pressures. This is a

---

29   Clare Hemmings, *Considering Emma Goldman* (Durham: Duke University Press, 2018), 25–26.

30   Clare Hemmings, "What is a Feminist Theorist," 70.

patient persona which is understanding and almost gentle with her textual needs and those of critics, colleagues, readers, or others.

The surprisingly compatible combination of intellectual curiosity and gentleness (of which de-authorization is but one example) is an inspiring perspective well worth imitating as a writing practice. Hemmings's embrace of discomfort and ambivalence, as well as her understanding of theory as storytelling, is fundamental for current feminist theory and cultural theory. This is especially true in the context of the neoliberal university and its increased pressures on productivity and "marketability" of scholarship. The kind of theory Hemmings proposes (and produces) asks us to sort through seemingly tidy cabinets and fold back things that are hidden. The overflowing boxes of the cabinet quickly become impossible to close. Feminist theory sprawls out of them, leaks into our lives in messy ways that inspire us, but also exhaust and challenge us. This is a rich scenario for cultural theory and feminist theory in the twenty-first century.

9. Affect, the Popular, and Vogues of Feeling in Pop Culture (Studies)
On Robyn Warhol's *Having a Good Cry* (2003)

Katja Kanzler

I sit on my couch, after a long day, and use my computer to watch an episode of *Clean House* before going to bed.[1] It is not the first episode of this show that I watch. I am well familiar with this and other formats in the genre: makeover shows that are about the cleaning and decluttering of messy homes. My habit of watching makeover shows is not something I talk about much. I do not enjoy talking about my viewing experience of this genre as I do with other TV shows, which I often love to discuss with others, further intensifying the pleasure I take in watching these shows. Not so with *Clean House*. I do not want to revisit my viewing pleasure in this show by talking about it; I do not want to bond over it with others. I really do not enjoy writing about it right now.

Clearly, what makes me come back to *Clean House* has nothing to do with its narrative. The show's storytelling is minimal and utterly predictable: a team of experts come to a messy house, they find out why it is messy (usually because of some unacknowledged emotional issues on the part of its inhabitants), they fix this cause of the messiness, clean the house, and that's the happy end. What makes me come back to such shows are the equally formulaic images of messiness that they showcase—usually mediated by camera work with lots of lingering shots, sometimes featuring ominous music, always accompanied by responses of the expert-characters who hyperbolically enact the visceral responses I observe in myself (albeit in more subdued

---

1   *Clean House*, presented by Niecy Nash and Tempest Bledsoe (Style Network, 2003–2011).

and self-conscious fashion): widely opened eyes of excitement, various formations of sneering that perform contempt or disgust. *Clean House* works for
me—in ways that *Hoarders*[2], for example, does not—because it showcases just
the right amount of messiness: not too much; not a pathological messiness
that could make me self-conscious about my own act of staring, exploding
the tacit rationalizations that allow me to tolerate my staring. The messiness
in *Hoarders* makes me feel compassion—a double compassion—for the people
living in such environments: one for the medical and social conditions that
contribute to their living situations, and an additional one for being exploited
by the television show (tied, of course, to feelings of guilt on my part). When
watching *Clean House*, I do not usually feel compassion for the contestants:
the show's narrative tells me that they are fine, they just cannot get their act
together for reasons that can be easily fixed. Their messiness is baroque and
impressive, for sure, but it is still a "regular" messiness, like the one in my own
home (which appears more orderly in comparison, making me feel smugly organized). So I feel licensed to sneer, to maybe even shake my head a little, to
enjoy a feeling of distance between me and the contestants who cannot get
their act together.

The preceding paragraphs are inspired by the preface that opens Robyn
Warhol's *Having a Good Cry: Effeminate Feelings and Pop-Culture Forms*: a set of
six testimonials in which readers talk about "what their bodies do when they
are reading" popular genres, the final vignette being by Warhol herself and in
the first person (ix).[3] The materials they discuss are quite different from the
TV format I address; also the viewing experiences are different, less shameful
than mine. Yet Warhol shares a shameful viewing experience later in the book.
Warhol uses these testimonials in the preface to scaffold her book's inquiry
into what it feels like to read popular narratives—setting the stage for the
book's thematic focus on structures of feeling in popular culture, along with
a somatic approach to such feelings, and for a method that combines body-
conscious self-observation with both narratological analysis and an inquiry
into the gender politics of popular culture.

Robyn Warhol is best known for her groundbreaking work in feminist
narratology. *Having a Good Cry* certainly contributes to this line of her work.

---

2   *Hoarders*, produced by Dave Severson et al. (A&E Networks, 2009–present).

3   All parenthetical citations in the text refer to Robyn Warhol, *Having a Good Cry: Effeminate Feelings and Pop-Culture Forms* (Columbus: Ohio State University Press, 2003).

However, in the following, I want to approach the book as the groundbreaking contribution to affect theory and popular culture studies that it also is. Warhol's study is a vanguard work in the much belabored "affective turn" that has been sweeping the humanities since the turn of the millennium, written at a time when the formation of affect studies as a recognizable school of inquiry was still very much under way. *Having a Good Cry* participated in these emerging conversations in ways that deserve more attention and that continue to be stimulating as the new millennium progresses, especially for someone who, like me, is interested in the structures of feeling that govern commercial popular culture. I thus want to read the book as an affect-attuned intervention in popular culture studies. In a reading that seeks to be receptive to the resonances and associations that *Having a Good Cry* evokes for me, I am interested in where and how it intervenes in scholarly conversations about affect and/in popular culture. Taking my cue from Warhol's emphatic and self-observant use of the first-person pronoun, I am also interested in where and how the book speaks to the affective dimensions of cultural inquiry. Finally, I am interested in using the book's impulses to think about structures of feeling in US popular culture at the time I am writing this, the end of the twenty-first century's second decade: are tears still such a central element in the matrix of popular affects? What other elements are coming to the fore, and what would it mean to think about them from the vantage point of Warhol's book? For this final question, I will come back to the uncomfortable viewing experience I just sketched.

A recent handbook article on "Affect and Narratology" is one of the few pieces I am aware of that acknowledges *Having a Good Cry*'s contribution to affect studies. Within it, Claudia Breger frames the book as a pioneering intervention that "forcefully connected narrative theory to the emerging paradigm of affect studies."[4] Breger notes how the book ventures beyond the psychoanalytic approaches that used to channel much of the engagement with affect in literary, cultural, and media studies, instead taking conceptual cues from Eve Kosofsky Sedgwick and Silvan Tomkins who would become major theoretical touchstones in what Patricia Clough, a few years later, labels the "affective

---

4   Claudia Breger, "Affect and Narratology," in *The Palgrave Handbook of Affect Studies and Textual Criticism*, ed. Donald R. Wehrs and Thomas Blake (London: Palgrave Macmillan, 2017), 237.

turn."[5] In vanguard fashion, Warhol focuses her attention on the body as the medium of feelings, approaching its somatic states as practices that performatively generate what we call emotions or feelings, rather than as expressions of feelings that exist prior to some bodily reflection. This move allows her to collapse the distinction between "real" and "fake" feelings that regularly animates the dismissal of popular culture's emotional effects. According to Warhol, the titular "good cry" that is ritually indulged in when one watches a soap opera is as "real" as any other instance of tears. Precisely because the emotional effects of popular culture tend to be tied to formulaic textual structures and to ritualistic media practices, they are of particular cultural import. Warhol describes popular narratives as key "technologies of affect" that "mark readers' bodies" (7) with somatic effects whose signatures accumulate over time: "Figuratively speaking, those patterns mold the body's plasticity, leaving the marks and shapes characteristic of the feelings their genres typically bring up" (8). As technologies of affect, popular narratives thus "work through readers' bodily feelings to produce and reproduce the physical fact of bourgeois subjectivity" (8). It is particularly the gendered dimension of this subjectivity which interests Warhol and which she explores in a set of affective configurations (sentimentalism, the marriage plot, seriality, soap operas).

In unfolding this argument, Warhol emphatically includes her own embodied self among the subjects molded by popular feelings: from her testimonial in the book's preface to the many moments when she addresses her own affects and feelings, making a point in using them as a resource for her inquiry, she carves for herself the textual persona of a "feeling scholar." This positioning is a key move for her book's project in popular culture studies, in ways I will address in a moment. Yet it also impacts the book's contribution to an emerging affect studies paradigm: taking on the long shadow of the New Criticism's "affective fallacy," this positioning speaks to affect studies' core argument about the interdependency (rather than antagonism) of cognition and feeling, highlighting the epistemic productivity of feelings in and through the book's own critical practice. Warhol's writing is naturally selective in the structures of feeling she self-reflexively explores, setting clear priorities, but I feel invited to appreciate criticism as a practice in which cognition and feeling intertwine beyond these instances of explicit self-reflection

---

5   Patricia Ticinento Clough and Jean Halley, eds., *The Affective Turn: Theorizing the Social* (Durham: Duke University Press, 2007).

to the more tacit, or more tacitly addressed, affective structures in her book and to the knowledge work that they mobilize (or immobilize).

In this spirit, I note, for example, how Warhol evokes a blend of intellectual frustrations and desires when outlining the motivation for her project. One of the frustrations she articulates concerns the slow and inconsistent de-essentializing of feminist studies which, despite mantras to the opposite, still often conceptualizes gender as tied to binarily sexed bodies. Even if not fleshed out in bold emotive colors, this frustration fuels one of the key conceptual moves of the book: to forgo the terms "feminine" and "masculine" for the denotation of gendered structures of feeling and to introduce an alternative terminology of "effeminate," "non-effeminate," and "antieffeminate" feelings. To me, this is one of the most interesting moves of the book, not primarily because it opens up a space to think gender independent of binary sex categories, but because it lays bare the affective signatures of disdain that are "stuck" onto several expressions of the feminine, to use Sara Ahmed's conceptual figure of "sticky feelings,"[6] and how this "sticking" affects the conceptual registers we have at our disposal as cultural critics. The pejorative coloration of "effeminate" connects the word with other ideas or phenomena that are dominantly conceptualized as associated with women and/or metaphorically feminized—ideas and phenomena that concern Warhol throughout her book, such as "sentimentalism" or, even more broadly, "popular culture." Arguably, Warhol's professed goal to "rehabilitat[e] effeminacy from the pejorative status it currently holds" (10) did not materialize in the book's aftermath, but I find exactly this failure productive: it highlights just how firmly the registers of disdain stick to some signifiers of the feminine and feminized, in ways that reach well into cultural inquiry. Perhaps what could be instructive here are the feminist efforts to recode sentimentalism from pejoratively framed beacon of cultural worthlessness to complex phenomenon very much worthy of sustained attention—efforts that started several decades ago with publications like Jane Tompkins's *Sensational Designs*:[7] Critical concepts come with their own structures of feeling, and while our scholarly conversations routinely shift the ideas that are attached to concepts, it takes more time and work to change how people feel about them. Feelings are stickier than ideas, also in academia.

---

6   Sara Ahmed, *The Cultural Politics of Emotion* (New York: Routledge, 2004), 89–92.
7   Jane Tompkins, *Sensational Designs: The Cultural Work of American Fiction, 1790–1860* (New York: Oxford University Press, 1986).

While the invocation of intellectual frustrations and desires marks an affective structure that Warhol's book probably shares with many pieces of cultural inquiry, there is one common structure that the book makes a point in complicating: the aloof distancing of the critic from the phenomena and subjects they critique, a scholarly self-fashioning whose distinct "passions and pleasures" Rita Felski so poignantly discussed.[8] Warhol's writing actively works on reducing the distance between herself as critic and the implied and actual readers of the popular narratives she examines, conspicuously including herself in this readership, in ways she makes explicit as a conceptual move in her chapter on soap operas: "soap opera scholars have commonly referred to the viewers of daytime serials as 'them'" (105), she notes, "construct[ing] the perspective of longtime viewers of soap opera as 'other' ... in opposition to the scholarly perspective that centers each study" (106). To counter this othering, Warhol calls on "feminist scholars to begin 'speaking of soap operas' still more frankly in the first person" (107).

In articulating this call, she invokes other feminist scholars of popular culture. Of course, such programmatic self-positionings of the critic as part of a social group of women have been a key move of feminist standpoint epistemology. Yet such self-positionings also are a distinct signature in popular culture studies, where Henry Jenkins has arguably been the most vocal proponent of the positionality of an "aca-fan," i.e., an academic who also identifies as a fan and who embraces these two entry points into cultural materials as mutually enriching. Jenkins describes this positionality in *Textual Poachers*, without using the term "aca-fan" yet, as he reminisces in the introduction to book's twentieth-anniversary edition.[9] Later, Jenkins prominently deployed the term to label his influential blog, "Confessions of an Aca-Fan," and he has continued to reflect on and practice this reading position throughout his publications.

Jenkins's self-positioning as an aca-fan and Warhol's programmatic gesture of discussing soap operas in the first person resonate with each other in interesting ways. A good way to trace the commonalities and differences in how the two operate their reading positions is to put Warhol's book in conversation with Jenkins's *The Wow Climax*, a book that shares with Warhol's an interest in the affective dimensions of popular culture, while proceeding

---

8   Rita Felski, *The Limits of Critique* (Chicago: University of Chicago Press, 2015), 10.
9   Henry Jenkins, *Textual Poachers: Television Fans and Participatory Culture*, updated ed., (New York: Routledge, 2013), viii.

from different conceptual vantage points and engaging with different cultural materials: Jenkins comes from a background in media-cultural studies rather than feminist narratology.[10] For example, his book is primarily interested in the Vaudeville tradition and its legacies in popular culture, it explores spectacle more than narrative, and it pays particular attention to the affective work of moments when popular materials violate the formulas that underwrite them. Like Warhol, Jenkins regularly uses his own affective responses as a resource for critical inquiry, pairing them with metacritical reflections that emphasize the surplus knowledge that becomes available when popular culture is engaged from up close rather than from a distance: "These aspects of popular culture are difficult to understand from a stance of contemplative distance. To understand how popular culture works on our emotions, we have to pull it close, get intimate with it, let it work its magic on us, and then write about our own engagement."[11] Such a position of closeness not only provides Jenkins with empirical data that he can use, in autobiographical fashion, for his cultural analysis. Such closeness also allows the fan-literate scholar to fully understand the cultural dynamics of popular materials, including the ways in which they theorize themselves.[12] Jenkins's chief horizon for his self-positioning in this book thus is an intervention in the methodology of popular culture studies. In the spirit of the figure of the aca-fan, he highlights how he understands his role as cultural critic as one of mediating between the epistemological regimes of vernacular and academic cultures, moving back and forth between the immersion and distance they respectively require.

Warhol operates her critical position using a similar movement back and forth, but she describes it in different ways and ultimately develops it to make a powerful argument about gendered structures of feeling. Warhol discusses this back and forth in her reading of the blockbuster movie *Pretty Woman*, where her concern is not an exploration of sentimentalism, as in the chapter on soap operas, but the structures of feeling that are tied to the conventional marriage plot. Warhol frames her reading of the film, from the start, as full of "discomforts" (64) that she describes in terms of an oscillation between

---

10   Henry Jenkins, *The Wow Climax: Tracing the Emotional Impact of Popular Culture* (New York: New York University Press, 2007).

11   Jenkins, *Wow*, 10.

12   Jenkins, 3–11. For an extended discussion of pop-cultural practices of self-observation, see Frank Kelleter, "Five Ways of Looking at Popular Seriality," in *Media of Serial Narrative*, ed. Frank Kelleter (Columbus: Ohio State University Press, 2017), 16–18, 22–26.

excitement and shame: "If, as a feminist reader, I feel shame in getting excited about marriage plots, *Pretty Woman* brings me to the point of humiliation" (64). With great attention to detail, Warhol tracks the somatic responses that perform shame and excitement in her practice of reading the movie, and the specific dimensions of the film that trigger them:

> The accelerated pulse and pleasure of the interest and enjoyment alternate with the mild nausea of shame, depending whether I'm attending to the text's overt narrative or to my almost compulsively experienced ideological critique, both of the text and of my enjoyment. ... [I]nterest and enjoyment mark my face when I am responding to the intradiegetic level of the action, the exchanges among the characters; to the extent that I can participate at the extradiegetic level as a member of the film's intended audience, I feel the widening up and out of my lips, the absorbed track-look-listen signifying excitement. But at a metadiegetic level that opens up when I adopt the perverse strategy of self-conscious, self-consciously feminist close reading, my eyes lower, my head is down, shame sets in (67).

Warhol goes on to discuss, by way of example, a set of moments in the movie that induce this mixture of excitement and shame for her. In doing so, she makes a point in highlighting the productivity of both feelings, those of pleasure and those of discomfort. More precisely, she highlights the productivity of their interplay, when it is engaged on a metaconscious level which she describes as that of "the perverse lover of marriage plots, the self-consciously feminist close reader" (69). This oscillation between excitement and shame, she argues, constitutes a uniquely gendered—"effeminate"—structure of feeling fueled by popular culture, "inscrib[ed] on the faces of effeminate viewers of 'chick flicks,' again and again, every time devotees of this genre read another marriage plot" (69). Reflecting on these structures of feeling, which only becomes possible when the critic owns and embraces them through a "body-conscious reading strategy" (70), provides a unique access point for critiquing these very structures, as she demonstrates in her reading of *Pretty Woman*. Not a position of aloof critical distance, but a closeness that is willing and agile enough to observe itself fuels the kind of critique that she outlines—a critique both of the gender politics of commercial popular culture and of the feelings that structure gendered existence. Elsewhere in the book, when Warhol discusses sentimental narratives, she carves out a similar reading position that oscillates between closeness and self-observation. There, she does not so much tie it to discussions of critical method, but much more broadly to reflections that go into the direction of a public pedagogy:

> As for the effeminate readers who love "having a good cry," I envision a community empowered by a relationship to sentimental texts that is both visceral and self-aware, fully conscious of how strategies "get us," and free to enjoy the physical act of crying. If we can dispel this sense of embarrassment and isolation associated with textually induced tears, our potential for participating in the transformation of culture and society will be that much more powerful. (57)

These remarks about embarrassment at "textually induced" affect, about the oscillation between excitement and shame bring me back to my testimonial from this essay's beginning—although I want to note that my sense of embarrassment and shame is different from the ones described by Warhol, because I observed myself responding to a TV show's invitation to look down on its characters. I want to conclude this essay by bringing some of the thoughts triggered by my reading of Warhol's book to bear on the experience I sketched in this testimonial—an embodied reading experience like the ones that fuel Warhol's analysis, yet one that is embedded in a pop-cultural ecosystem that has considerably changed in the seventeen years since the publication of *Having a Good Cry*. *As the World Turns*, the soap opera that takes center stage in one of the book's chapters, came to an end in 2010, after a run of 43 years.[13] This cancellation is part of a larger pattern that sees especially the daytime soap opera in decline, replaced by other formats that bring their own affective signatures to US popular culture. *As the World Turns* was replaced by a talk show (*The Talk*, currently in its tenth season).[14] Additionally, reality TV has become increasingly dominant in the field of daytime entertainment and beyond—though this dominance might already be on the decline, too (the Style Network that aired *Clean House*, for example, was discontinued in 2017). The "good cry" that inspired the title of Warhol's book still plays a significant role in these formats and genres—within the genre of reality TV, for example, the *Queer Eye* reboot has brought "good cry"-techniques to a new level of mastery.[15] But more and other structures of feeling have come to prominence in recent popular culture, and my personal viewing experience of *Clean*

---

13   *As the World Turns*, created by Irna Phillips (CBS, 1956–2010).

14   *The Talk*, created by Sara Gilbert (CBS, 2010–present).

15   *Queer Eye*, created by David Collins (Netflix, 2018–present).

House might offer a platform for thinking about them. When approaching this viewing experience as a historically situated instance of a body-conscious engagement of popular culture, which structures of feeling are particularly noteworthy?

One structure I find noteworthy is the guilty pleasure that resonates throughout my testimonial: the way in which I am self-censoring about the pleasure I take in watching *Clean House*, how I strive to keep it secret, hesitate to own it and feel vaguely nauseous when I do by writing about it; how I develop rationalizations for why staring and sneering are not so bad in watching this—as compared to other—shows. "Guilty pleasure" has, of course, become a canonized trope in recent popular culture practices, a trope that makes it possible to simultaneously own and disown types of pleasure that, for whatever reason, seem illicit. I find it stimulating to think about "guilty pleasure" against the backdrop of Warhol's remarks about the "alternation of excitement and shame" she discerns in "effeminate emotional experience" (65). On the one hand, experiences of guilty pleasure echo the oscillation between reading positions that Warhol outlines: an oscillation between a responsiveness to the appeal that pop-cultural materials extend to their intended audiences, and a self-conscious critique of this appeal (and one's own response), possibly due to its politics, possibly due to other reasons. In this sense, the formation of guilty pleasure into a ready-made trope could be seen as signaling a new cultural recognition and awareness of the "perverse" reading positions into which popular culture invites (some of) its consumers, especially those who identify as feminist or along other non- or anti-hegemonic lines. This trope could be seen as an instance of popular culture observing itself, theorizing itself, and, through the vernacular circulation of this theorizing, providing participants in the culture with better tools to productively navigate the contradictory affective structures in which commercial popular culture places them.[16]

Conversely, this might not be how the trope works, at least not in many instances of its use. When the sociologists Charles McCoy and Roscoe Scarborough conducted a set of interviews with television viewers who used the discourse of guilty pleasure, they found that the trope was primarily employed as a coping mechanism: viewers used it to deal with the "normative contradiction" they experienced when consuming TV content that they "know" to be "bad": "while they have created or embraced a symbolic boundary between

---

16   On self-observation in popular culture, see Kelleter, "Five Ways," 18.

'good' and 'bad' television, they find themselves transgressing that boundary by consuming and, in some cases, enjoying the shows they condemn."[17] In such constellations of use, then, the discourse of guilty pleasure serves to soothe precisely the discomfort that Warhol frames as productive in her reading of *Pretty Woman*. As a ready-made and recognizable trope, guilty pleasure calms the nausea that attends sensations of shame, translating them into a talking point that no longer has to be physically felt. It allows readers to take themselves out of the equation, to withdraw to a position of jaded superawareness, in which affective states and feelings tend to be citational performances rather than bodily realities—the opposite of a "body-conscious reading strategy."

A second affective structure I find noteworthy when I look at my viewing experience of *Clean House* is how it revolves around feelings of distance and disapproval: I caught myself enjoying how the show made me disidentify with the characters, how it encouraged me to judge them, providing me with plenty of narrative details to sanction my judgmental stance (in the particular episode I watched, the husband of the family was so negatively drawn, so nasty to his wife *and* responsible for most of the mess in the house that I gladly looked down on him). I enjoyed when the experts in the diegesis verbalized my visceral disapproval, because I thought the man deserved it. In fact, my knowledge of the genre's formula assured me that such sneering and chastising would do the man good: it would catalyze his and his home's makeover into better versions of themselves. So the distance I felt was only temporary, a phase in the progression of the episode whose second half veers into sentimentalism (where we are told that the man suffers from separation anxiety because he lost a sibling and that this anxiety governs his behavior, where we see him commit to working through it, to being nicer to his wife, etc.). The later acts of the episode's dramaturgy asked me to feel with and for the man, but what sticks with me are the earlier moments where the episode took me through the moves of looking down on him.

Sentimentalism's structures of feeling are quite dominant in the forms of effeminate culture that Warhol's book discusses. These structures, to a significant extent, revolve around affective attunement. *Clean House* and several other formats of recent US popular culture are, at least partly, designed to generate seemingly opposite structures of feeling, structures that build on

---

17   Charles Allan McCoy and Roscoe C. Scarborough, "Watching 'Bad' Television: Ironic Consumption, Camp, and Guilty Pleasure," *Poetics* 47 (2014): 41–59, here 41.

affective distance and dissociation, on disdain rather than affection. With regard to *Clean House*, it could be argued that moments of affective distance serve as a mere prelude to the attunement that marks each episode's narrative closure; that they are merely one move in an intricate choreography that modulates the implied viewer's affective proximity to the characters in the diegesis. Yet even there, these moments stand out: they are tied to spectacular images of domestic disorder that work independent of the episodes' narratives of transformation and their carefully delayed sentimentalism—spectacles that Jayne Raisborough aptly describes as "clutter porn."[18] They are additionally tied to resourceful and creative performances of disapproval by the expert-characters, performances in which verbal and non-verbal invective intertwine, and which unfold an appeal of their own that, too, is independent of their narrative embedding.

One could furthermore argue that these moments of affective distancing work to intensify the show's delayed sentimentalism, expanding the emotional space that viewers are called upon to travel as each episode asks them to feel compassion for characters they had initially been positioned to dismiss and dislike. Or it could be argued that moments of affective distancing only facilitate the show's sentimentalism—a facilitating that might have become necessary in a pop-cultural ecosystem affected by the long-lasting contempt for sentimentalism in the broader culture. Maybe the emotional dramaturgy of makeover shows exemplifies how, at least in this segment of contemporary popular culture, sentimentalism's strong emotions of affection need to be balanced by strong emotions of a different sort, emotions of disaffection; how materials that showcase the sentimental "good cry" now require some dose of "invective relief" that provokes sensations of disdain capable of offsetting sentimentalism's calls to empathy.

Yet it is also possible to approach these processes from a reverse perspective, asking how the show's sentimentalism might serve its moments of affective distancing. The sentimental wrap-up that the makeover show's conventions provide for could be read as legitimizing the performances of distance and dislike in which such shows indulge. Sentimental closures can provide such legitimization by giving performances of depreciation a goal and a purpose, claiming that they serve as catalysts in the personal transformation of allegedly suffering contestants. Such strategies of self-legitimization

---

18   Jayne Raisborough, *Lifestyle Media and the Formation of the Self* (London: Palgrave Macmillan, 2011), 66.

are not a new phenomenon in commercial popular culture. They recall, for example, twentieth-century exploitation films and their forerunners in nine-teenth-century exposé novels, which sought to authorize their graphic depictions of sex and violence by claiming to serve an educational purpose.[19] My clandestinely enjoyed makeover shows might similarly build their appeal on the promise of scenes that transgress the boundaries of what is deemed socially and medially acceptable—compared to the exploitation genre, the rather mild transgression of incivility, both enacted in the diegesis and encouraged in the sneering target viewer; and they might similarly seek to legitimize this transgressiveness by framing it as instrumental in projects of reform.

The kind of transgressiveness that makeover shows feature seems to enjoy a particular currency at the present moment. It has been observed in various contexts, described in various grades of emotional intensity, and conceptualized by way of various paradigms—from Berry and Sobieraj's "new incivility" to Higgins et al.'s "belligerent broadcasting."[20] The latter is particularly instructive in the context of my viewing experience of *Clean House*: Michael Higgins and his colleagues use this term to describe a distinctly "hot" version of conspicuous incivility they observe on US and UK television. They note:

> in a variety of genres, ... there has been a move in recent years to stage in-creasingly aggressive, and sometimes violent, forms of verbal confrontation. These genres range from talk shows which specialize in "confrontainment" ... through instances of "lifestyle" and "reality" TV, to adversarial forms of ac-countability interviewing.... The verbal confrontations that occur here often include forms of language not previously (or very exceptionally) heard in public discourse such as swearing and direct, unmitigated insults.[21]

While the "belligerence" they describe is certainly more aggressive than the moments of performative disdain in *Clean House*, I would insist that these

---

19   See Eric Schaefer, *Bold! Daring! Shocking! True!: A History of Exploitation Films, 1919–1959* (Durham: Duke University Press, 1999).

20   Jeffrey M. Berry and Sarah Sovieraj, *The Outrage Industry: Political Opinion Media and the New Incivility* (Oxford University Press, 2014); Michael Higgins et al., "Belligerent Broadcasting and Makeover Television: Professional Incivility in *Ramsay's Kitchen Night-mares*," *International Journal of Cultural Studies* 15, no. 5 (2012): 501–518. Especially in the context of political entertainment, and in response to the eroding boundary between entertainment and politics in the wake of the Trump presidency, there have been nu-merous discussions of conspicuous incivility in media culture.

21   Higgins et al., 502.

are related—that they are different points on a spectrum of symbolic abuse. Robyn Warhol's *Having a Good Cry* offers valuable impulses for thinking through the structures of feeling that pervade the contemporary popular culture of symbolic abuse. It encourages us to look closely at the somatic effects that this culture's materials elicit in their readers and viewers and at how these affective structures shape the ideas that people take out of their engagement with the materials. It encourages us to examine the popular formulas that inscribe such affective structures on the bodies of readers and viewers, fortifying these structures through the repetitions that are built into them. It encourages us to ask how the affective structures of the materials mold the social bodies of their readers and viewers, their sense of social self. It encourages us to explore the signatures of gender and other categories of social identification in these structures of feeling. It encourages us to come close, to not rest on a position of enlightened disdain for this culture, to take seriously the feelings that people feel when they engage with it. And it encourages us to reflect on our own affective investments and entanglements when critiquing the popular culture of symbolic abuse—to reflect on, that is, the structures of feeling that pervade our scholarly practice, in which distance and disdain have signatures of their own.

Cruel Optimism

Every theory has its season. Spring: actor network something. Phenomenology is for the liberal summer. Marxism: true fall. Winter: hang on, it's coming.

the hegemony you break may be your own
@fkelleter

lauren berlant has died. can this be true? last month i did the final proofs of an essay on cruel optimism when someone told me berlant now uses they/them. i couldn't confirm this online so i asked lauren. here is what they replied. it was the nicest mail. i'm heartbroken.

Tweet übersetzen

Von:	Lauren Berlant <l957@uchicago.edu>
Datum:	Do, Mai 6, 2021 17:04
An:	"Frank Kelleter"
Optionen:	Alle Kopfzeilen anzeigen | Druckversion zeigen | Dies als Datei herunterladen Adressbuch hinzufügen

Dear Frank,
It's true that I use they/them but when I wrote Cruel Op I was all girl and it's fine to use she/her. Thank you for engaging the book!
All best, Lauren

Lauren Berlant
George M. Pullman
Distinguished Service Professor

3:42 nachm. · 28. Juni 2021 · Twitter Web App

ıll Tweet-Aktivität anzeigen

84 Retweets   **13** Zitierte Tweets   **835** „Gefällt mir"-Angaben

10. Style under Stress
Quotability and Disaster in Lauren Berlant's *Cruel Optimism* (2011)

Frank Kelleter

1.

How does it feel to write about a crisis so large that it calls into question the very possibility of critical writing? This question does not currently stand at the center of humanist discourse, but it seems to have animated some of the most innovative work done in this field since the turn of the millennium. "Those of us who think for a living" (124)—as Lauren Berlant characterizes herself and her readers—tend to live for thought, which is another way of saying that they ("we"?) are often among the first who get to name a crisis.[1] After all, this is what intellectuals do in market societies; this is the function they have evolved to serve: institutions of higher learning pay good money to an entire class of people for reading and writing (and flying to conferences), because these activities promise to render intelligible the collectivity and historicity of processes that might otherwise appear as mere accidents of social

1   All parenthetical citations in the text refer to Lauren Berlant, *Cruel Optimism* (Durham: Duke University Press, 2011). I would like to thank my readers Maxi Albrecht, Dustin Breitenwischer, Emmy Fu, Anja Johannsen, Till Kadritzke, Christian Klöckner, Susanne Krugmann, Fabius Mayland, Anthony Obst, Tabea Vohmann, and Stephan Porombka. I am especially grateful to Annelot Prins, Simon Strick, and Maria Sulimma; their suggestions and objections have greatly contributed to my understanding of Lauren Berlant. On Lauren Berlant's pronouns, see tweet on facing page and the "Entry" chapter in this volume. Research for this essay has been supported by the Deutsche Forschungsgemeinschaft (DFG, German Research Foundation) under Germany's Excellence Strategy in the context of the Cluster of Excellence *Temporal Communities: Doing Literature in a Global Perspective*—EXC 2020—Project ID 390608380.

life. In the humanities, intellection makes political sense of subjective experience. Traveling under the sign of "theory," this work often retains core traits of its forerunners, theology and philosophy—revelation, exegesis, scholasticism—but its rhetoric is essentially one of public analysis, sometimes in the organized mode of systemic critique, sometimes in the more managerial form of criticism, surveying never-ending publications and arranging them into constellations of order.

But what about the feelings involved? How does it *affect* critical writing when the crisis at hand is no singular catastrophe, no repressed trauma that could be cured or alleviated by disclosure, but a banal everyday reality? And what if the shape of our daily calamities remains unrecognized not because they are hidden away from inspection but because they are utterly commonplace, taken for granted like the air we breathe? These questions drive Lauren Berlant's *Cruel Optimism*, an eminently quotable book. In fact, *Cruel Optimism* may be one of the most frequently quoted books of Anglophone theory after 2011. In it, Berlant describes life under neoliberalism as a psycho-political disaster zone. While more or less avoiding the term "neoliberalism"—for reasons worth looking into—Berlant is in effect talking about a world ruled by transnational market extremism, a world in which "[c]ollective infrastructures are collapsing all over the United States and the globe" (154).

According to *Cruel Optimism*, the psychological and environmental costs of this situation are immense. The fact that they are nevertheless accepted by populations and governments worldwide poses a keen challenge to theories of popular agency (or as some call it: democracy). To make sense of this predicament, Berlant asks us to consider ordinary people's attachments to ways of life that at least hold a promise of happiness even when they fail to deliver it. For many contemporaries, she writes, living a "good life" means holding on to *something* regardless of its dependability. It means establishing a sense of belonging without necessarily belonging to something sensible. It means "proximity to a *whatever, wherever*" (63).

One feels reminded of modernist justifications of religious belief that stress the psychological utility of faith over its doctrinal content. Berlant's pleas for ordinary attachments follow a similar logic but, as a feminist critic of gendered normativity, she does not think that this settles anything. Rather, Berlant maintains that what she calls "the promise of the promise" (174) can have disastrous consequences further down the road. The cruel oxymoron of "cruel optimism" expresses as much: "A relation of cruel optimism exists when something you desire is actually an obstacle to your flourishing. ... These kinds of optimistic relation ... become cruel when the object that draws your attachment actively impedes the aim that brought you to it initially" (1).

An older brand of theory would have no qualms calling such detrimental beliefs by the simple name of ideology. And indeed, what is ideology if not a collectively shared and publicly reinforced system of subjective misapprehensions? Again, Berlant agrees but feels uneasy about imposing such terms on experiential realities that she characterizes as being aware of their plight, aware of what they are going through, and yet remote from such explanatory abstractions.

Berlant's wariness of judgment is not untypical of contemporary theory. One might ask how subjectivity is even thought to manifest itself here (ontologically? expressively? culturally?) and why the ordinariness of ordinary life should depend on a type of self-knowledge that is said to be averse to conceptual detachment. (Invoking the lexicon of ontological withdrawal, *Cruel Optimism* talks about "the hesitancy and recessiveness in ordinary being" (124).) But in view of the loaded history of Marxist vanguardism, contemporary theory has good reason, especially in its feminist and queer manifestations, to concentrate on other questions, many of them focused on its own assumptions of epistemological superiority. Berlant, too, seems to be acutely conscious of her institutional position and the privileges that come with it. Like many Anglophone thinkers of the twenty-first century, she suspects academic critique to hold a demeaning attitude toward "popular pleasures" (123). Deploring "the ease with which intellectuals shit on people who hold to a dream" (ibid.)—paraphrasing a complaint made by, not about, Adorno—she feels that there might be something wrong with the language that humanities scholars bring to bear on the crisis of neoliberalism.

Repeatedly, therefore, the voice speaking in *Cruel Optimism* is on the verge of charging its own diagnostic stance with improper motives. Determined to bypass the trap of condescension, Berlant carefully avoids blaming those who are trying to make the best of a bad situation—those who do not push for structural change but muddle through, on the search for "a less-bad experience" (117). Realizing that "ordinary" people may regard the institutionalized negativity of critical discourse as a luxury and a taunt, *Cruel Optimism* is as much a book about stressed-out subjects trying to get by as it is a book about its own work of academic theorizing. It is theory struggling with its own position of observation—and Berlant, in numerous self-referential asides, lets us know that this is the case.

For a text with deep roots in feminist and queer theory, this is unsurprising. Berlant's indebtedness to feminist standpoint theory and other forms of situated knowledge is obvious.[2] Still there is something special about Berlant's interest in positionality. I want to suggest that *Cruel Optimism*, rather than recommending situated knowledge as an unambiguous antidote to false universalisms, begins to probe and question the very distinction between (objective) universalism and (subjective) situatedness. Constantly reflecting on the terms and conditions of her writing, Berlant tries to locate an appropriate style for a genre of intellection that has evidently lost belief in the transformative power of (economic, historical, psycho) analysis, while she also casts doubt on the utopian potential of alternative epistemologies of embodiment, proposing instead "to desubjectivize queerness" (18).

Berlant's book thus captures the movement of a style of thought that finds it increasingly difficult to take political confidence, or hope, from its own dedication to standpoint theory. Early on, when Berlant delineates how *Cruel Optimism* differs from her previous work and the feminist/queer theories that animated it, she stresses the need to rethink heterodox optimisms of affect, any affect, in light of the disaster of the present: "I therefore make no claims about what specific experiential modes of emotional reflexivity, if any, are especially queer, cool, resistant, revolutionary, or not" (13). The phrase "if any" reveals the depth of historical despair that this theory confronts. And then something surprising happens: "Nonetheless," Berlant writes, she wants to acknowledge her debt and continued commitment to the styles of thought that brought her to this point—and in order to summarize their commonality, in order to introduce them by name and to pay homage to their shared intellectual work, their radical necessity, she invokes—Theodor Adorno, of all people. "Nonetheless, I could have had none of these thoughts ... without a training in multiple critical theories of what Adorno calls the 'it could have been otherwise' of commitment: queer theory, psychoanalysis, deconstruction, antiracist theory, subaltern studies, and other radical ethnographic historiographies of the present (anthropological, sociological, and journalistic)" (13).

In a way, my essay is about the little surprise of this little moment, which marks both a tribute and a departure. Or, in Berlant's disillusioned translation of my clichés: a cruel optimism and an impasse. I will return to Adorno as an unlikely patron saint of Berlant's productive theoretical despair. At this point,

2   Compare, e.g., Sandra Harding, ed., *The Feminist Standpoint Theory Reader: Intellectual and Political Controversies* (New York: Routledge, 2004).

let me simply say that, to me, this counter-intuitive moment encapsulates what is intellectually most original and historically most poignant about *Cruel Optimism*, the bleakest work of theory I have read in a long time. Its utter lack of rhetorical triumphalism strikes me as uniquely adequate to the anarcho-capitalist endgame it talks about, and at the same time inseparable from the book's inner linguistic conflict, its often frustrating and self-frustrated, fully self-aware, rhetorical non-triumph.

2.

Despite all its epistemological doubts, *Cruel Optimism* commits to one particular historical conclusion, which rings painfully true indeed. Berlant insists that scenarios of misplaced hope abound in a world organized around an impossible promise, which is the promise of capitalism as the best historical option for establishing "the good life." No matter whether this elusive goal is sought in orthodox expectations of upward mobility, or in the arrival of another person who will finally bring happiness, or in the simple act of eating tasty food, any vision of "the good life"—in fact, any moment of temporary enjoyment in a time of "crisis ordinariness" (that is, crisis as a way of life, not an event)—is already entangled, in Berlant's description, with a political economy that postpones and prevents the very satisfactions it promotes.[3] In other words, what Berlant at one point refers to by its most banal postwar name, "the American Dream" (29), is shown to be exactly that: a dream, wishful but unreal, and yet enabling peculiarly American realities (within and without the United States) ranging from profound trust in monogamous notions of sexual fulfillment to the industrial provision of sweet and fatty diets.

Ten years after the publication of *Cruel Optimism*, the urgency of this diagnosis—implying that the globalized production of pleasures in the twenty-first century is bound to harm the bodies it claims to serve, and likely to destroy the habitat that sustains them—has become even more dramatic amid pandemic shock and irreversible ecological devastation. "Infrastructural stress" (43) is now a common, indeed an inescapable, condition of life on earth. In writing about this situation, however, Berlant wants to distance herself from the "melodrama" of "symptomatic reading" (15). As a student of

---

3   On "crisis ordinariness," see: "[c]risis is not exceptional to history or consciousness but a process embedded in the ordinary" (10).

American sentimentalism—her previous work includes three interconnected volumes on national ideologies of intimacy—she has a fine-tuned ear for the workings of romantic victimization narratives in modern fields of knowledge (sociology, psychology, economics, etc.). Trauma theory, in particular, comes in for nuanced critique in *Cruel Optimism* because it privileges the idea of a singular rupture over the likelihood of therapeutic feedback loops and retrospective arrangements. (For reasons that I will discuss below, Berlant stops short of a more fundamental critique of "event" ontology; her vocabulary often holds on to a language of being and becoming, contending only that there is nothing extra-ordinary or transcendental about such moments of subjective instantiation.)

My point is that Berlant's frustrations with classical theory and structural critique are stylistic as much as they are substantial. There is a palpable sense of rhetorical, perhaps even aesthetic, dissatisfaction with a specific type of academic writing. Consider her objections to the word "neoliberalism," which she characterizes as a "heuristic" that tends to personify "impersonal forces" for the sake of some larger morality play about malign perpetrators and objectified dupes (15). While this is an odd take on existing studies of neoliberalism (including the term "heuristic"), what strikes me as important is how Berlant justifies her dislike of the concept: her aim, she says, is "to avoid the closures of symptomatic reading" (15). With this refusal *to close things down*, Berlant implies that the abstract moniker "neoliberalism" does not explain much if it is invoked as a final address of critical inquiry. Such concepts of last resort serve as short-cuts, she suggests, absolving academics from doing the hard work of what Hortense Spillers has called "writing as revision"—a type of minute redescription that "makes the 'discovery' all over again."[4]

This is a fair and important argument. It is also an argument against bad usage, not against the concept of neoliberalism as such. Above all, *avoiding closure* is a stylistic ideal. Its prevalence in postclassical theory seems to arise from concerns of professional rhetoric, which in turn are grounded in theory's growing awareness of its own institutional history. Note, for instance, that methodological debates in literary and cultural studies are virtually forced to describe themselves in pioneering terms. Typically in these self-reinforcing controversies, new methods of "reading" (always conveniently labeled: distant, surface, reparative, etc.) are offered on the strength of their power of

---

4   Hortense Spillers, "Mama's Baby, Papa's Maybe: An American Grammar Book," *Diacritics* 17, no. 2 (1987): 64–81, here 69.

programmatic innovation, usually more so than on the strength of their concrete performance. Their biggest *promise*, it seems, is the promise of field-
intrinsic renewal in a situation of institutional *crisis*.

In particular, debates about "postcritique" are inextricable from their academic sites of articulation. In fact, some of the most prominent interventions
in this vein seem to be less concerned with the epistemological validity of certain critical practices than with their grating effects on professional rhetoric
in a struggling discipline. Especially among US humanities scholars, there is
at the moment a strong tendency to think (and write) about critical detachment not as a cognitive tool but as an affective attitude. While this perspective
has illuminated the gendered bias of supposedly "universalist" epistemologies—that is, their foundation in white, masculine, heterosexual, bourgeois
power, made visible with far-reaching political ripple effects by critics like Eve
Kosofsky Sedgwick or Heather Love—such historicization takes a backseat in
the more aestheticist types of postcritical scholarship when they treat critical detachment as a deeply subjective, indeed competitively personal desire
(rather than, say, an affectively charged matter of intersubjective knowledge).
Framed like this, critique appears responsible for unpleasant social situations
in which other (mostly leftist) writers strike a pose of condescending "cool-
ness."[5] In other words, certain styles of writing have come to feel irritating,

---

5   An implicit tone of personal resentment is not uncommon in these exchanges, partic-
    ularly on Twitter, that invaluable source of academic affect performance. Entire social
    media accounts seem devoted to documenting imagined charges of naiveté and an-
    noying collegial affectations. A random but typical tweet in this vein calls critique "a
    stock reflexive gesture of distancing, disavowal, & self-protection" that serves to up-
    hold "the critic's image of themselves as resistant, discriminating, immune to charm,
    'cool'." The same author says that this attitude is particularly widespread among col-
    leagues who have read too much Frankfurt School "and think that if they just sound
    depressed and contemptuous enough at all times that that will also mean that what
    they are saying about Random Object X is smart, interesting & politically salient" (19
    April 2020). Berlant, by contrast, is more careful—and more understanding of the emo-
    tional dimension of critical distancing, which she, too, describes as a gesture of protec-
    tion, but without inveighing against this stance and without reducing epistemological
    concerns to attitudes of needy posturing. But institutional anxieties run high in many
    recent attempts to cultivate positivity and affirmation as counter-affects to negativity
    and critique. — Parts of the paragraph above are adapted from Frank Kelleter, "DIS-
    CIPLINE COOL. Notes, Quotes, Tweets, and Facebook Postings on the Study of Ameri-
    can Self-Studies (LookingForward Remix)," in *Projecting American Studies: Essays on The-*

boring, or inopportune within a highly specific, highly self-referential, and highly competitive professional ecology.

This state of affairs is reflected in *Cruel Optimism*. More than just an analysis of peak capitalism, Berlant's book performs reproductive labor for a communicative network worried about its survival. "The closures of symptomatic reading" are risky in this regard as they conflict with the requirements of knowledge production in the neoliberal university—but not because symptomatic closures are too radical but because they are too predictable. This raises an infrastructural question: could the awful tedium of systemic critique be related to the tedious awfulness of systemic realities? Indeed I argue that there is more at stake in Berlant's aversion to externalized judgment than the descent of academic writing into formulaic staleness—a fate that awaits any successful method. In the case of postcritique, scholarship's search for programmatic disruption also appears to be motivated by the very forces scholarship finds it increasingly boring to critique. How else to explain all the games of epistemological one-upmanship in which theoretical vocabularies compete about who still falsely believes in "hidden" causes (despite claims to the contrary) and who already addresses "immanent" potentials or defeats (despite practices that suggest otherwise)? Not paranoia but schizophrenia—or intense nervousness at least—seems to be the hallmark of the humanities in the age of disappearing resources.

Fully aware of such institutional background noise, *Cruel Optimism* registers the indispensability of materialist, constructivist, and Marxian modes of inquiry, but struggles with their socio-political futility, their sometimes compromised relationship to queer theory, and their retrograde reputation in literary studies. Berlant does not quite put it that way—in fact, she does not even address postcritique—but her subtle theoretical self-positioning, if not the title of her book, makes me wonder if the anti-hegemonic self-positioning of current discourses of attachment (countering the supposedly ruling negativity of critical thought with something more "positive") should be taken at face value. What if the much-quoted impact of Jameson's and Althusser's Hegelianism on literary studies was much exaggerated in the initial 1990s salvos against suspicious minds and paranoid readings? What if this exaggeration served to position more deeply entrenched philosophies, with

---

ory, Method, and Practice, ed. Frank Kelleter and Alexander Starre (Heidelberg: Winter, 2018), 287–307, here 298.

even stronger commitments to profundity, such as Deleuzianism and neo-Heideggerianism, as suppressed and novel? And what if feminism, queer theory, critical race studies, disability studies, and other anti-bourgeois epistemologies were implicated in these schisms not only as radical alternatives, but always also as partisan doubles, competitively aligned with critique or post-critique, socialism or liberalism, structural analysis or ontological philosophy, etc.?[6]

Berlant's place in these discussions is remarkable because her writing is structured by such a high degree of self-awareness. This prompts her to frequently shift perspectives, sometimes experimentally so. True, large parts of *Cruel Optimism* rely on styles of thought that regard talk of "immanence" and "intensity" as new and even newly materialist. But then, Berlant always stresses the ordinariness of immanent life, rejecting any assumption of unique transcendence. This puts her in an interesting and productive position toward classical modes of social critique. While avoiding, like most of her peers, the Marxist notion of false consciousness—which in the hands of theorists such as Theodor Adorno or Sara Ahmed has never been a moral but always a structural concept—she invokes Marxism's "long tradition" of connecting the study of material production and social reproduction with "the affective components of labor-related subjectivity" (64). Like Raymond Williams, then, Berlant holds that subjective feelings are tightly interwoven with trans-subjective arrangements of collective life: "The 'structure of feeling' is a residue of common historical experience sensed but not spoken in a social formation" (65). This, she says, is "why the phrase 'political economy' must thread throughout our analysis" (37). And so it happens that contemporary affect theory, with its interest in what is felt even when it is not known, can figure in *Cruel Optimism* as "another phase in the history of ideology theory" (53).

3.

Is this a way out of Anglophone theory's current field-intrinsic anxieties? "How does one go about defetishizing negation while remaining critical?"

---

6   For a famous example within Anglophone feminism, see the 1998 debate between Nancy Fraser and Judith Butler in *New Left Critique*, with Fraser mapping various cross-combinations of such competing theoretical perspectives.

(123), Berlant asks. Her answer is that critical writing can try "to formulate, *without closing down*, the investments and incoherence of political subjectivity and subjectification in relation to the world's disheveled but predictable dynamics" (53, my emphasis). In other words, Berlant's intellectual desire is for "nonuniversal but general abstraction" (44).[7] I take this to call for a language of objective research that can generalize subjective experiences, but without over-generalizing them into the false objectivity of historical determinism. How does this work in *Cruel Optimism*?

Evidently, Berlant's chief interest is in personal practices of *adjustment*. How do "we" continue to live, she asks, how is life being "reproduced" from day to day, when any hope for transformation is already compromised by its anticipated disappointment?[8] The answer provided by *Cruel Optimism*—the book as well as the concept—is: "We" do so by "fantasies" of protective composure and intuitive relief, which Berlant finds developed and explored in various cultural "genres" that provide a repertoire of more or less self-aware, more or less self-suspecting coping "styles." Her archive thus consists of novels, films, and works of art since the 1990s, but also of the conflicted habits of "everyday life" that are registered, simulated, or formalized in these sources.

This method of searching for "patterns of adjustment" (9) in artworks comes naturally to a literary scholar, but it is not without problems. Leaving aside the vexing question of representativeness (which is important, however, if one wants to identify patterns), there is the more basic difficulty that studying stories *about* feelings—or ideas *about* objects—or images *of* embodiment—is not the same as studying feelings, objects, embodiment. This is a recurring conundrum for literary studies whenever it tries to make use of philosophical or sociological knowledge. What results from such borrowings is often circular validation: first the translation of aesthetic practices into more universal meanings (as if theory provided a dictionary to the hieroglyphics of art) and then the self-recognition of interpretation in its material or its

---

7   Berlant's phrase chiastically recalls Édouard Glissant's idea of "a nongeneralizing universal"; see Glissant, *Poetics of Relation*, trans. Betsy Wing (Ann Arbor: University of Michigan Press, [1990] 1997), 34. But where Glissant is reaching for a holistic epistemological perspective on life's endless production of difference—similar, in this regard, to Sylvia Wynter and other postcolonial theorists—Berlant is skeptical about the possibility and desirability of such an overarching view. In this, her concerns are more explicitly compositional.

8   All terms in quotation marks in this paragraph are used repeatedly throughout *Cruel Optimism*; I refrain from citing individual occurrences.

philosophical tools. Of course, this is not what Berlant is aiming at. In fact, she emphasizes that her material provides "affective *scenarios*" (9), not pure affect. But since the idea of purity is central to the brand of affect theory she quotes—where it refers to a type of ontological immanence that is said to be pre-social, pre-linguistic, pre-conceptual, etc.—Berlant's contrapuntal stress on construction, arrangement, and history makes all the difference.

Once more, *Cruel Optimism* struggles with the conflicting demands of two established styles of writing. On the one hand, Berlant's interpretations of artworks follow an old and venerable tradition of scholarship that regards literary texts (and films) as empathetic windows onto diverse human realities. It was William Empson who declared in 1973 (in a *Festschrift* for I.A. Richards): "The main purpose of reading imaginative literature is to grasp a wide variety of experience, imagining people with codes and customs very unlike our own."[9] Empson's term "experience" intersects in telling ways with Berlant's project, but so does the expression "our own," spoken here with discreet class consciousness. The relationship between literary humanism and imperial ventures of (sensual, geographic, economic) expansion is certainly a complicated one, but it is no coincidence that empathy was a standard motif in colonial romanticism. Ever since, "understanding the feelings of another" has become an indispensable feature of Western theories of fiction, especially those which focus on that most bourgeois of aesthetic figures: the domestic reader, always in the singular, alone with his or her book. For such individuals, we are told time and again, stories of foreign experiential worlds allow for self-transcendence without self-loss. In the eighteenth and nineteenth centuries, this pleasing self-description of literature takes many forms but it always also responds to the historically novel feeling of travelers, merchants, missionaries, soldiers, social upstarts, lovers, and other Western subjects to find themselves in places where they suspect they may not belong.[10] Part of this problem still echoes in *Cruel Optimism*, when Berlant discusses lower class

---

9   William Empson, "The Hammer's Ring," in *I.A. Richards: Essays in His Honor*, ed. Reuben Brower, Helen Vendler, John Hollander (Oxford: Oxford University Press, 1973), 73–84, here 75.

10   Frank Kelleter, "Koloniale Körper, blutüberströmt: Siedlungslust und Siedlungshorror in James Fenimore Coopers *The Last of the Mohicans: A Narrative of 1757* (1826)," in *race & sex: Eine Geschichte der Neuzeit: 49 Schlüsseltexte aus vier Jahrzehnten neu gelesen*, ed. Olaf Stieglitz and Jürgen Martschukat (Berlin: Neofelis, 2016), 337–344.

adjustments to infrastructural stress—using as one of her key entryways into "worker subjectivity" (189) an art-house film.

On the other hand, institutional self-awareness becomes methodical in *Cruel Optimism*. Naturally, Berlant knows that the works she enlists to access affective realities "unlike our own" (in Empson's terms) are highly fashioned artifacts, not unadulterated pieces of documentary evidence. Her response to this problem is to fold her awareness of this fact back into her interpretation, making it analytically consequential. At one point, for example, she explains how an avant-garde video project protesting the US occupation of Iraq exemplifies "the sonic aspects of ambient citizenship" (232). Immediately after this interpretation, however, she gives a pointed assessment of *The PSA Project*'s production culture, reception history, and institutional ecosystem. Suddenly deploying vocabulary reminiscent of Bourdieu (an otherwise under-quoted source despite Berlant's interest in "habit"), she concludes:

> [T]he narrative avant-gardism and polytonal dissonance of *The PSA Project* confirm the audience's cultural and emotional capital. As such ... its aim is not to make its consumers more vulnerable, as they are already in some sense socially marginal, but to provide a scene for being together in the political. ... Not challenging its audience politically, but only aesthetically, *The PSA Project* preaches to the choir. (237–238)

The rhetorical strategy here is *to do both*: deal with the artwork in a humanistic fashion, then *follow up* this more philosophical approach with a cultural analysis that regards the artwork as a social agent in its own right. Berlant initially treats what the work *shows* as a screen of illumination, only to switch perspective in a next step, focusing on what the work *does* when it shows what it shows. Thus, phenomenological "trust in the potential exemplarity of any episode" (8) is brought together with the historical politics of mediation, yet not in an integrative manner, but conjunctively and chronologically: first one, then the other. The fact that this sequence is repeated so often in *Cruel Optimism* suggests that the voice speaking here is itself attached to certain intellectual styles of composure and adjustment that carry it through this effort to make sense—until even the wide-ranging optimism of humanist reading, tracking "resonances among many scenes" (12), reveals its severely disappointing limits. Perhaps this is why the cruel part of these interpretations, the one about political economy, usually comes after the narratives and the images and the installation pieces have been translated into high concepts of the mind. And yet the voice that speaks in *Cruel Optimism* never fully crosses over into critical pattern recognition, preferring instead to bring in the economic or cultural-ecological dimensions of its analyses as separate points of view. Berlant apparently worries that anything else would amount to structural cynicism or a disavowal of subjective self-presence. "Preaching to the choir," she says at the end of her critique of *The PSA Project*, "is always undervalued" (238).

I may be excused for finding something rather American in this attitude. There is an unmistakably Emersonian tone in Berlant's appreciation of the ordinary—and more than a touch of democratic populism in her tendency to think of individual agency as a counterforce to social structure. The chapter on "obesity" is a case in point. As an almost invisible "national epidemic" (103) that condemns entire sections of the population to "slow death" (38) because they lack access to regular infrastructures of welfare (time, money, information, suitable health services, but also certain types of stores and products), obesity in the United States is an almost perfect example of "crisis ordinariness." It is a crisis in which medical plight and socio-economic discrimination overlap and reinforce each other. Like many emergencies of everyday life, this crisis is "ordinary"—that is, widely taken for granted, including by many who suffer it—precisely in the sense that it relatively rarely affects upper- and middle-class people. During the coronavirus pandemic, obesity has been an important factor in the unduly high death rate among African Americans and poor people, but reports treating it as a cause (of sorts) could hardly conceal their racist foundations.[11] In this manner, body normativity is always doubly oppressive, and not only for people classified as overweight: it subjects living bodies of all varieties to impossible images of happiness through self-mastery—and simultaneously accelerates the physical damages resulting from these fantasies through an unjust allocation of health resources.[12]

It may be noted in passing that this situation illustrates how a traditional sense of crisis, in which "crisis" is understood as a collective emergency that requires immediate action, differs from neoliberalism's "crisis ordinariness":

11   On the close interrelation between infrastructural racism and "pre-existing illnesses," see Keeanga-Yamahtta Taylor, "The Black Plague," *The New Yorker*, 16 April, 2020, https://www.newyorker.com/news/our-columnists/the-black-plague.

12   See Amy Erdman Farrell, *Fat Shame: Stigma and the Fat Body in American Culture* (New York: New York University Press, 2011); Hannele Harjunen, *Neoliberal Bodies and the Gendered Fat Body* (London: Routledge, 2017). I thank Maria Sulimma for discussing fat studies with me.

the latter is recognized as an urgent disaster only when it begins to reach parts of the population that previously considered themselves immune to it. As long as this does not happen, both liberal and conservative observers will likely culturalize the troubles of the poor and structurally disadvantaged. In many Western countries, this class of people, suffering from chronic public disinvestment in the wellbeing of their bodies, is disproportionately non-white. Thus, discussions of obesity in the US are heavily inflected by racialism and classism, framing certain eating habits as lifestyle choices particularly prevalent in Black and Brown and poor neighborhoods.

Against such invocations of personal responsibility, Berlant forcefully insists that America's obesity crisis is inextricable from "the global circulation of unhealthy commodities" (104). But then her inclination to think about subjectivity as a realm of affective existence categorically distinct from, if not opposed to, political objectification qualifies this insight in interesting ways. Again, *Cruel Optimism* offers two perspectives side by side, this time, however, explicitly disconnecting them in terms of their cognitive jurisdiction, stressing that "obesity seen as a biopolitical event *needs to be separated from* eating as a phenomenological act, and from food as a space of expressivity" (115, my emphasis).

Does it? The prompt epistemological alliance of phenomenology and expressivity in this sentence, and their joint distinction from political economy, are worth pondering. Doesn't subjectivity in this constellation begin to look a lot like an upscale name for liberal individualism? Both concepts, after all, are primed to describe personal experience as a relief from the constraints of material power. One can appreciate the counter-hegemonic impulse of this model and still remain unconvinced by its political consequences, that is, the effects of its built-in idealism in the era of post-bourgeois capitalism. Put more concretely, one can share Berlant's distaste for "scandals of the appetite" (105) that curtail, censor, or criminalize non-bourgeois practices of eating, sex, self-medication, etc.—and even more so her conviction that one cannot talk about such moral panics "without talking about the temporality of the workday, the debt cycle, and consumer practice and fantasy" (105)—and still feel unsure about the rhetorical wisdom of conceptually separating structures of consumption that invite entire classes of people to "undermine their own health one bad decision at a time" (105) from a hopeful ontology of eating, which regards food as "one of the few spaces of controllable, reliable pleasure people have" (115).

Slow death by demographic belonging is difficult to translate into a cele-
bration of cultural expressivity, even when the subjects exposed to such conditions insist on individual dignity, as they regularly will, when they fight
against fat shaming no less than *for* better living options. Like poverty itself,
obesity is no ontology. Or rather, it becomes one only by way of ideology. Otherwise the poor like to leave their situation behind, just as racialized subjects
who embrace a common experience will, in all likelihood, still want to get rid
of racism. Identity, in this sense, is inevitably a political issue—and politics,
in these circumstances, by definition identity politics, occurring strategically
within a larger struggle against social degradation and physical harm.

Berlant, I think, would not disagree. In fact, she expresses similar
thoughts with much greater eloquence. "[T]here is nothing promising,
heroic, or critical," she writes, about "the malnourishment of the poor
throughout the contemporary world" (107). But then her analysis shifts
back and forth between critiquing "the inculcation in children of a taste for
salt, sugar, and fat" (112) and endorsements of the subjective "interruption"
and "intermission" inherent in eating, no matter which food. Apparently,
the phenomenological part of the argument becomes necessary because
Cruel Optimism feels that a structural critique of bad diet, by itself, would
be imposed on real people who are, after all, making real choices. On the
one hand, this scruple reflects the mixed historical record, to put it mildly,
of Marxist vanguardism. In this respect, Berlant's cautionary tone is fully
justified. On the other hand, phenomenological rhetoric is a tricky candidate
for making such corrections, perhaps even in its politicized queer versions,
because phenomenology strongly tends to privilege ontological over socio-
historical notions of identity.[13] Identifying subjects with their perceptions
and collectivities with their experiences, this style of thought typically measures lifeworlds by the instruments of their consciousness, locking identities
into the sensations and desires instantaneously available to them. In fact, the
mere act of feeling or desiring something often attains an aura of dissidence,
or at least obstinacy, in phenomenological writing. Hence all these invocations of interruption, singularity, event, encounter, epiphany—an entire

---

13   For heterodox revisions of phenomenology that try to deal with this problem, see Gail
     Weiss, *Body Images: Embodiment as Intercorporeality* (London: Routledge, 1999); Iris Mar-
     ion Young, *On Female Body Experience: "Throwing Like a Girl" and Other Essays* (Oxford:
     Oxford University Press, 2005); Sara Ahmed, *Queer Phenomenology: Orientations, Objects,
     Others* (Durham: Duke University Press, 2006).

metaphysics of the transformative moment, which has turned modernist ontology into an attractive alternative to materialist-historical analysis after all grand political utopias of modernity have been discredited.[14] Just like the attrition of society mobilizes ideologies of community, so the recession of credible images of a worthwhile future sustains philosophies that seek fulfillment in the *kairos* of the present—or what Benjamin, in an inaugural text of this tradition, called messianic "Jetztzeit."[15]

Many intellectual topoi and habits emit from here. One is the rhetoric of immanent life with its fondness for tautology—a stylistic quirk that indicates less a failure of logic than the emphasis of devotion. "[L]ived immanence" (28), writes Berlant, means "thinking about life during lived time" (59), as if there could be any other kind of living and thinking. Of course, the point of these redundancies is to shelve any notion of disinterested truth (whether it speaks in the language of scientific objectivity or theological authority) but their rhetorical effect can advance an involuntary mysticism of its own, a mysticism of the here and now.[16] Far from replacing the religious distinction of transcendence and immanence with something more appropriate, this philosophy of life often elevates immanence to the status of a transcendent force itself, with all the soteriological implications of such a move on stylistic display, as I will argue below.[17]

---

14   Ironically, one of the most influential sources of this mode of thought, Deleuze and Guattari's *Anti-Oedipus* (1972), can be read as warning against a too-idealistic notion of desire—or a too-subjectivist one, for that matter. Fascism, one reads in *Anti-Oedipus*, has never simply been forced on populations but always also affectively chosen by them. What people desire can be their own subjection: a thought with obvious connections to the idea of cruel optimism, but like most American readers of Deleuze and Guattari, Berlant focuses on affect's improvisational creativity in this regard (influentially celebrated in Brian Massumi's crypto-pragmatist introduction to his English translation of Deleuze and Guattari's *Mille Plateaux* in 1987).

15   Walter Benjamin, "Über den Begriff der Geschichte," in *Gesammelte Schriften*, vol. 1, no. 2, ed. Rolf Tiedemann and Herman Schweppenhäuser (Frankfurt am Main: Suhrkamp, [1940] 1980), 691–704, here 701.

16   Put differently: As a *terminus technicus* in phenomenology, "lived experience" is not illogical but philosophically significant. This does not mean that its tautological structure cannot be historicized or questioned—nor that such questioning devalues political appeals to "lived experience" (first-hand familiarity) as a foundation for subaltern knowledge.

17   Incidentally, a tautological epistemology that would not require belief in the single event—or a romance of subjectivity—is provided by Luhmann's systems theory, which

Another intellectual resource for the project of "figuring out how to stay attached to life from within it" (11)—and from where else?—is the psychoanalytic notion of object choice, which, especially in its poststructuralist versions, tends to demystify the object (always suspect of fetishism) while sublimating the subjective act of choosing. For instance, when Berlant notes that obese people are often scolded for undermining their health "one bad decision at a time" (105), the word "decision" is doing more work in this description than the word "bad." For what does it even mean to say that someone "decides" to damage their body with junk food? Does such wording indicate a "paranoid style" (105) or does it describe a matter of object choice? Asked differently: if bad but tasty food is "one of the few stress relievers" (116) in struggling households, in how far does the simplicity of this simple pleasure alleviate the cruel insight that there is really nothing simple about it, dependent as it is on global systems of production and depletion? In fact, the cruelest part of all these ordinary crises may well be their active *promotion* of everyday coping and adjustment. After all, this is how corporate providers advertise junk food and other hyper-artificial wares: not as utopian harbingers of permanent well-being but precisely as the kind of individual self-interruptions that affect theory proclaims them to be: stress relievers, small indulgences, guilty pleasures, makeshift improvisations, momentary acts of recovery, temporary respites from the burden of being oneself, everyday boosts to our *resilience* (a word dutifully avoided in *Cruel Optimism* although Berlant's entire theory seems to circle around it).[18] Some of the conceptual tools that this anti-normative theory brings to bear on the subjective dimension of "crisis ordinariness"—including the idea of adjustment itself—are strangely compatible with libertarian notions of lifestyle choice. Is this because these slogans preserve some residual idea of true fulfillment or because no vision of a better life is anymore possible without them?

---

stresses the autopoietic maintenance of social worlds. It is interesting to speculate how *Cruel Optimism* might have unfolded in dialogue with this theoretical framework. Perhaps "contingency"—an important term for Luhmann and Berlant alike—would have emerged more explicitly as a central concept, but not to stress the possibility of a change that finally sets things right, but to argue that nothing is stable without enormous present effort, because it always might have evolved differently in the past. Things could be otherwise—but not as a promise of redemption.

18   *Cruel Optimism* mentions "resilience" only once, early on, as part of a sequence that covers "dignity, resilience, desire, or optimism" (16).

Perhaps neither: if *Cruel Optimism* occasionally reads like deep philosophy triggered by the simple fact that commercial products never keep their promise—that the satisfactions provided by chain stores or corny illusions like "the American Dream" leave people feeling sick—this is so, I think, because Berlant's positive theory of attachment is predisposed (for good historical reason but potentially conflicting with her wish to "desubjectivize queerness") to deal with negative choices, whether queer or not, by honoring their romance of subjective experience. And is this not exactly how cruel optimism works, according to Berlant's definition and handling of it? At this meta-theoretical level, cruel optimism means making bad choices that may be no choices at all but that theory will allow itself to call "bad" only up to a point, because one can always turn the tables and reclaim their immanent pleasure as, somehow, liberating, in spite of everything. It is as if theory is having its critical cake and eating it too. What remains unclear is why human fulfillment should even depend on *attachment to something* or some *thing* (rather than, say, nourishment of life).[19] "[W]anting to be near *x*" (25) is presented by Berlant along psychoanalytic lines as a universal given of human existence, but then she also feels the need to discuss it as a historical contingency, dependent on complicated Western ideals of happiness that are inherently entangled with capitalist ideas of "objects" and liberal-democratic notions of "choice."

4.

Why go through all these moves? Why all these quotations from competing theories, conceptual frameworks, and master thinkers, in *Cruel Optimism* and other texts of its genre, including this reading of Berlant's readings? Speaking from within this self-referential field, one might feel tempted to say that

---

19   If the question of "what will secure one's happiness" (126) is bound to be disappointed, perhaps this has less to do with the elusiveness of a suitable "what" than with the assumption that happiness is a goal to be secured—and that doing so means encountering or choosing an object "so that we can imagine that someone or something can fulfill our desire" (122). For a critique of this belief system, see Sara Ahmed, *The Promise of Happiness* (Durham: Duke University Press, 2010), a book philosophically close to Berlant's discourse. For a discussion of other intellectual and ethic traditions (that do not rely on the idea of desire as something to be fulfilled), see François Jullien, *Vital Nourishment: Departing from Happiness*, trans. Arthur Goldhammer (New York: Zone Books, 2007).

most intuitions collected under the term "cruel optimism" have already been captured by Engels's idea of false consciousness. This would seem especially true when one relied on Sara Ahmed's understanding of false consciousness, which emphasizes "that we do not have to assume that consciousness is what belongs to an individual subject." According to Ahmed, false consciousness "might be about how the social is arranged through the sharing of deceptions that precede the arrival of subjects."[20] On this view, the analysis of consumer "choices" deserves the name of critique only when it abandons the idiom of personal disapprobation and starts speaking directly to the larger situation of the people involved (or what Ahmed calls the concrete arrangement of the social in which they find themselves).

Berlant would be correct to point out that this is exactly what *Cruel Optimism* is trying to do—and that one of her foremost aims in this regard, fully compatible with her previous work on heteronormative dictates of (un)happiness, is to highlight the *un-dramatic* nature of everyday suffering and adjustment: "being treads water" (10). I have already explained why I find this project compromised by certain populisms that I have termed, perhaps polemically but not without historical reflection, "American." At the same time, these American—or should I say: deeply liberal?—impulses are aided, as so often in Anglophone academia, by some of the most esoterically difficult—and originally conservative, even illiberal—varieties of European high theory. (The seemingly simple term "being" in the quotation above is a case in point.) In fact, there is nothing ordinary about the intellectual style of this book on ordinariness.

To make sense of this, one can apply Berlant to Berlant. I have suggested that her theory—or rather, her practice of theorizing—constitutes, in itself, a genre of affective composure and intellectual adaptation. In other words, Berlant's writing style affords and performs ways of coping that resemble the politico-emotional techniques of "living on" she recognizes in her material. This aspect of *Cruel Optimism* illuminates not only Berlant's use of quotations (from literary and theoretical works) but also the high degree of quotability of her own text. Anecdotally speaking, my impression is that the presence of *Cruel Optimism* in current academic discourse—but especially in keynote lectures, conference papers, classroom discussions, etc.—hinges on a register of *momentary insight*. Arresting turns of phrase or surprising re-descriptions

---

20   Ahmed, *The Promise of Happiness*, 165.

(quite in Luhmann's sense of the term) are singled out for quotation, sometimes preceded by the words "or as Lauren Berlant calls it ...." Apparently, one of the most widely appreciated virtues of this style is how it manages to re-animate ideas that in more established idiom would risk sounding formulaic or objectifying. If there is cognitive pleasure to a book as bleak as *Cruel Optimism*, it surely has to do with all these passages of sudden clarification, all the serendipitous conceptual combinations that you cannot avoid underlining, because they give a fresh sense of intellectual urgency to some of the oldest questions and answers of critical theory.

Some might say that this is simply memification, a process of breaking down theory into affectively charged instants of explanatory brilliance, underwritten by an academic star system. And true, Berlant's own politics of quotation can feel that way, often bypassing the nitty-gritty of bottom-up research and preferring instead the more rarefied company of a few master thinkers who are represented by memorable sayings ("Life has been interrupted and, as Badiou would say, settled by an event that demands fidelity," 32) or the unavoidable reference to some theoretical master text ("an under-heralded aspect of *The Political Unconscious* was the centrality of Deleuze's and Guattari's *Anti-Oedipus* to the working through of Jameson's three interpretive horizons ...", 67).[21] But this is grossly underselling the stylistic complexity of *Cruel Optimism*. Remarkably—even surprisingly, given Berlant's interest in the ordinary—her lively innervations of cultural theory do not simply *exemplify* abstract observations with poignant case stories. Instead, her style often works the other way round, *translating* cases (mostly culled from literature) into philosophical constellations that are enlightening precisely because they evade the trap of critical blueprints. Converting and continually re-converting narrative scenarios into conceptual sequences, *Cruel Optimism* produces event-like moments of insight that nevertheless refuse to converge into a systematic account of political economy. To me, this is largely a matter of syntax. Berlant's talent for brilliant aphorisms and her fondness of serial relative clauses need to be seen in this context. Here are two typical sentences from *Cruel Optimism*:

---

21   A point rarely reflected upon is how such academic quotation practices are a matter of professional *time*. The neoliberal university is draining the humanities not only of financial resources but also temporal ones. The resulting regime of research, writing, and publishing is usually not conducive to, say, detailed literature reports.

To be in crisis is not to have the privilege of the taken-for-granted: it is to bear an extended burden of vulnerability for an undetermined duration. To be in goes-without-saying ordinariness can only be an aspiration for those whose other option is to be overmastered by the moment of the event that began at a time that only retroactively leads one to diagnosis. (62)

Declaratory sentences dominated by the verb "to be" come naturally to the ontological mind, as Adorno has pointed out.[22] As a style of writing, modernist ontology is deeply invested in *identification*, but identification not of material objects or living creatures—this would mean to apprehend the merely "ontic"—but identification as the bringing-to-language of ontological truth, that is, life itself as revealed within or underneath social reality and physical matter.[23] Granted, what Heidegger, the most influential writer in this tradition, called "Being" can be translated into many different names. But what all these translations have in common is their principled disdain for referentiality. As identifications that refuse to identify, their highest ambition is to name that which is said to exist prior to the sociality of language: affect irreducible to emotion, the event out of history, the flesh before the body, the thing that is no mere object, etc. Concepts of this kind result not so much from performative contradictions as they call something into existence: a secularized mysticism, conjuring a "deeper" materialism, transcendence grounded in immanence. Grammatically, therefore, ontological writing has always been preoccupied with the conceit of *definition*, reproducing its linguistic features while denouncing its linguistic possibility. This style keeps returning to the syntax of "x is y" like a dog returns to its vomit, because y never simply concretizes x nor does it abstract from it. Rather, the mutual identification of two abstractions, each claiming to denote supreme concreteness, performs a moment of aphoristic truth. "No 'something,' only sentences could ever be ontological," says Adorno.[24]

Berlant often writes within this tradition. In the sentences quoted above, the near-tautological sequence of "the moment of the event," emphasizing its

---

22 See Theodor W. Adorno, *Negative Dialektik* (Frankfurt am Main: Suhrkamp, [1966] 1992). In the short passage above, "to be" / "is" occurs seven times.

23 On the "ontological difference," setting Being apart from beings, see Martin Heidegger, *Sein und Zeit* (Tübingen: Max Niemeyer, [1926] 1986).

24 Adorno, *Negative Dialektik*, 131 (my translation). E.B. Ashton translates: "nothing but propositions could be ontological," in Adorno, *Negative Dialectics* (London: Routledge, 1973), 125.

own need for emphasis, demonstrates as much. But gone are existentialism's claims for a philosophy that heroically "struggles" with "the unspeakable." Instead of the "jargon of authenticity" that Adorno found in Heidegger, *Cruel Optimism* offers ontology as a worried coping strategy, always distrustful of its own charisma, but also too prized, possibly too familiar, to be given up.[25] Avoiding anything that might resemble a transcendental signifier ("Being," "Capital," "Phallus," etc.), Berlant keeps converting critical vocabularies into each other, as if all of them intuited something important about the current world but none of them could exorcise what has befallen it. Sentences dread their ending because no promise of conclusion holds up. And yet the text pushes forward, stacking relative clauses onto each other, where earlier—or more doctrinaire—theorists would have put a full stop. Definitions are paradoxically serialized (*a* is *b*, which is *c*, because all *aa* are like some *d* that resembles *e*, or as X would call it, *f*), not because the writer cannot make up her mind, but because she senses that commitment to any one philosophical lexicon might imply the impossible claim of speaking from a position outside the mess of neoliberal living. Almost resignedly, then, but with the force of a temporary eye-opener, this style keeps falling back on that most common—that least imposing—of words: "something":

> If consumption promises satisfaction in substitution and then denies it because all objects are rest stops amid the process of remaining unsatisfied that counts for being alive under capitalism, in the impasse of desire, then hoarding seems like a solution to something. (42)

An American-type pragmatism of *"whatever, wherever"* (63) guides this sentence, but its intellectual point really comes with the anticlimactic ending. As a stylistic choice, to opt for shifting re-descriptions rather than settle into analytic closure fully accords with Berlant's theoretical gambit, when she characterizes the trajectory of postwar liberalism as a movement toward normalized precarity. Accordingly, the form of the sentence just quoted (substituting the word "consumption" with a series of conceptual replacements that decline to culminate in any satisfying explanation) mirrors its content (about the failing promises of substitution). The rest stops of the market are analogous here to the rest stops of the mind reflecting on them: the work of promise and disappointment occurs both at the level of the political economy and at the

---

25   Adorno, *Jargon der Eigentlichkeit: Zur deutschen Ideologie* (Frankfurt am Main: Suhrkamp, 1964).

level of its intellection. In fact, "hoarding"—the main clause's long-delayed subject—is not a bad term for Berlant's own theory with its huge archive of promising ideas and words, such as "impasse" or "desire." Not letting go of concepts that suggest, somehow, the possibility of reliable sense-making, this style nonetheless knows itself to be engaged in a cognitive "process of remaining unsatisfied" that counts for thinking under capitalism.

The high quotability of *Cruel Optimism* has everything to do with these "rest stops" of the critical mind, the hoarded-up self-reflections of a damaged and damaging modernity. We witness explanations that do not even claim to provide solutions, only momentary relief. When quoted, they are usually reproduced as expressions rather than propositions, because what impresses about them—and what satisfies for a while—is precisely what they perform: the wealth and ingenuity of a vocabulary. At least we have *that*, Berlant seems to suggest: a treasure trove of words—*ein Wortschatz*.

At times, this highly elaborate style even approaches classical effects of beauty, or a kind of word magic that can resemble poetry. Berlant is extremely fond of alliterations and puns. Expressions such as "being possessed by coming into possession of possessions" (39) abound. And before you know it, things start to rhyme: meaning unfolds "between Home, Hymn, and Hum" (32) when "the bourgeois ... carries his propriety onto property" (33). Meanwhile "labor fuels the shift from the concrete real to the soundtrack reel" (35) and "I am not the subject of a hymn but of a hum, the thing that resonates around me, which might be heaven or bees or labor or desires or electric wires" (33). Clearly, this writing aspires to be more than prose. Insights are literally *sounded out*, "between reverie and reverence," between "resonance and reverence" (32).

The lyricism of *Cruel Optimism* is fundamental to its rhetorical project—and this in a threefold sense. *Affectively*, it marks this style as reaching for epiphanic alleviation when nothing else seems trustworthy anymore. *Intellectually*, such lyricism points, again, to Berlant's deep investment in the onto-ideological tradition, with its affinity for etymology (be it Emersonian or Heideggerian).[26] About her own "punning," for instance, Berlant says that it constitutes a "Thoreauvian method" (35). This statement half-divulges, half-asserts the transcendentalism at the heart of Berlant's philosophy of immanence. It also illustrates how carefully this rhetoric-as-poetics incorporates its own self-intellection, or critique. And it does so—the third function

---

26   Sometimes etymology even alliterates: "ambit ... is akin to ambition" (230).

of such lyricism—*performatively*, that is, without dogmatic consequences. Almost like the subjectivities described, Berlant's text keeps holding on to illusions that it knows to be illusory—and then tells us that it is doing so. In this, it recalls modernism's faith in the saving grace of self-reference (think of Wallace Stevens's "supreme fiction"), but with all modernist confidence now re-routed into a much bleaker, much more distressed understanding of what it means to "believe in a fiction, which you know to be a fiction."[27]

Another way of putting this is to say that cruel optimism's "promise of the promise" is complemented by *Cruel Optimism*'s attachment to attachment. In her choice of material, Berlant is often drawn to stories and images about something that arrives or someone "who comes up to you" (34) and changes everything. True, the romanticism of "being open to an encounter that's potentially transformative" (35) is described as what it is—cruel, perhaps even prompting cruelty when finding itself disappointed—but *optimism*, in these narratives, typically means hope for the advent of a redeeming force: that extraordinary instant "when someone allows himself to be changed by an event of being with the object" (32). Both in the heteronormative psychology of object choice and the Judeo-Christian theologies that precede it, this hope to be "changed by an encounter" (34) is hope for *salvation* whenever the moment of ontological transformation promises to put all ontic transformations to rest. "Satisfaction" in these scenarios is essentially imagined as a change that ends all change, at least for a while. Hope, therefore, is not just hope for a better tomorrow but for a tomorrow that arises as an eternal today—what Reinhart Koselleck has called the "futureless future" of nineteenth-century European *Geschichtsphilosophie*, which has found a queer(ed) home in some of the most anti-bourgeois quarters of contemporary cultural studies.[28]

---

27   Wallace Stevens: "The final belief is to believe in a fiction, which you know to be a fiction, there being nothing else. The exquisite truth is to know that it is a fiction and that you believe in it willingly"; see *Collected Poetry and Prose* (New York: Library of America, 1997), 903.

28   Reinhart Koselleck, *Futures Past: On the Semantics of Historical Time*, trans. Keith Tribe (New York: Columbia University Press, [1979] 2004), 19. — Riffing on *Cruel Optimism*'s self-positioning toward queer theory, one might say that there is something odd, if historically intriguing, about reducing the idea of optimism to the mere presence of a rhetoric of futurity. To promote change as valuable in itself, one has to ignore a large number of credible versions of it: the unlucky, tragic, catastrophic ones. Thus, skepticism toward "change we can believe in" is not necessarily a sign of conservative attach-

Historically, the real-world cruelty of this soteriological desire has always resulted from its veiled imperative to *allow* oneself to be transformed: the soft coerciveness that asks people to *open* themselves to their own becoming ("Be open to the one who comes up to you," 34). My point is that all these fantasies, which Berlant characterizes as such, are not universal but particular. This is the dilemma of their theoretical disclosure: any language of disillusion prolongs the illusion if philosophy reinforces the existential charisma of situations that are really historical contingencies. Berlant's performative self-awareness reacts to this dilemma by making a move and then questioning it. It upholds a metaphysic of "the event," but only in cruelly optimistic quotations, collapsing the singularity of salvation into everyday attachments to "anything" (35), as if the falseness of the promise could be compensated by the universalism of its ordinariness.

5.

Analysis, philosophy, and self-reflection: these theoretical registers *take turn* in Berlant's writing. They exist side by side in *Cruel Optimism*—hoarded up, one might say—but their conjunctive presence produces an overall effect, a solution to something. To no small degree, this "something" is a professional crisis. Berlant says her aim is to "resist idealizing, even implicitly, any program of better thought or reading" (124). Reminiscent of Bruno Latour's suspicion that "powerful explanations" reveal the explainer's "lust for power," this mind-set—hyper-critical to the point of postcritique—conveys rather specific anxieties of institutional practice.[29] In Berlant's words, people who write within the genre of theory ("those of us who think for a living") are "too well-positioned to characterize certain acts of virtuous thought as dramatically powerful" (124). What *Cruel Optimism* offers in place of such virtuous thought is, ultimately, virtuosa thought: an intellectual style that reassures by the very skillfulness with which it disturbs "us." One feels that there is something extraordinary about the way this text keeps integrating "us," when any criticism "we" are disposed to bring up against it has already been included within it.

---

ment to the status quo; it can also express the perceived likelihood of things getting even worse.

29   Bruno Latour, *Reassembling the Social: An Introduction to Actor-Network-Theory* (Oxford: Oxford University Press, 2005), 85.

"We"? The first person plural is of central importance in *Cruel Optimism*. "We are set up to overestimate the proper clarity and destiny of an idea's effects and appropriate affects" (124), Berlant says. But who exactly is "set up" here, who is "too well-positioned"? If Berlant's study of neoliberal life performs affective work, it does so for a distinct subset of neoliberal subjects, namely, humanities scholars, and among them especially those who are attached to modernist philosophies of immanence (phenomenology, psychoanalysis, "new" materialisms, etc.) while feeling disenchanted by the failures, or bored by the routines, or exhausted by the demands, of materialist historical research. Again there is a strong correlation between these dispositions and the Americanness—or, at least, the Westernness—of the institutional frameworks called up in *Cruel Optimism*. Accordingly, I have put the word "we" in inverted commas above: it quotes Berlant's standard quotation of the generalized subject of phenomenological inquiry, which, outside this rhetorical field, always refers to particular populations and their contingent situations—in this case, as Berlant calls it, "a U.S. world" (69).

This is not a question of which scholar carries which passport. Rather, *Cruel Optimism* does its work of elucidation and consolation, agitation and reproduction, within and for an intellectual ecosystem that consists of professionals who interface with the world largely through American or Anglophone products of entertainment and learning—who convene around the globe to exchange second-order observations of mass-produced stories and songs—who watch films in order to "teach" them (and theory "through" them)—who have learned to experience poetry as a key to life, if not always living. Like any ecosystem, this one looks like the world to those who inhabit it. But never so thoughtlessly as not to require defense or justification: Social awareness runs high in the humanities, often expressed in the everyday (and social media) genre of rhetorically acknowledging one's privilege. Berlant is both more careful and more pointed in her critique of "the devastating failure of white, middle-class American subjectivity, whether feminist or not" (155), which I take to be her way of saying liberalism. Fully conscious that she is speaking about—and from within—a special demographic, she recognizes the danger of self-awareness turning rhetorical. Some anxiety of elitism remains. Perhaps this runs in the DNA of Western intellectualism: so many philosophies trying to get beyond philosophy, but never by way of ignoring it, rarely by way of deflating it. Berlant's juxtaposition of competing idioms feels like a timely strategy of relativization in this regard. Still her tools and their deployment are, by necessity, highly situated within the catastrophe of the contemporary, i.e., no longer ratified by expressivist acknowledgments of positionality, because these, too, are dependent now on increasingly pressured infrastructures and their (counter)norms of reproduction.

This raises the question of Berlant's own object of desire and its probable turn into a precarious object of disappointment. I suggest that in its widest designation, this object—postclassical theory's impossible love interest—is "ordinary life." Granted, this romance is as old as the institutionalization of thought itself. But in its neoliberal American version, as Berlant knows and demonstrates, the age-old dream of "intellection as the guardian of the bruised and disappointed self" (145) runs up against a global history of crimes carried out in the name—and often with the help of—grand intellectual systems of historiography and macro-analysis. Pragmatism and love of the ordinary are intuitive responses to this disturbing heritage in a social environment that is marked to equal degrees by populist dread of snobbery and liberal fear of "impasses" (a thoroughly negative term in *Cruel Optimism*, as far as I can see).[30] Under such circumstances, theory's desire for immanence is essentially the desire for immanent theory: a theory that would emerge directly from life as it is lived, with the subjectivity of self-present bodies offering a political solution in itself.

Against this background, the remarkable achievement of *Cruel Optimism* is to register from within American liberalism—and rehearsing some of its favorite vocabularies, including an entire lexicon of (lifestyle) "choice"—the manifold exhaustions and misrecognitions of this style of thought. Doing so in 2011, as a US intellectual, Berlant may be forgiven for largely sidelining a form of cruelty that is even more damaging than the cruelty of liberal disappointment, if one of its consequences. Since the publication of *Cruel Optimism* ten years ago, it has become increasingly clear that adjustment to infrastructural stress includes *ressentiments* that are "cruel" in a more literal, often lethal sense of the term. The rise of neofascism—this signature development of Western societies in the twenty-first century—is difficult (though not impossible) to reconcile with populist romances of the ordinary, even in the self-

---

30   Though not in other queer theories, including receptions of Berlant that aim to rethink "impasse" as a turning point or paradoxical opening; see Käthe von Bose et al., eds., *I Is for Impasse* (Berlin: b_books, 2015). I thank Simon Strick for discussing this point with me.

conflicted and disillusioned versions that Lauren Berlant works out so skill-
fully in the third year of the Obama presidency.[31]

Is this reading a critique of *Cruel Optimism*? I hope not in the sense of
proposing a more virtuous way of theorizing. Perhaps the important question, in terms of critique, is to reconstruct and recognize what *Cruel Optimism*
is doing for its readers and its time. I have tried to trace how Berlant's attachment to liberal notions of individual agency and to transcendental philosophies of affective immanence is tested by her simultaneous recognition of the
cruelty inherent in these optimisms. The result, as far as I can see, is twofold.
On the one hand, *Cruel Optimism* tries to *complement* phenomenological and
ontological styles of thought—which Berlant mainly calls up in their already
heterodox feminist and queer adaptations—with the sometimes conflicting
but increasingly urgent observational modes of Marxian or generally materialist-historical analysis, trying to do justice both to "the labor of disappointment and the disappointment of labor" (45). On the other hand, Berlant keeps
displacing her disapproval of the more metaphysical—or vitalist—aspects of
affect theory (most obviously in her dazzling critique of trauma discourse)
into the still onto-phenomenological notions of subjectivized "interruption"
and "intuition," which arguably serve to save rather than dispel many of the
cruel deceptions encapsulated in canonized high-theoretical concepts of "being," "experience," "encounter," "immanence," "the ordinary," "life," and "the
event."[32]

As a style under stress, however, Berlant's method offers guarded
promises of its own. Maybe these are more realistic than the righteous
utopias of earlier critical genres, including many that have habitually sub-
scribed to "historical materialism." No doubt, *Cruel Optimism* is saturated
with the political worries of its time; so much in Berlant's book makes sense
right now, but who knows how attachment to *these* attachments will look

---

31   See Frank Kelleter, "Hegemoronic Vistas: The Pseudo-Gramscian Right from the Pow-
      ell Memorandum to the 'Flight 93 Election,'" in *Trump's America: Political Culture and
      National Identity*, ed. Liam Kennedy (Edinburgh: University of Edinburgh Press, 2020),
      72–106.

32   For a similar argument, see Clare Hemmings's (explicitly feminist) critique of ontolog-
      ical affect theory's celebration of "the unexpected, the singular, or indeed the quirky,
      over the generally applicable, where the latter becomes associated with the pessimism
      of social determinist perspectives, and the former with the hope of freedom from so-
      cial constraint" ("Invoking Affect: Cultural Theory and the Ontological Turn," *Cultural
      Studies* 19, no. 5 (2005): 548-567, here 550).

like during the next war, or after it. And yet such style enables a wider perspective. This reader, at least, felt that Berlant's writing resembles an intellectual mode almost archived today as obsolete: the helpfully unhelpful, inconsolable but not even nihilistic reflection on "damaged life." Approaching this term from another quarter of the politico-philosophical field than Adorno, who coined it, *Cruel Optimism* gives a darkly Marxian inflection to many contemporary phenomenologies, essentially retro-aligning "queer theory, ... antiracist theory, subaltern studies, and other radical ethnographic historiographies of the present" (13) with a project that *Minima Moralia* in 1951 defined as social theory's unavoidable return to the always slippery concept of "individual experience," precisely because "the large historical categories" of Hegelian critique "are no longer above suspicion of fraud."[33] Out of this grew *Negative Dialektik* (1967), switching critical perspective once more (and again and again), arguing for "micrological" inquiry while dismissing any transcendently immanent lingo of subjectivity. My reservations about some of Berlant's theoretical commitments aside, I cannot help but read *Cruel Optimism* as the *Negative Dialektik* of our time, Western modernity's prewar present to its postwar past. The similarities between these texts are just too numerous. They share a sense of intellectual integrity premised on extreme self-awareness. Their ethics is one of minimizing status-quo morality. In the end, philosophy is all they have.

And so, almost uniquely among literary scholars today, Berlant, even when she critiques critique, does not claim to be practicing anything other than critique. In fact, her writing is at its most compelling when it demonstrates the necessity of not agreeing to a broken world—and not because such attitude would mend much, but because in a world without it, all agreement risks becoming false agreement. What is most productive, then, or most valuable, about *Cruel Optimism*'s interest in the positivity of attachment is precisely the inherent negativity of a style that never settles for, or with, its own conclusions—a style that always counters every move it makes. It is almost dialectics. But without devastating hope for synthesis. Or as Lauren Berlant puts it:

"And one might be wrong about everything." (158)

---

33   Theodor W. Adorno, *Minima Moralia: Reflexionen aus dem beschädigten Leben* (Frankfurt am Main: Suhrkamp, [1951] 1991), 10; translation by E.F.N. Jephcott in *Minima Moralia: Reflections on a Damaged Life* (London: Verso, 2005), 17.

11. Structures of the Impasse
Notes with and athwart Lauren Berlant's
Cruel Optimism (2011)

Samuel Zipp

"These new aesthetic forms ... emerge during the 1990s to register a shift in how the older state-liberal-capitalist fantasies shape adjustments to the structural pressures of crisis and loss that are wearing out the power of the good life's traditional fantasy bribe without wearing out the need for a good life." (7)[1]

Cruel optimism? For me it's those renderings you often see these days, the bright but just this side of indistinct promotional images rolled out to shill for a new urban development project—a mixed-use warehouse conversion or food hall or "luxury loft." Looming expanses of glass and undulating wood, reclaimed facades of distressed brick or concrete, carefully intricate plaza spaces dotted here and there with rigidly strolling figures, skin-toned in multi-hues from peach to brown, signage in Futura or Helvetica—COF-FEE—bare, hanging clear-wire teardrop bulbs, swelling bio-swales: Olmsted meets Jacobs meets Jobs.

They shimmer there on the page or the screen, the promise of life remade, the city reconciled with its natural underpinnings, brought to its fullest civic and predictably diverse fulfillment. It's a kind of fever dream for our times—the developer's utopia as mirage of public life. I'm often seduced by these images anyway—longing overcoming better judgment—and sometimes by the places themselves, even when they take shape in a form that is always somehow just a tad less shimmery and just-so than they appeared in prospect. They are relentlessly pleasant, even as one cannot help but feel they are something of a swindle—"the good life's traditional fantasy bribe," Lauren Berlant might call them.

---

1   All parenthetical citations in the text refer to Lauren Berlant, *Cruel Optimism* (Durham: Duke University Press, 2011).

They are cruel for the way they appear optimistic, a trick that's still possible, even fundamental.

"Given the multi- and trans-medial platforms that make contemporary political and intuitive disarray available to more people in diverse kinds of worlds, old structuralisms of the before and after are inadequate." (69)

To hear her tell it, the persistent desire for the always just withheld good life has displaced and overwhelmed the older wish for a public life through which a carefully delineated fraction of "everyone" was to be collected, cajoled, persuaded, even forced to participate with everyone else. The new ordinary, the new everyday, is not merely one of distraction, or mediation, or alienation that might dissolve those publics even as they form up, but one in which our shared "mass sensorium" swamps wishes for collectivity with constant hopes of a good life that themselves dissolve in the face of "newly proliferating pressures to scramble for modes of living on" (8).

"What is the good life when the world that was to have been delivered by upward mobility and collective uplift that national/capitalism promised goes awry in front of one?" (69)

There's a history here: an attempt to register the affective dimensions of the political and cultural moment emergent since the 1970s—the times after what historian Jefferson Cowie calls "the great exception" of the postwar boom years. Cruel optimism is the way we experience our times of perpetual crisis: we continue to produce fantasies of the "good life," even as our longing for that good life stands in the way of ever actually achieving the justice and pleasure it promises. With "the retraction, during the last three decades, of the social democratic promise of the post-Second World War period in the United States and Europe," the "fantasy bribe" of the good life displaces the welfare state—which itself traded the possibility of structural societal transformation for relative affluence and stability based on exclusion (3).

But the good life survives on fumes now, too, promising something that it can evermore rarely deliver, a state that, as it becomes increasingly precarious and further out of reach, results in an aesthetics not of future-oriented anticipation—of "growth," to use the term that structured politics, culture, and economics during the age of the great exception, but of perpetual repetition, of unfolding stasis, of "ongoingness."

"... the present moment increasingly imposes itself on consciousness as a moment in extended crisis, with one happening piling on another..." (7)

What does ongoingness feel like?

For me it appeared in soft fits and starts, and then all at once—in what now seems like a blur of headlines and ordinary crises, the usual shocks of adult-hood and the decay that accompanies growth. Time's relentless forward inch a mere blip in retrospect.

First, there were the hesitant alarm bells, stuttering to life: the false crisis of Y2K, apocalypse forestalled, and then the odd horror of an election that felt, well, stolen: lawyers, Florida, hanging chads.

Then: all at once, some months later, sometime in the first months of 2001. It came by phone, sudden and unexpected, as these things have to: my father on the phone—something like, "it's about mom, we've just come back from the doctor, and she has a brain tumor, she'll have an operation tomorrow." Alright, his mom, my grandmother, at that point on the cusp of 95, so anything could happen. But no, it suddenly rushed over me, he meant my mother, just past sixty, and still a kind of adult abstraction for me just pulling up on thirty. She was not supposed to be near any kind of end. Six months later though that end arrived, and a new shadowy time arrived too, for me at least.

After that the shocks mounted up, slowly "piling on" with abrupt unexpected interruptions that feel now, in retrospect, like an onrushing smeary surge.

What used to feel like the big one: a bright clear New York mid-morning, late summer almost fall. A distant boom. In my head it was a sound from just outside, a block away: one of those huge unwieldy metal plates dropped suddenly from its swinging chain onto the street below. Minutes later, the swell of sirens suggested something else. With the TV on, then up on our roof looking out toward Manhattan, we watched the same "thing" everyone else did. But what was this improbable "thing" that we were watching. I'm still not sure. First one tower, then the next. No need to describe it—you all know.

The days after that return in montage: fighter jets circling in the eerie blue skies stained only by that tailing, wind-driven tan plume; Humvees and body armor at the Brooklyn Bridge crossing; flags on the highways; eyes meeting and soft nods on the subway hurtling under closed streets and shuttered stops; the smell of burned cement and people coming unexpectedly around corners; a quivering red glow south amongst the spared towers from the rail of the Manhattan Bridge bike lane. One day on the Brooklyn Heights promenade we ran into a friend for the first time since the attack: you've had a hard year, he said.

A year became a decade, and then two, it seemed, all of it montage now:

Just get it over with, a friend sighed in exasperation, let the inevitable bombing begin. Get it over with, and then we can all fulfill our predetermined roles: nationalist bloodlust, pacifist protestors, two halves of the same expected coin. But then: Tora Bora. The agreed-upon malefactor disappeared, slipped away, the greatest military on earth apparently buffaloed.

And then: the long slow idiotic roll towards catastrophe: WMDs; "shock and awe"; the rout of Baghdad; the oil ministry ringed with troops while the museum was sacked; the strange, giddy, pathetic release on the streets of Baghdad and screens everywhere, the toppling of a hollow sheet metal statue, strongman no more. "We're an empire now, and when we act, we create our own reality."

And then: life in the "reality-based community": a stack of naked prisoners, wires, a hooded man spread-eagle standing on a box. Something called waterboarding: a whole new vocabulary for imperial false innocence turned to dust. (Renewed, not so much as new, it turned out, from imperial adventures a century before, but forgotten, hidden from most of us, like so much else.)

And then: a few years later, standing in my office, finding myself screaming at the radio: reports of a whole city, just one more "reality-based community," caught beneath the storm surge, levees given way, whole families on rooftops looking up, mouthing words that must be help.

In between there were other floods, and wildfires, and mass shootings, and earthquakes, and landslides, the expected disasters, the ones that always seemed to happen elsewhere. But then: hurrying to get a train, the last one north out of Manhattan it turned out, before the floodwaters rose there, too, and the "superstorm" sent the harbor into the subway tunnels.

Somewhere in there, too, a more gradual unraveling, marked here and there by signs: great rafts of foreclosures, falling financial institutions, bailouts and no bailouts, and new jargon: credit default swaps, collateralized debt obligations, tranches. One day, on a visit to Michigan, just outside Detroit, beyond Eight Mile, just off a blurry suburban strip, a whole street of brick and siding bungalows, almost every one with a "for sale" sign—the curbside scrim of quiet, all pervasive devastation. You can measure the decade-plus since by the occupations, the chokeholds and knees on necks, the always recurring litany of names, the tear-gassed plazas and stormed capitol buildings, each a surprise that was somehow also expected.

A succession of headlines, mostly, from where I sat, so many symptoms of larger crises, traumatic for those whose lives they laid to waste, but a collective shock because we'd been unevenly spared for so long, now just so many chickens coming home to roost, as they say. Welcome to the world, white man.

"... most of what we call events are not of the scale of memorable impact but rather are episodes, that is, occasions that frame experience while not changing much of anything ..." (101)

"The vague expectations of normative optimism produce small self-interruptions as the heterotopias of sovereignty amid structural inequality, political depression, and other intimate disappointments." (49)

Each of these disturbances felt singular in the moment of their occurrence. They erupted, receded, and reverberated, and for a while they seemed to exist only for themselves—singular tragedies and catastrophes, each one ripping open all anew each time. In between something like regularity resumed, as if each shock could be contained, smoothed out by the "vague expectations of normative optimism." Perhaps it should have occurred to me that each episode of restored "sovereignty"—of even-keeled course correction—was in fact a "heterotopia"—a frantic rush to restore untroubled momentum amidst an unfolding furrow in the roiling sea. In retrospect, of course, all of them seem of a piece, or at least connected and cumulative—a series of scenes that add up to one great, splitting rupture.

"... a moment on the verge of a post-normative phase, in which fantasmatic clarities about the conditions for enduring collectivity, historical continuity, and infrastructural stability have melted away, along with predictable relations between event and affect." (225)

We might have told ourselves, though, that moments of crisis are also moments of possibility, when broken things might form up again in unexpected ways, reconfigured in shapes that combine otherwise from their normally enforced structure.

"It is a sign of how desperately overwhelming the infrastructural processes are now—from environmental to economic disparities and depletion—that localism and xenophobias are resurfacing in the political at the same time as more inclusive forms of popular imaginary emerge." (262)

But then—symptom and shock all at once: another grim election season, surely a foregone conclusion. "It's her turn," they said, a new political dynasty in the making, until it wasn't. Polling broken, conventional wisdom ruptured, the "popular imaginary" lurched hard the other way, the rupture seemingly swallowing all possibility.

Somewhere there must be a list of all the fresh outrages—or a Twitter thread more likely, constantly updating—every little always popping scandal, each one simultaneously petty and all-consuming, even as no list could capture the sheer engulfing totality of the new newsfeed life. Every moment now, if you let it, becomes like the past decade in miniature, compressed, multiplied, and constant.

All the Trump-clysms of course, but also the odd portents: the ones that arrive as absurdist horror: The Chinese government actually calls its AI-fueled surveillance system "Skynet." Here in the US, when you get a new "Real ID" driver's license, you know it's "real" because it has a yellow-outlined star in the upper right corner. When will our Elie Wiesel arrive? Our Sarah Connor?

And finally: the cruelest answer. The great closing in swept across the globe over the course of a surprised winter, a vast ravening we all knew was coming but could never admit was on its way just yet. Now there are tons stacked on the lungs of the world, pressing the stretched breath out of each frail husk, thinning out the already unraveling future. All hopes now like the dusty film of a convenience store plastic bag, second-generation downcycled to ward off the inevitable: it will end caught in a tree and blown to shreds or swept downstream to dissolve and settle, undying, in the stomachs of turtles, the gills of fish, and back again to line our own guts. Now there are retreats to already-stocked bunkers, hunkering down in the swell-calculated niche markets shaped by our own heedless patterns.

The plague will pass, of course, but not without having revealed with brutal clarity the truth on which it has preyed and lived: social distance was already the everyday algorithm of collective life. We are all in this together going it alone.

"In scenarios of cruel optimism we are forced to suspend ordinary notions of repair and flourishing to ask whether the survival scenarios we attach to those affects weren't the problem in the first place." (49)

All along, of course, has been the slow dawning of what we might call the cruelty of optimism—the stepwise, oblique, but steadily emerging unwinding of an old atmosphere of surety. Once we thought we could be sure that just making a way in the world, working and buying and spending, was part of a pact, an agreement to just keep making and buying more, to expand the stores of prosperity, to let growth eventually fill up the world with enough for all.

Somewhere along the way that began to unravel, to fray; now every act is a little wound in the flesh of the world, every thing, every box of stuff in the cupboard, is a *resource*, seemingly a frail, disappearing material in over-demand headed for depletion, or an over-processed product of some toxic assembly, one more tax on the world's tipped balance, tied eventually and inevitably, somehow, to the great procession of disasters: the glaciers sliding into the sea, the storms battering the cities, the floods and fires, the waters and mercury inching up again each year inexorably. Were we just doomed to kill ourselves and the planet, simply by the cruelty of our optimism, "in the first place"?

"... what thriving might entail amid a mounting sense of contingency ..." (11)

A conundrum: thriving is now disaster. But things continue, nonetheless:

"A situation is a state of things in which something that will perhaps matter is unfolding amid the usual activity of life." (5)

Things as we know them, Berlant tells us, always remain "a genre of unforeclosed experience" (5). They are always in this sense in emergence, as Raymond Williams might have had it, always unfolding, always in a state of "ongoingness." If nothing can quite fully cohere then neither can it be pinned down or defined, made the basis of a position or a surety, an action. Tarrying in this ongoingness, Berlant advises, means dithering in constant "impasse," while all around demands, declarations, relentless positions are pitched on the mere pulse of fleeting but relentless sensation.

And yet:

"... the energy that generates this sustaining commitment to the work of undoing a world while making one requires fantasy to motor programs of action, to distort the present on behalf of what the present can become ... [A]ny action of making a claim on the present involves bruising processes of detachment from anchors in the world, along with optimistic projections of a world that is worth our attachment to it." (263)

"Bruising processes of detachment" and "optimistic projections": The usual utopia of critical theory remains undisturbed, at the end, clung to as stubbornly as to any other status quo. Has Berlant described not just the "impasse" of the current moment, but the impasse of critical theory too?

"... cruel optimism's double bind: ... it is awkward and it is threatening to detach from what is already not working." (263)

Old habits die hard. Has Berlant described the prevailing structure of feeling afresh but prescribed the same remedy? Cruel optimism, indeed. Once it was "the popular" in its wild state, repository of pleasure and jouissance that would disrupt rationality. Then it was "affect," source of non-normative desire that would scramble the circuits of normativity. Theorized correctly, of course. Each, it's now painfully clear, theory or no, will break left or right as a matter of course. And that resurfaced "localism and xenophobia" lays claim to unruly feeling without the benefit of theory at all.

But, along the way:

"... to understand collective attachments to fundamentally stressful conventional lives, we need to think about normativity as aspirational and as an evolving and incoherent cluster of hegemonic promises about the present and future experience of social belonging that can be entered into in a number of ways, in affective transactions that take place alongside the more instrumental ones." (167)

Or:

"To see hegemony as domination and subordination is to disavow how much of dependable life relies on the sheerly optimistic formalism of attachment." (185)

What if normativity is not, or not only, "authoritarian desire," but also the "optimistic formalism of attachment"? (186)

To what extent is the wish for sociality, for attachment of all sorts always and inevitably, to some degree we can't necessarily predict, encompass, or ward off, an implicit, even unwilled plan also for normativity, even if only in its minimal form as shape or binding, the minor coercions constitutive of working to live together? Is to "tarry" with the impasse also to tarry with normativity, the expected bête noire of "theory"?

Perhaps it is folly, mere cruel optimism, to continually expect the sleek and designed spaces of contemporary social belonging—with their top-heavy wobble, carefully providing reassurance to the already assured—to deliver even the feeling of a just public life. No doubt. But has theory, too, reached its own state of cruel optimism?

How to convince those with "fundamentally stressful conventional lives" to imagine otherwise? (167) The world that once needed disruption—playful subversion, radical transgression—is now always in constant disruption, harnessed as business-class mantra or unleashed as sheer and constant threat of precarity. All bets are off, for some, left and right—and no tarrying will do. Fury has the hour and optimism results only in cruelty.

But can the road back to a just sociality keep running through disruption of the already disrupting? Somewhere along the way a new normativity will have to cohere—what new worlds can be made without the balm of some assembled form of "normative optimism?"

We are all at an impasse now.

Inter Disciplinary Anxieties

Funhouse fact: "Ghost Science" actually *is* the best translation of the German word *Geisteswissenschaft*.

12. A Connexionist Bartleby?
A Melvillean Reading of Luc Boltanski and Ève Chiapello's *The New Spirit of Capitalism* (1999/2005)

Stefanie Mueller

"I would prefer not to."

In the aftermath of the financial crisis of 2007/08, the protagonist of Herman Melville's "Bartleby, the Scrivener: A Story of Wallstreet" (1853) became an icon of the Occupy Wall Street movement. Even at the time, commentators pointed out that this made a lot of sense given that Bartleby's story is about his occupation of a lawyer's office located somewhere on Wall Street. Despite the lawyer's best efforts at removing Bartleby, a copyist who (for mysterious reasons) stops reading and writing and hence becomes unemployable, Bartleby does not budge, but continues to inhabit the lawyer's premises until the latter is forced to move. (Bartleby's "cadaverously gentlemanly *nonchalance*" proves bad for business.)[1] By choosing Bartleby as their "patron saint," Occupy Wall Street imagined a genealogy of Wall Street occupations in which Wall Street moves rather than the protestors.[2]

In addition to the motif of passive yet physical resistance (refusing to be moved), Bartleby also became an icon of symbolic resistance to the pervasive ideology of capitalism. Bartleby's famous tagline, "I would prefer not to," featured prominently, for example, on a poster that showed the silhouettes of a wheel, with a hamster standing (contemplatively) in front of it. Adopting Bartleby's indirect mode of resistance was not simply a statement of refusal

---

1   Herman Melville, "Bartleby, The Scrivener: A Story of Wall-street," *Melville's Short Novels*, ed. Dan McCall (New York: Norton, [1853] 2002), 16.

2   Nina Martyris, "A Patron Saint for Occupy Wall Street," *The New Republic*, October 15, 2011, https://newrepublic.com/article/96276/nina-martyris-ows-and-bartleby-the-sc rivener.

to return to everyday capitalist routines and one's place in the system, but it also opened—as it does in Melville's text—a space for criticism that could not be coopted or assimilated. In this sense, Bartleby became a model for Occupy Wall Street because he appeared to represent a way of criticizing the status quo that did not contribute to the ideological feedback-loop. His language of preference left nothing for capitalism to coopt or assimilate.

"[S]ay now that in a day or two you will begin to be a little reasonable:—say so, Bartleby," the lawyer implores. To which Bartleby replies: "At present, I would prefer not to be a little reasonable."[3]

Making Connections

As a scholar of US literature and culture, I read *The New Spirit of Capitalism* as part of this cultural moment in the late 2000s. While the study was first published in 1999 in France and translated into English in 2005, its significance became apparent most forcefully during the aftermath of the financial crisis and during the formation of what has been called the economic turn or, more recently, the economic humanities. One of the key insights of Luc Boltanski and Ève Chiapello's study is that the contemporary capitalist regime has emerged fortified from the attacks of the '68 movement by incorporating and adapting the social and artistic critique levelled at it. If the bureaucratic capitalism of the sixties in France had been charged with restricting liberty and authenticity, the corporate capitalism of the nineties had not just learned but benefitted from offering employees more self-organized, creative, and fulfilling labor. To stay with Melville, Bartleby's colleagues Nippers and Turkey had finally gotten what they *really* needed: flexible working hours and adjustable standing desks. At a time of economic crisis, *The New Spirit of Capitalism* offered an analysis of how the capitalist regime continued to justify and thereby maintain itself.

As their title suggests, Boltanski and Chiapello's study is indebted to Max Weber's *The Protestant Ethic and the Spirit of Capitalism* (1905), and in particular to Weber's thesis that profit-seeking and self-interest are not enough to motivate people to operate within a capitalist system but "that people need

---

3   Melville, "Bartleby," 20.

powerful moral reasons for rallying to capitalism" (9).[4] Yet, instead of Weber's religious framework, Boltanski and Chiapello make use of Albert Hirschman's secular one: the idea that Enlightenment thought justified profit-seeking "in terms of society's common good" (9). Combining Weber's and Hirschman's insights into what motivates capitalism's subjects, Boltanski and Chiapello look for contemporary capitalism's justifications both in terms of individual and general motives—and how these have changed over time. As both Weber and Hirschman suggested, capitalism cannot of itself find reasons for people to participate nor grounds for a moral justification of its system (8–9). It has to find these elsewhere.

While Boltanski and Chiapello's focus is on the spirit of capitalism that began to emerge during the 1990s, their book also includes an analysis of the second spirit (1930s to 1960s) and some brief references to the first. The first spirit is embodied in the captains of industry and a form of capitalism that is often described as proprietary and which Boltanski and Chiapello characterize as domestic and patrimonial. The sacrifices that were made to afford the rise of large industrial corporations in the late nineteenth and early twentieth centuries were justified by a "vulgar utilitarianism," they write: "a belief in progress, the future, science, technology, and the benefits of industry" (17). The crisis of legitimation from which the second spirit emerges is inaugurated by the stock market crash of 1929. No longer owned and controlled by a single individual or family, the company itself becomes the narrative center of this new ethos, with the manager as its "heroic" protagonist (18).[5] The impersonal, bureaucratic organization emerges as a model for "social justice" in the management discourse of this period because it appears to operate on

---

4   All parenthetical citations in the text refer to Luc Boltanski and Ève Chiapello, *The New Spirit of Capitalism* (London: Verso, 2005).

5   Boltanski and Chiapello write that this is also the period "of the birth of management literature" (59). While Boltanski and Chiapello consistently foreground the role of economic crises (such as in 1929) and "the emergence of the new social body of salaried managers and administrators" (59), I would argue that the fundamental shift in operative power plays a much more important role in this period, that is, the separation of ownership and control in corporations that takes place during the first decades of the twentieth century. This legal development entails a fundamental shift in the nature of corporate property and to no little extent contributes to the rise of corporate storytelling. See, for example, Roland Marchand, *Creating the Corporate Soul: The Rise of Public Relations and Corporate Imagery in American Big Business* (Berkeley: University of California Press, [1998] 2001).

objective and rational criteria: "The new system will be more just, and hence more conducive to everyone's benefit, because people in firms will be assessed according to objective criteria, and there will be an end to nepotism, favours, 'string-pulling,' 'the grapevine.' As for society as a whole, the 'rational management' proposed here, by making firms more efficient, serves economic and social progress, the two terms not being dissociated at the time" (86). In this way, the second spirit of capitalism gives meaning to the work of the French *cadres* (the management elites) until May 1968, when the social and artistic critique leveled against it requires a fundamental reorganization of corporate and ideological structures.

This is one of Boltanski and Chiapello's central tenets: that capitalism has a "surprising capacity for survival by absorbing part of the critique" directed against it (27). Critique thus works as a "motor in changes in the spirit of capitalism," which means that criticizing capitalism runs the danger of contributing to a feedback-loop (27). The key aspects of the artistic and the social critique levelled against capitalism in 1968 consisted in charges that "capitalism [is] a source of *disenchantment* and *inauthenticity*," and that it is "opposed to the freedom, autonomy and creativity of ... human beings" (37). Looking at the management literature of the 1990s, Boltanski and Chiapello find evidence that the third spirit of capitalism has successfully acculturated this critique. How else to explain, they ask, the rejection of hierarchical organization, the endorsement of flexible and creative work (or rather, "projects"), and the high priority of personal self-fulfillment in work? The protagonist of this narrative is the project manager, who has learned to live in networks, collaborating and connecting with colleagues, clients, and experts. The name that Boltanski and Chiapello give this logic of capitalism is "connexionist" (136).

While many scholars in 2008 and after may have turned to *The New Spirit of Capitalism* to better understand capitalism's "surprising capacity for survival," part of the book's relevance may stem from the fact that it is not *radically* new. In particular, the study's reference to Max Weber's work provides a familiar angle on capitalism. In *The Protestant Ethic and the Spirit of Capitalism*, Weber discusses US American life writing and advice literature, such as Benjamin Franklin's "Necessary Hints to those that Would Be Rich." In *The New Spirit of Capitalism*, Boltanski and Chiapello analyze management literature from the 1960s and 1990s, which they understand as the modern version of those earlier "works of advice and edification concerning the conduct of business (or the family economy)" (59). Overall, therefore, their book is making connections to texts that—for a long time—formed part of the canon of American Studies.

Moreover, what Boltanski and Chiapello describe as a new spirit of capitalism seemed to some like old news. After all, whereas corporate capitalism of the "connexionist" kind may have been new to France in the 1990s, in the United States it had been in the making for much longer. As one reviewer puts it, "one-third of the book is devoted to a portrait of a new capitalism that, for Americans, is hardly new. We have had our fill of baloney about project-oriented and communal workplaces, 'the creative class,' flexible production, so-called lifetime learning, [and so forth]."[6] Yet, nonetheless, a study of the kind that Boltanski and Chiapello provided for the French case was still missing for the US at the time

Because it is in a sense both new and old, *The New Spirit of Capitalism* ultimately confronts us with the question of what is new (or old) about the economic humanities that took shape in the years after the financial crisis. In itself, the combined study of literature and economics is hardly new either. As recently as the 1990s, scholars in literary and cultural studies engaged in what Martha Woodmansee and Mark Osteen called in a collection of the same name "New Economic Criticism." Scholarship that contributed to this approach included works such as Walter Benn Michaels's *The Gold Standard and the Logic of Naturalism* (1987) and Marc Shell's *Money, Language, and Thought* (1982). In a recent article for *American Literary History*, Paul Crosthwaite, Peter Knight, and Nicky Marsh have argued that, while these works have become associated largely with a focus on the homology between language and money, the "Economic Humanities" were much more heterogeneous and ultimately prescient. However, it is the "label," they argue, the conjunctive nature of "literature and economics," that has proven constraining.[7]

"I like to be stationary."

Approaching the question of what kind of research and what goals the Economic Humanities should pursue, Crosthwaite, Knight, and Marsh urge us

---

6   Wallace Katz, "Democracy and the New Capitalism," review of *The New Spirit of Capitalism*, by Luc Boltanski and Ève Chiapello, trans. Gregory Elliott, *New Labor Forum* 16, no. 2 (Spring 2007): 126–130, here 126.

7   Paul Crosthwaite, Peter Knight, and Nicky Marsh, "The Economic Humanities and the History of Financial Advice," *American Literary History* 31, no. 4 (2019): 661–686, here 664.

not to leave the field of economics to "the self-designated experts."[8] The humanities are "needed," they maintain, "to remedy the technocratic 'tunnel vision'" that had contributed so evidently to the financial crisis.[9] In this sense, the major challenge of the Economic Humanities is to "demystify" and denaturalize "the categories of economic knowledge" by historicizing them: "to consider the narratives, tropes, and foundational metaphors—as well as the institutional contexts and representational technologies—that have made particular modes of economic knowledge and discourse dominant in different historical moments."[10] Importantly, this project is not about narrowly "dissecting ... technical assumptions," but about studying "the broader historical imaginary through an anatomy of the necessary fictions underpinning economics."[11]

What are "the narratives, tropes, and foundational metaphors" that afford and shape economic knowledge? Perhaps Bartleby can help us out here. From the perspective of the new spirit of capitalism, Bartleby is obviously the epitome of the wage-laborer who has *not* "learn[ed] to live 'in a network'" (85). Boltanski and Chiapello describe the ideal habitus constructed by management literature as one that is embodied in "*creative* beings" who are "proficient at numerous tasks, constantly educating themselves, adaptable, with a capacity for self-organization and working with very different people" (76). Bartleby, of course, is none of these. What is more, Bartleby does not let himself be mobilized—neiter literally nor figuratively. Mobilization, Boltanski and Chiapello explain, is the preferred term for motivation in management discourse in the 1990s, because it suggests movement without a mover. While "'motivation' ... connotes a form of control they endeavour to reject, [managers] prefer 'mobilization,' which refers to an attempt at motivation supposedly devoid of any manipulation" (80). Nobody needs to motivate the perfect laborer, they are intrinsically mobilized. But Bartleby refuses any form of mobility, resisting both the lawyer's attempts to get him to vacate the premises and his attempts to find Bartleby a new job. "I like to be stationary," Bartleby tells his confounded employer. "But I'm not particular."[12]

8   Crosthwaite, Knight, and Marsh, "The Economic Humanities," 664.
9   Crosthwaite, Knight, and Marsh, 665.
10   Ibid.
11   Ibid.
12   Melville, "Bartleby," 30.

Taking a more historical approach, we could say that "Bartleby the Scrivener" can provide us with a literary example of the industrialist-capitalist habitus, which Boltanski and Chiapello describe as characteristic of the first spirit of capitalism. The lawyer's office and his management practices are exemplary in this way for "the essentially familiar forms of capitalism," for "patrimony," "hierarchy," and "domestic" arrangements (19). But that is not what should interest us here. What is more important is that Melville's text gives us access to some controlling metaphors of the industrialist-capitalist imagination, such as, for example, the metaphor of the wall. As many scholars, most famously Leo Marx, have pointed out, the story is about Bartleby's confinement and isolation: walls, screens, closed doors, and eventually a prison yard keep Bartleby confined and separated from his fellow human beings. These spatial metaphors build on the association between Wall Street and capitalism that was already established by the time of Melville's writing, but they go beyond metonymy. They revolve around the pivotal role of property in the antebellum economy, suggesting all kinds of containers and enclosures. In other words, they evoke a world that is (in this respect) precisely defined by stationariness and confinement.

A Connexionist Bartleby?

As critics and reviewers have suggested over the years, the value of *The New Spirit of Capitalism* rests in how it provides us with a better understanding of the development of the institutional contexts of three distinct spirits of capitalism, each the result of capitalism's ability to incorporate non-economic motives and each expressing its own logic of justification. But I want to suggest that the book's significance for the twenty-first century—its value as a key-work—derives from an aspect of Boltanski and Chiapello's study that is rarely if noticed or commented on[13]: its observations on the role of the imag-

---

13 And if critics do, they usually do so negatively: "Another possible strategy for losing weight might be to ditch the textual materials that form the basis of a 'corpus' of work from the 1960s and from the 1990s." Martin Parker, "The Seventh City," review of *The New Spirit of Capitalism*, by Luc Boltanski and Ève Chiapello, *Organization* 15, no. 4 (2008): 610–614, here 611.

ination in the transformations described, and, following from this, how it draws our attention to the "traveling" forms of corporate storytelling.[14]

At first sight, *The New Spirit of Capitalism* is not a work that invites interdisciplinary research with the humanities, at least not when we consider its assessment of "artistic critique." Boltanski and Chiapello argue that, while the social critique of capitalism (i.e., demands for solidarity, equality, and most of all security) lost momentum and influence in the seventies and eighties on account of political changes, the artistic critique, which demanded liberation, autonomy, and authenticity, was incorporated into capitalist discourses themselves. This happened, first, by way of a commodification of authenticity (primarily by offering goods that had hitherto been excluded from the commodity sphere), and, second, by way of philosophy's and sociology's discrediting of the very notion of authenticity and hence the subject (445). Boltanski and Chiapello refer to the work of Pierre Bourdieu, Jacques Derrida, and Gilles Deleuze to illustrate the latter argument, and it is clear that this second critique weighs much heavier in their eyes because, they contend, it leaves no position from which to criticize capitalism. In the same vein, they suggest that it has been the work of philosophy and sociology (Deleuze, Latour, Callon) in the seventies that has helped to detach the concept of the network from its earlier (criminal) associations and redefine it in the language of liberation (145–146).

My point here is not to discuss the validity of their argument since that has already been done: The idea of the artistic critique's complicity has been challenged by Maurizio Lazzarato, among others, and it has been revisited in more nuanced ways by recent analysts of creativity and authenticity, such as Andreas Reckwitz.[15] But despite their critical, at times negative, perspective on some theoretical frameworks of twentieth-century cultural studies, Boltanski and Chiapello nonetheless provide the outline of a cultural studies analysis. It is in the context of their discussion of the genre of management literature that they refer to "the connexionist imagination" and its wider significance beyond this corpus of texts.

---

14   For the idea of forms as traveling, see Caroline Levine, *Forms: Whole, Rhythm, Hierarchy, Network* (Princeton: Princeton University Press, 2015).

15   Maurizio Lazzarato, "The Misfortunes of the 'Artistic Critique' and of Cultural Employment," trans. Mary O'Neill, *Transversal*, January 2007, https://transversal.at/transversal/0207/lazzarato/en; Andreas Reckwitz, *The Invention of Creativity: Modern Society and the Culture of the New*, trans. Steven Black (Cambridge: Polity, 2017).

The New Spirit of Capitalism is based on a qualitative and quantitative analysis of French management literature from the 1960s through the 1990s; metaphors and tropes play a central role in these texts. While the comparatively small number of selected documents has been criticized, Boltanski and Chiapello describe management literature as a coherent genre that is related to the "edifying books or manuals of moral instruction" (58) studied by Max Weber as accompanying the rise of the managerial class since the beginning of the twentieth century. As a genre, management literature is characterized by its "prescriptive," normative style (58)—"[the books'] aim is to state what should be, not what is" (59)—as well as by its occasionally "lyrical, even heroic style" (59). Somewhat apologetically, they twice admit "that realism is not a major feature of the texts studied" (59, 58). What is a major feature instead is intertextuality, and in particular, intertextual references to the metaphor of the network in writings from the humanities and natural sciences. "This is how the forms of capitalist production accede to representation in each epoch, by mobilizing concepts and tools that were initially developed largely autonomously in the theoretical sphere or domain of basic scientific research" (104). Moreover, this incorporation of non-economic usages of the network-metaphor is not unidirectional. Instead, the network-metaphor proves to be a traveling concept, a form that—as they note with some reservation—"is gradually taking on the task of a new general representation of societies" (138).

Ultimately, Boltanski and Chiapello suggest that their findings about management literature and the changes in corporate culture illustrate a larger socio-cultural transformation at the end of the twentieth century. As such, what they have described is not limited to this corpus of texts or to companies' internal communications, but shapes culture at large. Boltanski and Chiapello call this "the connexionist imagination" (140): "As disclosed by novelistic, cinematic or TV fiction, an investment of the imagination by the social in the shape of dramas, tensions, complexes or dilemmas associated with the question of class and social origins ... thus tends to be replaced today by a focus on the question of bonds, which are grasped as invariably problematic, fragile, to be created or re-created" (138).

This is a claim that is grand and narrow at the same time. Yet it nonetheless suggests the contours of an interdisciplinary research agenda for the twenty-first century. This is not to say, of course, that there is no cultural studies scholarship available on networks: Jonathan Grossman's *Charles Dickens's Networks* (2012) and Wesley Beal's *Networks of Modernism: Reorganizing American*

Narrative (2015) come to mind, as well as the special issue of *Amerikastudien/ American Studies, Network Theory and American Studies* (2012), edited by Ulfried Reicherdt und Regina Schober. But I want to briefly suggest a different direction of research, one in which Boltanski and Chiapello already take the first steps.

Using Boltanski and Chiapello's observations on the genre of management literature as a starting point, such research could focus on the varieties of corporate storytelling in US culture. Corporate storytelling is a term that refers to the managerial narratives that companies use to provide their employees not just with motivation and inspiration, but more practically with the rules and norms that should guide their decisions when working for the company (corporate philosophies, memos, etc.). But it is also increasingly used for external communications with customers and partners to contribute to the brand value, such as in mission statements, advertisements, and so forth. Moreover, various forms of life writing, such as the autobiographies of founders or CEOs, have become an important genre for both internal and external communications, as have TED talks. But corporate storytelling, in my definition here, is not limited to this (largely) factual variety of memos and autobiographies. It also includes a growing body of fictional narratives that practice and explore corporate storytelling as expression of the connexionist imagination, such as Joshua Ferris's *Then We Came to the End* (2007), Jennifer Egan's *Visit from the Goon Squad* (2010), or, more recently, Elvia Wilk's *Oval: A Novel* (2019). Such works go far beyond a preoccupation with "bonds" and relationships, as Boltanski and Chiapello suggest, and significantly add to our understanding—in the spirit of Economic Humanities—of how aesthetic and social forms interact and afford "particular modes of economic knowledge."[16]

"Ah Bartleby! Ah humanity!"

One question remains to be answered, however: the question of the goal of Economic Humanities in the face of capitalism's ability to incorporate critique. "I would prefer not to," says Bartleby, but should this be the critic's tagline too? Recently, Rita Felski and Elizabeth Anker have called this type of "self-questioning" a "generic feature of critique": a habit that comes with the

---

16   Crosthwaite, Knight, and Marsh, "The Economic Humanities," 665.

project.[17] Yet as an analytical disposition, it seems more than appropriate at the beginning of an interdisciplinary endeavor if we consider, as Crosthwaite, Knight, and Marsh do, that "[t]o be taken seriously by those within economics, finance, and business studies, the Economic Humanities will need to become intimately familiar with research in those disciplines."[18] Faced with such a task, Michelle Chihara and Matt Seybold have recently wondered about the danger of complicity: "But, by spending so many hours engaging with what might be compellingly be characterized as capitalist apologia, mustn't we also ask: Are we complicit, just as economists are, in rationalizing and normalizing an unsound and exploitative ideology?"[19]

The Economic Humanities are not the first interdisciplinary project in the Humanities that grapples with the task of defining its relationship to another discipline, of course. Crosthwaite, Knight, and Marsh have looked to the Environmental Humanities for a model, and they have specifically highlighted how "our understanding of both the environment and the economy—and our ability to avert catastrophe—will be greatly improved if we resist regarding these as narrowly technological fields best left to the self-designated experts."[20] While I agree that the Environmental Humanities provide a positive example (even though the relationship to science is not untroubled), we can also turn to Law and Literature for a more cautionary tale. As an approach to teaching in US law schools, Law and Literature sought to counter the growing influence of the Law and Economics school (spearheaded by Ronald Coase and Richard Posner, for example) in the 1970s. The latter stood for the idea that the tools and frameworks of economic theory can be applied to law and make legal practice more consistent, transparent, and ultimately just. In an effort to retain the idea of equity in legal training, Law and Literature sought to provide what seemed to be missing: "Literature could save law from itself by reminding it of its lost humanity, infusing it with the human in order to grant it a new reality."[21] Even though Law and Literature has since developed into

---

17   Elizabeth Anker and Rita Felski, "Introduction," in *Critique and Postcritique*, ed. Elizabeth Anker and Rita Felski (Durham: Duke University Press, 2017), 8.

18   Crosthwaite, Knight, and Marsh, "The Economic Humanities," 665.

19   Matt Seybold and Michelle Chihara, "Introduction," in *The Routledge Companion to Literature and Economics*, ed. Matt Seybold and Michelle Chihara (New York: Routledge, 2019), 3.

20   Crosthwaite, Knight, and Marsh, "The Economic Humanities," 664.

21   Julie Stone Peters, "Law, Literature, and the Vanishing Real," *PMLA* 120, no. 2 (2005): 442–453, here 445. Peters's argument is much more complex and bidirectional in that

a heterogenous field that is engaged in a debate over critique of its own, it has still not fully come to terms with these questions of interdisciplinarity.[22] This is also the question that Economic Humanities must continue to address, and it will not be an easy one to settle. "Ah Bartleby!", the lawyer sighs, and we may, too. "Ah humanity!"[23]

she points out what literary studies hoped to gain from the interdisciplinary project: "At the same time, speaking truth to power, literature could at last do something real" (445).

22   See Elizabeth Anker and Bernadette Meyler, eds., *New Directions in Law and Literature* (New York: Oxford University Press, 2017).

23   Melville, "Bartleby," 34.

13. Of Apes and Children
Communication, Interdisciplinarity, and Michael Tomasello's *Why We Cooperate* (2009)

Philipp Löffler

1. Introduction

We have all learned to value interdisciplinarity.[1] No grant application will be successful without it. Today, many of the most important academic institutions are sponsored on the premise that they foster collaborations between fields and subfields. My own discipline, American studies, "has held up interdisciplinarity as a sign of its own maverick status" since its inception.[2] And it is not likely that the "enormous amount of genre mixing in intellectual life" that has been going on for the past couple of decades will lose its original appeal anytime soon.[3] However, while most academics will hold on to the promise of interdisciplinary work, few of them are prepared to probe the conditions of their optimism. Why do scholars believe in the success of communication between academic fields? What are the conditions that allow us to assume that transfer of knowledge within and across disciplines is fea-

---

1   On the significance of interdisciplinarity since the 1960s, see Louis Menand, *The Market-place of Ideas: Reform and Resistance in the American University* (New York: Norton, 2010), 93–126; David Alworth, "Hip to Post45," *Contemporary Literature* 54, no. 3 (2013): 621–33; Rebecca Hill, "What Is This Thing Called Interdisciplinarity? Teaching Interdisciplinary Methods Courses in American Studies," *American Quarterly* 68, no. 2 (2016): 361–65.

2   Hill, "This Thing Called Interdisciplinarity," 361. Within the German American Studies context, we may think of such institutions as the John F. Kennedy Institute for North American Studies at Freie Universität Berlin, The Obama Institute for Transnational American Studies in Mainz, or the Heidelberg Center for American Studies.

3   Clifford Geertz, "Blurred Genres: The Refiguration of Social Thought," *The American Scholar* 49, no. 2 (1980): 165–79, here 165.

sible and/or productive? What do scholars do when they communicate with one another? Why do they get along? What is their language?

Reluctant to predict definite answers, I want to engage with these questions in a discussion of Michael Tomasello's book *Why We Cooperate*, an abridged version of his 2008 "Tanner Lectures on Human Values" at Stanford University.[4] Given the rich diversity of approaches and methodologies within literary and cultural studies, Tomasello's slim book on evolutionary anthropology may not be the most likely choice, to be sure. But its location within the world of academic knowledge might also be its greatest asset: interdisciplinary consultation as a method to gauge the limits and possibilities of interdisciplinarity on a more general scale.

To be more precise: Tomasello's work enables us to imagine what literary and cultural studies can learn from the behavioral sciences. In particular, it might help us circumnavigate some of the impasses that occur when literary scholars speak about the social. Based on empirical research on human infants and chimpanzees, Tomasello's findings on how and why human individuals cooperate complements and challenges sociology-inspired scholarship in the Humanities and its continued strong emphasis on the work of Pierre Bourdieu. What Tomasello shows is that there exists a dimension of mutual understanding in processes of social interaction that need not be learned nor rehearsed. Rather, cooperation and interaction are behavioral expressions of a natural, pre-linguistic state of being, available already to infants at age one. I would like to speculate about the consequences of this claim. My intuition is that if we take seriously the suggested dialogue between the fields and Tomasello's notion of a pre-discursive, naturalized concept of human interaction, we will have to reconsider the idea of interdisciplinarity as such. Let's take a closer look at the problem at stake.

2. Translation, Translatability, Interdisciplinarity

Interdisciplinarity has become so ubiquitous within the Humanities—literary and cultural studies in particular—that many would hesitate to call it a concept at all, let alone spend time on theorizing it or turning it into a problem. The question, however, is not whether joint or multidisciplinary scholarship

---

4   All parenthetical citations in the text refer to Michael Tomasello, *Why We Cooperate* (Cambridge, MA: MIT Press, 2009).

produces valuable results, nor whether those engaged in interdisciplinary collaborations are qualified or entitled to tap into other disciplinary territories, even if it is only to trump "one's disciplinary mates by importing prestigious ideas from unrelated disciplines."[5] We do not need to speak about the "potential" of interdisciplinarity, as if that has ever been questioned.[6] The current crisis of scholarship in the Humanities makes conversations across disciplines and academic fields almost imperative—not least in order to generate third-party funding as a way of keeping scholarship financially viable.

Inasmuch, however, as there is widespread agreement about the necessity to collaborate with colleagues working in neighboring academic fields, there has been little concern about the theoretical conditions that would enable this kind of exchange. What, for example, is the meta-language that allows scholars of various disciplines to engage in joint scholarship without compromising or obscuring the premises of their own disciplinary homelands? I will return to the question a bit further down. Scientific paradigms are not necessarily compatible with one another, and finding a language to facilitate communication between fields comes with a baggage of tricky questions about the practices of scholarship itself. We may briefly turn to philosopher Donald Davidson to get an idea of what the issue is. In a much-quoted essay, he writes:

> Philosophers of many persuasions are prone to talk of conceptual schemes. Conceptual schemes, we are told, are ways of organizing experience; they are systems of categories that give form to the data of sensation; they are points of view from which individuals, cultures, or periods survey the passing scene. There may be no translating from one scheme to another, in which case the beliefs, desires, hopes and bits of knowledge that characterize one person have no true counterparts for the subscriber to another scheme. Re-

---

5   Marshall Sahlins, "The Conflicts of the Faculty," *Critical Inquiry* 35, no. 4 (2009): 997–1018, here 1014.

6   On the "potential" of interdisciplinarity as a method in American studies, see Simon Wendt, "American Studies as a Multi/Inter/Transdisciplinary Endeavor? Problems, Challenges, and the Potential of Heroism for Collaborative Research," in *Projecting American Studies: Essays on Theory, Method, and Practice*, ed. Frank Kelleter and Alexander Starre (Heidelberg: Universitätsverlag Winter, 2018), 197–205.

ality itself is relative to a scheme: what counts as real in one system may not in another.[7]

Davidson's observation builds on a longer scholarly tradition seeking to emphasize the historical and methodological idiosyncrasies of scientific discourse.[8] It also rephrases a point well known among literary scholars with Derridean leanings: the non-identity of languages and sign systems and the untranslatability of individual experience. For academics socialized in the 1980s and 1990s, broadly committed to the project of deconstruction, the unreliability of codes and referencing systems represented a somewhat liberating, subversive potential because linguistic unreliability seemed to suggest resistance to hegemonic control and political cooptation. This was the identitarian promise of theory's golden age. Postcolonial, critical race, queer and gender studies became dominant as their proponents fused the allure of high theory with liberal, progressive political programs. The revisionist turns of the past four decades within American studies reflect this commitment in exemplary fashion.[9]

At the same time, however, that Davidson's observation seems compatible with theory production in literary and cultural studies, it also calls into question the premises upon which the notion of non-translatability and the arguments derived from it may become meaningful. Insisting on the idea of linguistic and conceptual non-identity between languages (and identities) builds on a sense of relativism that cannot be logically maintained: "The dominant metaphor of conceptual relativism, that of differing points of view, seems to betray an underlying paradox. Different points of view make sense, but only if there is a common coordinate system on which to plot them; yet the existence of a common system belies the claim of dramatic incomparability."[10]

---

7   Donald Davidson, "On the Very Idea of a Conceptual Scheme," *Proceedings and Addresses of the American Philosophical Association* 47 (1973–1974): 5–20, here 5.

8   See Ludwik Fleck, *Genesis and Development of a Scientific Fact*, trans. Frederick Bradley (Chicago: University of Chicago Press, [1935] 1979); Thomas S. Kuhn, *The Structure of Scientific Revolutions* (Cambridge, MA: MIT Press, 1964); Karl Popper, *The Logic of Scientific Discovery*, trans. Karl Popper (London: Routledge, [1935] 1999).

9   On the institutional history of American studies as a discipline and its various political turns, see Lucy Maddox, *Locating American Studies: The Evolution of a Discipline* (Baltimore: Johns Hopkins University Press, 1998).

10   Davidson, "Conceptual Scheme," 6.

For Davidson, sharing a conceptual scheme is thus related to sharing a language. "The relation may be supposed to be this: if conceptual schemes differ, so do languages. But speakers of different languages may share a conceptual scheme provided there is a way of translating one language into the other."[11]

For the purposes of our discussion, the key phrase in the above quote is "provided there is." For it is neither clear whether translation between disciplines is possible, nor whether it should be desirable. When scholars of different fields attempt to speak to one another about a problem or a cluster of questions they think is pertinent to their scholarly communities, they must assume that both sides have something to offer that neither of them could generate alone. Examples abound. We may think of fields that have traditionally been located at the opposite ends of the disciplinary curriculum, as in recent attempts to make neuro-science and biology adaptable to cultural studies and vice versa. But it may also be fields of inquiry that have evolved in close proximity to one another and that seem to share a good deal of common ground with regard to both methodology and thematic orientation: philosophy and the arts; literature and the social sciences; history and political science.

The more intricate problem, I believe, is to explain the conceptual grounds upon which communication between disciplines succeeds in the first place. Davidson himself has introduced the "principle of charity," describing a mutually dependent need for interpretative compensation among practitioners of different occupations and speakers of different languages.[12] Paul Grice's "cooperative principle" has usefully alerted us that interaction amongst humans is successful as long as we assume an underlying purpose and the acceptance of a shared set of conversational maxims and implicatures.[13] Margaret Gilbert and John Searle have advanced the idea of a "shared intentionality," which Tomasello heavily relies on.[14] And Jürgen Habermas has variously defended

---

11   Davidson, 7.

12   See Davidson, "Conceptual Scheme," 18–19.

13   See H. Paul Grice, "Logic and Conversation," in *Syntax and Semantics* 3, ed. Peter Cole and Jerry L. Morgan (New York: Academic Press, 1975): 41–58, here 45.

14   See Margaret Gilbert, *On Social Facts* (Princeton: Princeton University Press, 1989), 154–203; John Searle, *The Construction of Social Reality* (New York: The Free Press, 1995), 1–30; Michael Tomasello, *The Cultural Origins of Human Cognition* (Cambridge, MA: Harvard University Press, 1999), 56–93; Tomasello, *The Origins of Communication* (Cambridge, MA: MIT Press, 2008), 342–47; Tomasello, *Why We Cooperate*, 1–48.

his notion of "communicative rationality" to explain meaningful social inter-action in what he defines as a "post-metaphysical world."[15]

These (and other) approaches describe the discursive conditions for suc-cessful interaction, but in so doing, they must rely—for better or worse—on a set of abstract principles that necessarily precede the moment of communica-tive action itself. In other words: these theories acknowledge the particularity of different (communicative) practices but only in so far as they assume a common linguistic/conceptual backdrop against which differences manifest themselves and can be smoothed out. If this is the precondition for interdis-ciplinarity as a method—that we can reach that common ground—then the practical question has to be: how can we get there? I ask this question as a literary scholar and will use Michael Tomasello's arguments to help me frame a tentative solution.

3. Literature, Communication, Exchange

If culture and literature are man-made, as few would dispute, there must be a quintessentially human, non-discursive dimension to reading and writing, preceding literature's appropriation within the theory world of English de-partments or in fact any other professional-academic terrain. There must, in other words, be a dimension to literary production that, in John Dewey's sense of "experience," helps us to understand the artwork before it is framed and categorized conceptually; the consequence of an "impulsion," an almost phys-ical reaction to the materials of our everyday environments: "On the lower scale, air and food materials are such things; on the higher, tools, whether the pen of the writer or the anvil of the blacksmith, utensils and furnishings, property, friends, and institutions, all the support and sustenances without which a civilized life cannot be."[16]

For Tomasello, these fundamental forms of human interaction and the experience of a shared object world become meaningful and authoritative through the work of social institutions. This should not come as a surprise.

---

15   See Jürgen Habermas, *Theorie des kommunikativen Handelns, Band. 1: Handlungsrational-ität und gesellschaftliche Rationalisierung* (Frankfurt am Main: Suhrkamp, 1981), 369–409; Jürgen Habermas, *Zwischen Naturalismus und Religion* (Frankfurt am Main: Suhrkamp, 2005), 27–83.

16   John Dewey, *Art as Experience* (New York: Penguin, [1934] 2005), 61.

"Social institutions are sets of behavioral practices governed by various kinds of mutually recognized norms and rules" (xi). What might be somewhat more astonishing in Tomasello's account of institutionality is the age at which a sense of social cooperation evolves amongst humans. Social practices, as well as the "norms and rules" necessary to preform them successfully, are acquired at the earliest stages of infancy, "pre-linguistically, at twelve to four-teen months of age" (18). Reminiscent of Paul Grice's "cooperative principle," human infants "not only inform others of things helpfully and accurately interpret informative intentions directed at them, they even understand imperatives in cooperative fashion" (19).

Though for different reasons, these processes of meaningful interaction are observable in groups of human infants but also amongst communities of great apes. The difference lies in what Tomasello calls "directed" or "shared intentionality" (39). Whereas chimpanzees cooperate exclusively to gratify im-mediate personal needs, human infants are "part of some larger we-intention-ality" (ibid.), that is, they are naturally prone to identify with others and thus produce "a conception of the self as one among others" (40). Importantly, this sense of solidarity exists prior to infants entering systematic regimens of so-cial normalization; the notion of a "we-ness" exists as a bio-genetically deter-mined constant, available to all human individuals and developing only later into more specifically coded social and disciplinary norms. What this means, essentially, is that no matter where we come from and regardless of our pro-fessional occupations, there exists a propensity amongst humans to enforce socially cooperative behavior independently of "the fear of authority" and "the promise of reciprocity" (38). In other words, human individuals are born as social animals before institutionally controlled modes of habitualization and rehearsals of social practices can be set in motion. What are the implications of this argument for the ways in which we conduct research as members of scientific communities? And in how far may it be helpful for explaining the alleged success of interdisciplinary work?

Let's return to the analogy of conceptual schemes and languages. For Tomasello, languages are used to perform complex practices; they attain significance within concrete institutional settings, where they are employed to ensure and regulate cooperative practices of a certain kind: there is a certain way of doing things, that is, using language, in particular fields of practice that are specific to the site of practice itself. Of course, this applies to all areas of social life and cannot be reduced to fields of cultural production: if I walk into the super-market, "my entering the store subjects me to a whole range of rules and obligations" (56), most of which I expect to be in place and most of which I comply with without ever thinking about them. There are goods to be purchased; I am not allowed to steal; I'll have to wait in line at the checkout counter; if the goods that I bought are damaged in any way I can return them. "What is common to all of these institutional phenomena is a uniquely human sense of 'we'" (57). Supermarkets work because there is a shared agreement about the premises that govern behavior once you have entered the supermarket world. The supermarket world as any institutionalized site of practice is defined by "joint goals and distinct and generalized roles, with participants mutually aware" that "they are dependent on one another for success" (99). These practices, Tomasello maintains, entail "the seeds of generalized, agent-neutral normative judgments of rights and responsibilities (99) that can also be found "in social institutions" (99).

Here, Tomasello seems deceptively close to scholars endorsing Bourdieu-derived descriptions of the art world, or more conventional theories of social practice.[17] But this is only a first impression. Traditional sociological accounts of practice assume an institutionally grounded dialectic between the incorporation and the performance of social scripts.[18] We routinize a set of moves within the bounds of a particular social setting, say, the university classroom. The validity of our (incorporated) knowledge is perpetually affirmed and tested by our peers, fellow academics, as they engage with what we do (as advisors, competitors, peer-reviewers, etc). And of course, the same mechanisms may be assumed to govern other fields of social practice from the local sports club to the administration of professional organizations.

Tomasello's view is notably different; his notion of "we-ness," or "shared intentionality" (57) is not bound to any institutional setting: "it does not come only from the collective, institutional world of supermarkets, private property, health departments, and the like" (57). Rather, as Tomasello's research group has found in a string of experiments on the acquisition of socially normative behavior, cooperative action and its implicit set of rules precede the coming

---

17   On the practice turn within the social sciences, see Andreas Reckwitz, "Towards a Theory of Social Practices: A Development in Cultural Theorizing," *European Journal of Social Theory* 5, no. 2 (2002): 243–63; Karl H. Hörning and Julia Reuter, eds., *Doing Culture: Neue Positionen zum Verhältnis von Kultur und sozialer Praxis* (Bielefeld: transcript, 2004).

18   On the reciprocity of incorporation and performance, see Pierre Bourdieu, *The Logic of Practice*, trans. Richard Nice (Cambridge: Polity Press, [1980] 1990), 52–65; Pierre Bourdieu, *Pascalian Meditations*, trans. Richard Nice (Stanford: Stanford University Press, 2000), 138–42.

into being of social institutions; the belief in cooperation resembles a natural intuition that human infants are equipped with before they enter contexts of social interaction. All "human cultures have rules and norms for sharing or possibly trading food and other valuable objects" (XII).

This is not, however, because individual human beings enter the world unbeknownst of the existence of social institutions, the functions of which they learn in a tedious process of adaptation as they grow up. The opposite seems to be true, as Tomasello maintains. It is as if they already knew the rules of the game before entering the playing field. While scholars trained in cultural sociology feel inclined to explain normative social practices as the consequence of historically and institutionally specific forms of learning, Tomasello stresses almost the opposite: children are endowed with an innate ability to cooperate in ways that other, non-human primates are not. "They form with others joint goals to which both parties are normatively committed, they establish with others domains of joint attention and common conceptual ground, and they create with others symbolic, institutional realities that assign deontic powers to otherwise inert entities" (105). Let's speculate a bit about the consequences of this claim for our understanding of what interdisciplinary could mean.

If we remained radically Wittgensteinean and assumed that scientific disciplines are organized much like "private languages" ("Privatsprachen"), idiosyncratic and non-translatable into other registers of scientific discourse, we would still need what Davidson describes as a conceptual scheme on the basis of which we could speak about the issue of non-translatability.[19] Take the world of literature and literary studies. The trouble of describing the field and its various areas consists precisely in accounting for both a continued sense of systemic cohesion—historically and institutionally—and a simultaneous series of moments of conflict and antagonism among the field's most pertinent practitioners: writers, readers, editors, retailers, professional academic interpreters, and many more. It is almost impossible to describe the multiple levels of practice in and through which they communicate and exchange goods (printed matter) and ideas (at very specific moments in history), while maintaining the long durée narratives of traditional literary-historical

---

19   On "Privatsprachen," see Wittgenstein: "The words of this language are to refer to what only the speaker can know—to his immediate private sensations. So another person cannot understand the language." Ludwig Wittgenstein, *Philosophical Investigations*, trans. G.E.M. Anscombe (London: Pearson, [1953] 1973), §243.

scholarship. Studies in the history of the book have made that point particularly clear.

Even if we had a basic literary-geographic map at hand, we would still be participants in the very world we are trying to describe. The problem is familiar enough. The point here, however, is not to insist on the subjectivity of perspective and the impossibility of a neutral scientific gaze.[20] That is, our interest should not be in the fallibility of field descriptions, if fallibility is used as a concept to discredit the reliability of scholarly perspectives on the grounds of their embeddedness in the discourse they profess to analyze. What appears to be more relevant for the purpose of this discussion are situations in which our sense of direction clashes with that of our peers, when the books we write or read—as literary authors *and* as scholars—simply do not speak to those we deem most important, when communication seems to fail and we feel pressured to account for these moments of failure. These discrepancies, that is, moments in which what we think we are doing clashes with our interlocutor's sense of action, become even more apparent in cross-disciplinary perspective. Just imagine an evolutionary anthropologist and a cognitive linguist, committed to Chomsky's generative grammar, discussing language and language acquisition: a clash of scientific cultures in the most literal sense of the term. It is in those situations that we are in dire need of communicative practices that would enable translation.

The history of science has produced multiple examples in which practitioners of different fields, facing that kind of impasse, have produced marvelously innovative solutions, "puzzle-solving strategies," as Thomas Kuhn famously called them.[21] But these moments of mutual understanding did not come about as the consequence of a planned encounter of different scientific cultures. Progress cannot be planned as such; it can only be hoped for. In most of the cases, chance, unpredictability, and what Tomasello calls a "drift to the arbitrary" have dominated human puzzle-solving activities.[22] In order to understand why communication and translation seem to work out nonetheless, we need to return to Tomasello's notion of a shared intentionality, a quality that we bring into the world before we are socialized as individuals and before

---

20   This aspect is fleshed out with enviable clarity in the conclusion of Foucault's *Archeology of Knowledge*. See Michel Foucault, *Archeology of Knowledge*, trans. A. M. Sheridan Smith (New York: Pantheon Books, [1969] 1972), 199–211.

21   Kuhn, *Scientific Revolutions*, 35–42.

22   Tomasello, *Origins of Communication*, 220–21.

we become members of particular cultural or scientific communities: the innate belief that human behavior is group-oriented and goal-driven, whatever the exact outcome may be. Infants "do not learn this from adults; it comes naturally" (4). And if it comes naturally, then this, rather than an intricate metalanguage, should be the natural bond between scholars of different fields.

It is a truism, to be sure, that forms of interaction are likely to become increasingly complex and intricate over time, especially as they go along with the evolution of symbolic sign systems, that is, languages and the institutional spaces in which languages and practices become meaningful. It's just that the mechanisms that allow for goal-oriented cooperative behavior exist independently of the various contexts of social (and scientific) practice in which they become manifest. And the same holds true for our capacity to use languages. This uniquely human ability is part of what psychologist Elisabeth Spelke, in a response to *Why We Cooperate*, calls a "cognitive core system" which "emerges early in infancy" and is "universal across our species, despite the many differences in the practices and belief systems of people in different cultural groups."[23] As Spelke's research has shown, "members of distant cultures," just like infants, "perform the same object-representation tasks with similar results," enacting a pre-social, pre-discursive capacity to work together.[24] It is this insight into the human capacity to enforce and regulate joint action that—by analogy—might help to explain some of the more obscure theoretical aspects involved in interdisciplinarity, not least the challenge of translatability.

4. Scholars and Sandboxes

What, then, can we learn from the behavioral sciences that we did not already know? What is the value of Tomasello's work for our understanding of what interdisciplinarity should or could accomplish? The answer that I feel confident with feels somewhat vague and may disappoint, at least at first glance: interdisciplinary communication works—somehow. But we knew that before. The truly interesting point is this: *Why We Cooperate* shows that we have to

---

23   Elisabeth S. Spelke, "Forum: Why We Cooperate," in *Why We Cooperate*, Michael Tomasello (Cambridge, MA: MIT Press, 2009), 157. See also Elisabeth S. Spelke and Katherine D. Kinzler, "Core Knowledge," *Developmental Science* 10, no. 1 (2007): 89–96.

24   Spelke, "Forum," 159.

think in new ways about *why* cross-disciplinary exchange works and what the implications of these exchanges are—even if we don't like them. Put most simply, and somewhat provocatively: the reason why conversations between scholars of different disciplines are bound to succeed has nothing to do with their creativity or their expertise at finding hitherto undiscovered disciplinary synergies. Scientific languages, just like natural languages, emerge as the consequence of a shared desire amongst humans for joint action, traceable ontogenetically to the earliest years of infancy. If we extrapolate from Tomasello's findings, we may conclude that scholars engaged in interdisciplinary work are like toddlers seeking help from their mates (and expecting the fulfillment of their request) as they struggle to accomplish a given task (e.g., finish a puzzle, build a sand castle). Whether or not the expected collaboration turns out to be productive is independent of the foregoing moment of bonding and the intuitive commitment to working together. That point is crucial: there will never be a reliable scholarly meta-language, only mutual conceptual approximations to a shared problem. There is a sandbox, there is a red shovel and a blue bucket, but that's about it.

The analogy between infants and scholars may no doubt seem inappropriate on a number of levels. After all, academic professionals are hyper-specialists in their fields, experienced intellectual workers, trained at all sorts of institutional levels within and without the academic world. Their professional experience seems to stand in almost diametrical opposition to the pre-discursive naiveté of the toddler, making progress in tedious trial-and-error experiments conducted in the sandbox. But then again, are we not still taking similarly clumsy baby steps in our daily professional lives, testing out what is and what isn't possible within the academic domains we inhabit?

There are, however, some more reliable conclusions that we may derive from Tomasello's work as presented in *Why We Cooperate*. These are more serious for contemporary debates about the future of the research university: interdisciplinarity cannot simply be planned as if collaborations between scholars of different fields would be meaningful and valuable in and of themselves. If they occur, such moments of collaboration should emerge spontaneously, that is, in response to a given problem the solution of which resists predictability and control. Sometimes such endeavors simply do not yield any useful data or insights at all. The outcome of scholarship has never been foreseeable, not even within individual disciplines. Hence, it does not make sense to assume that work across disciplinary borders promises results that are more valuable than those produced within the confines of traditional academic core disciplines. Interdisciplinarity should not be used as a normative scholarly method to constrain the freedom of scientific inquiry.

And yet, for a number of familiar political and economic reasons, interdisciplinarity will continue to shape academic curricula, M.A. and PhD programs, and entire clusters of research. "Claims that interdisciplinarity is vital to the twenty-first-century university are heralded at a moment when 'tectonic change' is not simply economic hyperbole but may well be upon us."[25] Jacobs's words resonate. If this is a reality, however, that we cannot evade, then the least we can do is to acknowledge what interdisciplinarity truly means, namely a bunch of kids getting together, driven by a sense of community, a "we-ness" that is much stronger than that created by academic departmental affiliations. This is why we cooperate. And this is why the work of Michael Tomasello matters. Do we have to understand each other? No, not necessarily. Will the neuro-sciences help us develop a better understanding of Emily Dickinson's poetry? I truly doubt it. Can medical doctors help literary scholars describe more accurately representations of illness or health in literature? I am positive they can't. But that has never been the goal in the first place. And it shouldn't be.

What should be endorsed, by contrast, is a trust-based curiosity about the unpredictability of conceptual-scientific progress, the belief that things will work out—somehow. And again, I am suggesting this point as a member of a scholarly community that has always felt strong about the permeability of its own disciplinary demarcations. Given its tumultuous institutional history, American Studies is a good place to start thinking about the benefits of interdisciplinary work. But not because that particular field has produced results that would be superior to competing scientific-academic accomplishments. Rather, it's a field that has been invested in the potentials of an open, critical conversation about the very notion of what it means to speak about America as a cultural-political formation. In that sense, reading Tomasello's *Why We Cooperate* may serve as a very timely reminder to re-embrace what one of the field's founders once wrote about the problem of method:

Method in scholarship grows out of practice, or rather out of repeated criticism of practice intended to remedy observed shortcomings.... A new

---

25   Jerry Jacobs, *In Defense of Disciplines: Interdisciplinarity and Specialization in the Research University* (Chicago: University of Chicago Press, 2013), 5.

method will have to come piecemeal, through a kind of principled oppor-
tunism, in the course of daily struggles with our various tasks. No one man
will be able to redesign the whole enterprise. What will count is the image
in our minds of the structure we believe we are helping to build.[26]

What matters is not how that "structure" looks like, in the words of Smith;
it's the belief that scholars are able to work together, "helping to build" it,
irrespective of its final shape.

---

26   Henry Nash Smith, "Can 'American Studies' Develop a Method?" *American Quarterly* 9,
       no. 2 (1957): 197–208, here 207.

American Redescriptions

Society must be described or else there is no such thing as society.

14. Polarization and the Limits of Empathy
On Arlie Russell Hochschild's *Strangers in Their Own Land* (2016)

Johannes Voelz

1.

In March 2020, as the coronavirus spread throughout the United States, political scientists and commentators began to speculate on the ramifications the pandemic would have for the polarized state of US society.[1] In the past, national crises, such as the attacks of September 11, 2001, had tended to rally the nation behind the administration. Public health crises in particular had had the effect of bringing people together across the political divide. "Facing a public health threat," the *New York Times* summarizes the findings of quantitative scholarship on the issue, "the more anxious Democrats and Republicans became, the more likely they both were to trust expert sources like the Centers for Disease Control and Prevention."[2] Elsewhere, this rule of thumb seemed to apply to the coronavirus as well. Though post-Brexit Britain is politically, socially, and culturally deeply divided, the response to the pandemic was not.[3]

And in the United States? Pollsters found that through mid-March 2020, the response to the virus differed sharply between Democratic and Republican voters. Echoing the stance of Trump and Trump-loyal media such as Fox News, Republicans expressed significantly less concern about the pandemic than did Democrats. An NBC News/Wall Street Journal poll, conducted from

---

1   I am grateful to Martin Stempfhuber for his comments on a draft version of this essay.
2   Emily Badger and Kevin Quealy, "Red vs. Blue on Coronavirus Concern: The Gap Is Still Big but Closing," *New York Times*, March 21, 2020, https://www.nytimes.com/interactiv e/2020/03/21/upshot/coronavirus-public-opinion.html.
3   Badger and Quealy, "Red vs. Blue."

March 11 to 13, found that "68 percent of Democrats are worried that some-one in their family could catch the virus, while just 40 percent of Republicans and 45 percent of independents share that concern."[4] Apparently, these results were not a mere matter of partisans proudly touting the party line when approached by pollsters. Indeed, it seemed that in response to the coronavirus, Republicans and Democrats *acted* differently. Setting out to study differences in behavior rather than in professed opinion, political scientist Brian Schaffner analyzed Google searches for "hand sanitizer" and found that from March 1 to 12, 2020, "places that were more Republican were much less likely to search for hand sanitizer."[5] These polling results seemed to justify claims by some political scientists who have proposed that Republicans and Democrats increasingly live in separate realities, that polarization is no longer a matter merely of politics or social sorting but of epistemology.[6]

Things, however, changed in the second half of March, 2020. As Trump, the Republican Party, and their affiliated media channels began to take the crisis more seriously, the stark partisan differences in the reaction to the crisis diminished. For many political pundits and scientists, this was a sign that polarization was subsiding. In the *L.A. Times*, Kevin Collins, chief research officer of the polling organization Survey 160, stated that "while partisanship continues to structure public opinion, the facts on the ground can ultimately break through when the situation is grave enough."[7] On this reading, reality, boosted by the deadly force of the virus, was finally able to cut through and liberate itself from the constructions which partisans had imposed on it.

However, it would seem that this was an unduly hopeful interpretation, given the fact that the change of heart among Republicans did not come in spite of, but following, the swift turnaround of Trump and his media mouthpieces. The convergence of Democrats and Republicans in their responses to the virus may not have been an indicator that the nation was coming to its (nonpartisan) senses but that Republicans are so beholden to their authority

4   Jay J. Van Bavel, "In a pandemic, political polarization could kill people," *The Washington Post*, March 22, 2020, https://www.washingtonpost.com/outlook/2020/03/23/coronavirus-polarization-political-exaggeration/.

5   Badger and Quealy, "Red vs. Blue."

6   Morgan Marietta and David C. Barker, *One Nation, Two Realities: Dueling Facts in American Democracy* (Oxford: Oxford University Press, 2019).

7   Janet Hook, "Even the coronavirus crisis can't bridge America's partisan divide," *Los Angeles Times*, March 20, 2020, https://www.latimes.com/politics/story/2020-03-20/coronavirus-crisis-cant-bridge-partisan-divide.

figures that they are willing to follow wherever they lead them. One day, the pandemic is a joke, the next day it is an existential crisis. It takes extraordinary commitment and identification with one's political leadership to be able to instantly adjust one's outlook to such drastic changes of perspective. Or, as Paul Krugman put it on March 31, "as far as I know there haven't been any howls of protest from Fox viewers, or Rush Limbaugh listeners, who are now being told something completely different from what they were hearing three weeks ago. Their trust in Fox, their disdain for *The New York Times* and *The Washington Post*, and, above all, their faith in Donald Trump are apparently unshaken."[8]

What's more, even as Trump's about-face temporarily lined up his view of the crisis with that of experts (and with Democratic politicians and their followers), Trump made sure not to let the coronavirus crisis go to waste. As the *New York Times* reported, on March 29, Trump "repeated a complaint that Democratic governors had insulted him and said he would delegate calls with those officials to other people in the White House ... 'Because when they disrespect me, they're disrespecting our government,' he said."[9] Indeed, Trump, barred from holding rallies, found a new forum in his daily televised coronavirus briefings. Not only did the epidemic provide his broadcasts with urgency. The epidemic provided material ideally suited for his signature style made up of praise, insult, insinuation, and speculation. Polarization doesn't run out of steam just because there is general agreement on an issue. As long as that issue offers room for voicing grievances and threats, as long as agreement leaves the grammar of resentment intact, polarization—it seems at the time I'm writing this piece in early April 2020—will not loosen its grip on the United States just because tens of thousands of people are dying from a virus.

Polarization has been on the upswing in America for a long time now. Historians and political scientists trace it back to the break-up of the New Deal coalition in response to the Democratic Party's embrace of the Civil Rights

---

8   Paul Krugman, Opinion Newsletter, New York Times, March 31, 2020, https://messagi ng-custom-newsletters.nytimes.com/template/oakv2?uri=nyt://newsletter/79cb9e21-0 e7e-478e-bcec-f726db9d36e5&productCode=PK&te=1&nl=paul-krugman&emc=edit_p k_20200411

9   Michael D. Shear, "Trump Extends Social Distancing Guidelines Through End of April," *New York Times*, March 29, 2020, https://www.nytimes.com/2020/03/29/us/politics/tru mp-coronavirus-guidelines.html?searchResultPosition=1.

Movement in the 1960s.[10] Apparently, the lack of polarization during the extended New Deal era had something to do with the New Deal consensus about the desirability of economic redistribution and the welfare state. But the fact that the New Deal coalition broke apart over the Civil Rights Movement makes the story more complicated and should warn us against idealizations of a pre-polarized past. In the United States, nonpartisanship came at the price of across-the-board acceptance of systematic Jim Crow racism. Alas, in the United States everything is tainted by racism, even the very thing a European observer might be inclined to embrace whole-heartedly: the New Deal.

But neither is it quite right to say that the United States has been polarized since the late 1960s. Polarization is a development that has continued to grow increasingly severe and encompassing.[11] By now, polarization is no longer simply a matter of stark political disagreement. It is a matter of overarching identities—conservative versus liberal, Republican versus Democrat—that inflect entire ways of life, value systems, ideologies, aesthetic sensibilities, and vocabularies of affective expressivity. Not since before the Civil War have Americans experienced a divide this intense and unforgiving. Not only do they perceive those who think differently as strangers, or, indeed, as enemies. They have effectively reduced a complex and pluralistic society into two identity camps. Any aspect of life, from the most banal (do you prefer a Prius or a Pick-Up?) to the existential (isn't the coronavirus just another attempt get rid of Trump?), has the potential of serving as a shibboleth in the Manichean reordering of life.[12]

It almost goes without saying (though political and social scientists say it over and over again, and now—you are my witness—they are joined by colleagues from cultural and literary studies) that with the presidential election of 2016, polarization of US society reached a new level. Trump's whole approach to politics is built on the conflictual surplus that he extracts from

---

10   Sam Rosenfeld, *The Polarizers: Postwar Architects of Our Partisan Era* (Chicago: University of Chicago Press, 2018).

11   See James E. Campbell, *Polarized: Making Sense of a Divided America* (Princeton: Princeton University Press, 2016); Alan I. Abramowitz, *The Great Alignment: Race, Party Transformation, and the Rise of Donald Trump* (New Haven: Yale University Press, 2018).

12   See Marc Hetherington and Jonathan Weiler, *Prius or Pickup? How the Answers to Four Simple Questions Explain America's Great Divide* (Boston: Houghton Mifflin Harcourt, 2018); Lilliana Mason, *Uncivil Agreement: How Politics Became Our Identity* (Chicago: University of Chicago Press, 2018); Ezra Klein, *Why We're Polarized* (New York: Avid Readers Press, 2020).

an us-versus-them logic. His electoral college success did not just catapult a populist to the White House who understands how to elicit and absorb a resentment mix generated by economic inequality, deep-seated racism, and empire-in-decline anxieties. His ascent to the presidency also cemented the polarization of the social world by effectively imposing it on those who voted for him and those who did not. Trump literally polarizes by forcing you to take sides.

What has been less often remarked on is that the rise of Trump, in pushing polarization to the next level, also raised the awareness of polarization, as well as the desire to overcome it. Americans are not only more divided than before. They are also more preoccupied with—and more concerned about—that divide. Strictly speaking, registering new levels of polarization as a problem, and wanting to solve that problem, are two separate issues. In practice, these two issues tend to blend together. What I want to call "the concern with polarization" has a dual meaning—the awareness of increasing polarization and the desire to undo it. No single book exemplifies this twofold concern more strikingly than Arlie Russell Hochschild's *Strangers in their Own Land: Anger and Mourning on the American Right*, which appeared just a few weeks before the 2016 presidential elections.[13] It is this twofold concern to which Hochschild's book owes its remarkable success. It is the conflation of the two dimensions of *concern* that blunts its analytical force. It is the blind spot of the dual concern that makes the book end up as a symptom rather than an analysis of polarization in America. And finally, it is the earnestness of the concern that allows us to see clearer why it is so difficult to find a way out of polarization.

2.

Strangers in their Own Land is a piece of fieldwork sociology written expressly for the general reader. Hochschild, a self-proclaimed progressive from Berkeley, spent five years (roughly from 2010 and 2015) with Tea Party supporters in Louisiana in order to gain an understanding of their outlook on the world. In the aftermath of the 2016 election, her book promised to provide an answer to the question haunting liberal America: who were these people that voted Trump into the White House—against nearly all predictions?

---

13   All parenthetical citations in the text refer to Arlie Russell Hochschild, *Strangers in Their Own Land: Anger and Mourning on the American Right* (New York: The New Press, 2016).

Hochschild's book wasn't the only 2016 offering that liberal readers turned to for answers. A whole number of authors—most, but not all of them, academic—published non-fiction bestsellers that made credible bids in the contest for the most plausible account of what had been going on under the radar of the pollsters. Strikingly, most of them stressed the centrality of class. What needed to be explained, it seemed, was how there had emerged a new identity group—"the white working class"—that was particularly receptive to the appeal of a right-wing populist, and that had made the difference in the unexpected electoral outcome. Perhaps closest to the explanation offered by Hochschild came Katherine Cramer's book, *The Politics of Resentment: Rural Consciousness in Wisconsin and the Rise of Scott Walker*.[14] Cramer, a political scientist at the University of Wisconsin-Madison, did not, however, appeal to a broader public in the same way as Hochschild. To be sure, this was a matter of language (Cramer stays clear of jargon but doesn't make use of narrative), but also of focus. Like Hochschild, Cramer conducted interviews with rural conservatives. But whereas Hochschild aimed to offer an insight into conservatives' *emotions* by climbing what she called the "empathy wall" separating conservatives from liberals, Cramer instead tried to capture the "rural *consciousness*" of her Wisconsin subjects (her title is a bit misleading: the book does not offer any conceptual, phenomenological, or sociological discussion of the *feeling* of resentment). Telling a story about her subject's feelings and telling a story about how she felt about their feelings—this is the textual formula of Hochschild's narrative sociology that is thrown into relief when her book is compared to Cramer's.

The emphasis on first-person narrative put Hochschild's book in the vicinity of long-form reportage, but in the book market of 2016, it also made *Strangers in Their Own Land* resonate with J.D. Vance's *Hillbilly Elegy*, a Kentucky-Ohio family memoir that offered a first-person glimpse into rustbelt consciousness.[15] Vance's book presented the reader with the feelings of inferiority that beset the protagonist as he moved up from his rural working-class family background to the high-earning, cosmopolitan world of business consulting. *Hillbilly Elegy* faintly recalls Didier Eribon's *Returning to Reims* (which appeared in English translation in 2013), not only because it presents

---

14   Katherine J. Cramer, *The Politics of Resentment: Rural Consciousness in Wisconsin and the Rise of Scott Walker* (Chicago: The University of Chicago Press, 2016).

15   J.D. Vance, *Hillbilly Elegy: A Memoir of a Family and a Culture in Crisis* (New York: Harper Collins, 2016).

a first-person account of the challenges posed by social climbing, but also because Vance tried to articulate sociological explanations of his subjective experiences.[16] And yet, Vance's book is equally distant from *Returning to Reims* as it is from *Strangers in their Own Land* because it demonstrates—rather painfully—just how much training is required to be able to credibly don the sociologist's hat. Vance aimed to turn this shortcoming into an asset by venting his discontentment with any scholarly approach to his hillbilly life: "No single book, or expert, or field could fully explain the problems of hillbillies in modern America," he insisted. "Our elegy is a sociological one, yes, but it is also about psychology and community and culture and faith."[17] Vance's insistence that he could only open the hillbilly world to the reader by shining a light on those dimensions of existence that purportedly lie outside of sociological analysis—psychology, community, culture, and faith—makes sense as a memoirist's pitch. But his anti-sociological stance also took away from the larger explanatory value of his story. Particularly regarding the concern with polarization, *Hillbilly Elegy* has little to offer.

3.

Hochschild, on the other hand, addresses polarization head on in the very first sentence of her preface.

> When I began this research five years ago, I was becoming alarmed at the increasingly hostile split in our nation between two political camps. ... I had some understanding of the liberal left camp, I thought, but what was happening on the right? Most people who ask this question come at it from a political perspective. And while I have my views too, as a sociologist I had a keen interest in how life *feels* to people on the right—that is, in the emotion that underlies politics. To understand their emotions, I had to imagine myself into their shoes. Trying this, I came upon their "deep story," a narrative *as felt*. (ix, emphasis in original)

To reconstruct this "deep story," Hochschild met with forty Tea Party supporters from Lake Charles, Louisiana, and "accumulated over four thousand pages

---

16   Didier Eribon, *Returning to Reims*, trans. Michael Lucey (Los Angeles: Semiotext(e), [2009] 2013).

17   Vance, *Hillbilly Elegy*, 145.

of transcribed interviews" (248). She asked them about their political views, about specific policies, about how they coped with the ecological devastation around them, and, most crucially, she inquired into their moral imagination. Having immersed herself in their world, she tried to come up with a narrative, structured around a single metaphor—people waiting in line—that aimed to capture how they experienced their lives. In the next step, she tested out the deep story with her interviewees. Lo and behold, they all attested that she had really nailed it. This was their story.

Here are its opening paragraphs:

> You are patiently standing in a long line leading up a hill, as in a pilgrimage. You are situated in the middle of this line, along with others who are also white, older, Christian, and predominantly male, some with college degrees, some not.
>
> Just over the brow of the hill is the American Dream, the goal of everyone waiting in line. Many in the back of the line are people of color—poor, young and old, mainly without college degrees. It's scary to look back; there are so many behind you, and in principle you wish them well. Still, you've waited a long time, worked hard, and the line is barely moving. You deserve to move forward a little faster. You're patient but weary. You focus ahead, especially on those at the very top of the hill. (136)

Hochschild's rendition of her Tea Party subjects' deep story mixes the sociologically specific ("white, older, Christian, and predominantly male, some with college degrees, some not" versus "people of color—poor, young and old, mainly without college degrees") with the mythically sedimented. The myth she invokes (by name) is none other than the American Dream, which in this case refers to an economic success story according to which your self-reliant and self-disciplined efforts will eventually be rewarded. The American Dream myth has always been most powerful when brought up as a reminder of how things should be, but are not. So it is in this case: the deep story Hochschild constructs is one of frustration and resentment. It accentuates the disappointment and anger elicited by the feeling that the rewards you were promised for all your good, hard work are being withheld. Frustration, anger, resentment, betrayal: the deep story assembles the emotional underside of the American Dream, the ensemble of affects awaiting those who realize that a dream is just a dream.

The ingenuity of the metaphor of "waiting in line" lies in the way it opens up a plurality of causes for being stuck. There are at least three responses you might develop while ruminating on why the line isn't getting any shorter, only one of which crops up in Hochschild's rendition. You might begin to wonder, firstly, whether perhaps someone is responsible for keeping the line from moving ahead. There might be gatekeepers up ahead, beyond the hill, that do not let enough people through. Or perhaps it isn't the gatekeepers themselves who are the problem; maybe there simply aren't enough gates. Put differently, there might be a systemic problem with access to the rewards deserved by the righteous and hard-working.

Secondly, you might begin to wonder whether the problem lies in the very act of waiting in line. Perhaps rather than worry about access, you begin to worry about your decision to get in line in the first place. Maybe you begin to see that waiting in line isn't worth it, that the ideal you are after isn't as glamorous as you thought. The dream you are waiting in line to realize might begin to appear bankrupt. Maybe, you realize while waiting, the vision of the good life conveyed by the American myth of success doesn't seem all that good anymore. Maybe you begin to imagine a different structure of society, built on more communal, less competitive and less materialistic values.

The third option, however, sees the cause of the problem neither in a broken system, nor in broken ideals, but rather in individualized villains who keep you from getting what you deserve. This is the explanation that features in Hochschild's resentment story. As a metaphor, she introduces "the line cutters."

> Look! You see people *cutting in line ahead of you!* You're following the rules. They aren't. As they cut in, it feels like you are being moved back. How can they just do that? Who are they? Some are black. Through affirmative action plans, pushed by the federal government, they are being given preference for places in colleges and universities, apprenticeships, jobs, welfare payments, and free lunches, and they hold a certain secret place in people's minds, as we see below. Women, immigrants, refugees, public sector workers—where will it end? ... It's not fair.

> And President Obama: how did he rise so high? The biracial son of a low-income single mother becomes president of the most powerful country in the world; you didn't see that coming. And if he's there, what kind of a slouch does his rise make you feel like, you who are supposed to be so much more privileged? (137)

For Hochschild's "Tea Party friends," as she calls them, the only thing that comes to mind while being stuck in line is that someone else is moving past them. Sure, any reader with even a minimal capacity for empathy can understand that this is an experience that feels unjust, and that it will make you want to cry out in anger and frustration. We have all been children at some point, after all. To develop an even deeper empathy—to begin to believe that this story gets the problem right, that there is indeed no other way of responding, yes, that this response is justified—requires the willful negation of responses one and two. Which is probably the reason why they have no place in Hochschild's book.

And yet, Hochschild herself is ultimately at odds with herself about how to treat the deep story, and in particular the portion about line-cutters. Reading the above paragraph out loud, it remains unclear whether Hochschild is really buying into her goal of adopting the perspective of her Louisiana subjects—or whether she is in fact making fun of them. Adopting a second-person free indirect discourse, she conveys characters full of petty resentment. The whining tone ("it's not fair"), the obtuseness ("you didn't see that coming"), the openly expressed envy ("how did *he* rise so high?")—none of this appears to achieve what Hochschild sets out to do: to see the world through the eyes of those who are on the other side of the partisan divide; to muster enough empathy to grant their perspective an inner moral logic and coherence. It's not that Hochschild isn't sincerely trying. It's rather that there is a fundamental logical flaw in trying to gain an understanding of polarization and at the same time work against polarization—all with the help of empathy. In passages such as the above, the contradictions of her project come to the fore.

4.

This brings us to the problem of the dual concern of polarization—the desire to understand and simultaneously to undo it. Not only do these two goals turn out to be incompatible. Like a ping pong player who tries to hit two balls and ends up hitting neither, the sociologist who banks on empathy to explain and help undo polarization will miss both marks at once.

Let's take these targets one at a time. If the goal is to make us understand why people who are economically suffering from the Republican Party's anti-government policies support a political movement that wants to minimize government even further, then comprehending the story these people tell themselves is certainly helpful. The story that Hochschild's Louisiana Tea Partiers recognize as their own is suggestive of how they perceive themselves and the world around them. But what people tell themselves about their views and behavior is not a sufficient explanation of their behavior, nor of the adequacy of their views. A rather old-fashioned term comes to mind here. By exploring a deep story people claim as their own, one may in fact be doing no more than bring to light their false consciousness.

Hochschild is not entirely unaware of this problem. While she wants to avoid explaining her subjects' mindset as false consciousness, she notes that the deep story she reconstructs from the many, many interviews she has led is also the story told day in and day out by Fox News: "Fox commentators reflect your feelings, for your deep story is also the Fox News deep story" (139). But if the deep story is in fact the ideological narrative disseminated by partisan media, then how can Hochschild benefit from feeling her way into her subjects' point of view? Indeed, she would have most likely come up with a similar rendition of the deep story had she skipped the laborious work of interviewing forty Tea Party supporters and had she only worked from the scripts of Fox News and Rush Limbaugh. In which case it would become obvious that the task at hand has nothing to do with empathy, but merely with recording—and decoding—an ideological framework designed to produce nothing if not false consciousness.

One of the books Hochschild briefly discusses in a sort of literature review early on in *Strangers in Their Own Land* is Thomas Frank's *What's the Matter with Kansas? How Conservatives Won the Heart of America* from 2004. Though Hochschild doesn't acknowledge this, Frank starts out by proposing what amounts to various deep stories. He doesn't do any field research to assemble them but simply picks up ideological narratives floating around in the mediasphere. Here are some of the differently accentuated—but interconnected—deep stories offered by Frank.

> Or perhaps you are one of those many, many millions of average-income Americans who see nothing deranged about this at all [the insistence on a conservatism based on free market policies and conservative values]. For you this picture of hard-times conservatism makes perfect sense, and it is the opposite phenomenon—working-class people who insist on voting for liberals—that strikes you as an indecipherable puzzlement. ... Maybe you were one of those who stood up for America way back in 1968, sick of hearing those rich kids in beads badmouth the country every night on TV. Maybe you knew

exactly what Richard Nixon meant when he talked about the "silent majority," the people whose hard work was rewarded with constant insults from
the network news, the Hollywood movies, and the know-it-all college professors, none of them interested in anything you had to say. Or maybe it was
the liberal judges who got you mad as hell, casually rewriting the laws of
your state according to some daft idea they had picked up at a cocktail party,
or ordering your town to shoulder some billion-dollar desegregation scheme
that they had dreamed up on their own, or turning criminals loose to prey
on the hardworking and the industrious. Or perhaps it was the drive for gun
control, which was obviously directed toward the same end of disarming and
ultimately disempowering people like you.[18]

Frank's hypothetical stories are immediately related to Hochschild's deep
story. Indeed, the phrase "hard work was rewarded with constant insults from
the network news" could be lifted directly from *Strangers in Their Own Land*. All
the various versions assembled by Frank in this paragraph emphasize cultural
reasons for "converting" to conservatism, and indeed, it is his argument that
the answer to what Hochschild calls "the great paradox"—why do middle-
and working-class people embrace economic policies that are opposed to
their interests?—lies in the strategic use which economic elites make of
conservative cultural politics. By offering them cultural conservatism, Frank
argues, these elites hoodwink middle- and working-class Americans into
agreeing to economic policies that hurt them.

There may be good reasons for Hochschild to reject Frank's argument.
In fact, her study gives us the valuable insight that the policies of deregula-
tion detrimental to middle- and working-class Americans aren't sold to them
by diverting their attention away from economics to cultural issues, but that
free-market, pro-corporate economic policies are themselves perceived—and
embraced—as cultural issues. But the reason I bring up Frank's book is not to
show how his argument differs from Hochschild's, but to point to a methodological problem of the deep story. I would venture to say that Hochschild's
subjects would have reacted just as approvingly had she come back to them
with the paragraph composed by Frank. Here, too, they would have likely cried
out, like one of the Tea Partiers of her book, "You've read my mind" (145). The

18   Thomas Frank, *What's the Matter with Kansas? How Conservatives Won the Heart of America*
(New York: Henry Holt, 2004), 2–3.

fact that Frank can come up with a comparable version of the deep story simply by reproducing widespread cultural narratives of the American right poses
the question what precisely Hochschild has actually achieved by spending five
years with her "Tea Party friends."

In one of the most trenchant reviews of Hochschild's book, sociologist
Harel Shapira contrasts Hochschild's method with Clifford Geertz's "thick description":

> Geertz does something that Hochschild fails to do: he objectifies his research
> subjects; he turns them into an object of analysis. In so doing, Geertz es-
> tablishes an important and necessary epistemological gap between himself
> and the people he writes about. It is not an empathy gap; it is a gap in what
> it means to understand, in what it is that the researcher understands and
> what it is that people we write about understand.[19]

The knowledge gap between the sociologist (or anthropologist) and the subject
studied by the sociologist hinges on the status of the deep story as ideology.
For the sociologist, reconstructing an ideological narrative is a first, necessary step. But resting there would mean falsely elevating ideology to sociological insight. Suddenly, the Fox News narrative is claimed to be something
more—something deeper—than what it is, although the narrative itself stays
exactly what it was before. It's a magic trick that allows Hochschild to produce effects of epiphany for her interviewees, herself, and a good many of her
readers. To move from magic trick to insight, empathy becomes an obstacle.
As Shapira puts it: "While empathy can help us understand our informants'
truth, it is important to distinguish our informants' truth from sociological
truth—a truth that asks us to make visible the social forces that others are
often blind to."[20]

Hochschild, I take it, both is and is not conscious of the pitfalls that come
with her call for empathy as a sociological method. In its almost parodic tone,
the language she uses in her rendition of the line-cutters portion of the deep
story (quoted above) signals that she is putting herself at a distance from her
subjects, that she cannot make their resentment her own. But rather than own

---

19   Harel Shapira, "Who Cares What They Think? Going About the Right the Wrong Way,"
      review of *Strangers in Their Own Land: Anger and Mourning on the American Right*, by Arlie
      Russell Hochschild, *Contemporary Sociology* 46, no.5 (September 2017): 512–517, here
      515.
20   Shapira, "Who Cares," 516–517.

the distance as an epistemological necessity for reaching sociological truth, she reprimands herself for her moral failure of not living up to her own empathy imperative. "[T]he empathy wall was higher than I'd imagined," she admits repeatedly. "I could see what they couldn't see, but not—as Yogi Berra might say—what I couldn't see. I still felt blind to what they saw and honored" (82). It is as if her analysis were not trying to establish sociological insights about her subjects—seeing what they can't see, for her, isn't of any use—but insights that ultimately relate to herself.

But what kind of insights are these? It is not that she is really writing a sociological account of a Berkeley progressive as she purportedly offers an account of Louisiana Tea Party supporters. Rather, she seems to be subjecting herself to an experiment, the goal of which is to immerse herself so deeply in her subjects' worldviews that she throws overboard all of her excess knowledge and becomes like them. It is an experiment that smacks of controlled spiritual conversion. She calls it "getting in the spirit of things." Thus, as she is pondering the contradictions of industrial expansion in light of radical environmental devastation in the Lake Charles area, she reports on her thought process: "As I was trying to climb this slippery empathy wall, a subversive thought occurred to me: do we need all the new plastic the American Chemical Association is promising us? ... We'll throw away more plastic bottles, buy more, and further expand the market for plastic, the production of which pollutes water. But I was straying from my goal, getting into the spirit of things" (91-92). It is a true dilemma in which Hochschild finds herself. Not only does the empathy wall remain slippery; so do the sociological insights her book promises to yield. Put differently, empathy is keeping her from gaining the distance from her subjects that she would need to decode their deep story, while the ethnographic starting point of her study—she may have found new friends in Louisiana, but she remains a visitor from California—bars her from fulfilling her goal of total empathetic immersion.

5.

It may ultimately be beside the point, however, to criticize Hochschild for failing to produce any deep sociological knowledge about her subjects. After all, it is reasonable to suggest that Hochschild's dual concern with polarization is not so much directed at sociologically decoding the worldview of the right, but at finding a way of engaging with people on the other side of the divide. The task of public sociology, from this view, prioritizes the public over sociology. *Strangers in their Own Land* would have to be seen as an exercise in civility, as practical guide to revitalize a democratic public in the stranglehold of polarization.

In her response to a review by William Davies, Hochschild indeed seems to measure the success of her book by its effect on bipartisan discourse: "Given the split between sectors and classes, it is all the more important to try to heal the political breach, especially given a president who has shown himself to be both divisive and volatile. ... Almost as if in answer to all this, a grassroots nationwide movement is on the rise."[21] The task of her book, we may infer, is to provide material for this new grassroots movement that is trying to heal the nation. In fact, she characterizes the strategy of the bipartisan movement in the very terms she used for explaining the rationale of her book. In the Preface to *Strangers*, she writes, "I have lived most of my life in the progressive camp but in recent years I began to want to better understand those on the right. How did they come to hold their views? Could we make common cause on some issues?" (xi). That same hope to come together on shared issues, she claims, mobilizes the new anti-polarization movement she has made out: "Deep political differences remain, of course, but efforts in this nationwide, grassroots movement to heal the rift have revealed a series of specific 'cross-over' issues—the reduction of prison populations, the importance of clean energy, peace."[22]

While Hochschild, writing in 2017, puts her hope in an allegedly emerging non-partisan movement, the majority of recent studies by political scientists point out that the United States continues to become more intensely polarized.[23] As I pointed out at the beginning of this essay, not even the coronavirus epidemic seems to be able to fundamentally change this. The question I wish to pose, however, is not whether the grassroots movement in which Hochschild puts her hope, and to which she clearly wants to belong, has gained any discernible traction or not. The question is rather whether Hochschild's idea of how to overcome polarization can work. The answer hinges on our understanding of contemporary polarization.

---

21   Arlie Russel Hochschild, "A Response to William Davies' 'A Review of Arlie Russell Hochschild's *Strangers in Their Own Land: Anger and Mourning on the American Right*,'" *International Journal of Politics, Culture, and Society* 30 (2017): 421–423, here 422.

22   Hochschild, "Response," 423.

23   For a good overview of the scholarship, see Klein, *Why We're Polarized*.

No doubt, Hochschild is very earnest in her hopes that by learning to understand the other side, Americans will be able to rekindle bi-partisan conversations. With enough empathy, they will feel how the other sides sees and experiences the world. Without empathizing away all disagreement, their new understanding and appreciation of the people in the other camp will allow them to come together on issues that they are equally invested in. They will, Hochschild hopes, form coalitions in fighting for fewer prison inmates, less pollution, and peace.

Ultimately, Hochschild seems right to suggest that any way out of polarization will have to involve a rekindling of the democratic public sphere. Overcoming the partisan splits that endanger US democracy will have to involve that people begin to re-learn how to talk to one another. In that sense, the grassroots movement on whose burgeoning she insists (whether rightly or wrongly) cannot be entirely on the wrong track. And yet, I'm afraid that the path on which Hochschild has set out to reach a democratic rebirth will prove a dead end. This is the case because she gets wrong what is currently driving polarization, and how empathy reinforces rather than offsets this dynamic.

Political scientists such as Bill Bishop, Matthew Levendusky, and Lilliana Mason have shown that polarization in the United States has turned all politics into identity politics.[24] Not the type of identity politics that pushes for the recognition of marginalized groups, but one in which taking sides in political struggles is a matter of your identity as a liberal or conservative, or better: Democrat of Republican. In this process, what political scientists call "ideology"—the set of policy positions held by voters—becomes subservient to party identification. As Levendusky puts it, "voters typically shift their ideology to fit with their party identification."[25]

As they turn politics into identity politics, Americans begin to reduce the complexity of a highly differentiated and pluralized society into exactly two camps. As Mason observes: "Across the electorate, Americans have been dividing with increasing distinction into two partisan teams. Emerging research has shown that members of both parties negatively stereotype members of the opposing party, and the extent of this partisan stereotyping has increased

---

24   See Bill Bishop, *The Big Sort: Why the Clustering of Like-Minded America is Tearing Us Apart* (Boston: Houghton Mifflin, 2008); Matthew Levendusky, *The Partisan Sort: How Liberals Became Democrats and Conservatives Became Republicans* (Chicago: University of Chicago Press, 2009); Mason, *Uncivil Agreement*.

25   Levendusky, *The Partisan Sort*, 3.

by 50 percent between 1960 and 2010. They view the other party as more extreme than their own, while they view their own party as not at all extreme."[26] The dynamic in which people behave when their identity comes up against the other camp's identity takes on characteristics that are difficult to square with the requirements of a democratic public. As they create enmity with the other team—which is partially imaginary but by no means illusory since its effects are all too real—Americans begin to succumb to a zero-sum logic of conflict, in which victory becomes the greatest aspiration and defeat the greatest fear. "Group victory is a powerful prize, and American partisans have increasingly seen that goal as more important than the practical matters of governing a nation," writes Mason.[27] As she points out, Trump is particularly adept at cashing in on the currency of group victory. Not for nothing did he promise crowds early on during his campaign in 2015, "We will have so much winning if I get elected that you may get bored with the winning."[28]

With politics having become a matter of identity, political allegiance not only predetermines a whole package of increasingly polarized policy positions any given individual is likely to buy into; political identity also becomes a matter of a whole way of life, seeping into where you do your grocery shopping, what car you drive, how you comport yourself, etc. In other words, in the type of polarized society exemplified and spearheaded by the United States, political identity becomes cultural identity.

Another useful way of understanding this is to describe cultural identity as an overarching "mega-identity," as Mason calls it. She distinguishes between political identity—defined by the question, which party do you belong to?—and social identities, such as religion, race, class, etc. In the current process of polarization, it isn't just that political identities move further apart. They also begin to snowball, attaching to themselves those social identities that initially had to be considered separate from political identities.

> Religion and race, as well as class, geography, and culture, are dividing the parties in such a way that the effect of party identity is magnified. The competition is no longer between Democrats and Republicans. A single vote can now indicate a person's partisan preference as well as his or her religion, race, ethnicity, gender, neighborhood, and favorite grocery store. This is no longer

---

26   Mason, *Uncivil Agreement*, 3.

27   Mason, 4.

28   Mason, 2.

a single social identity. Partisanship can now be thought of as a mega-identity, with all the psychological and behavioral magnifications that implies.[29]

To be sure, social identity components were always attached to political identities. For instance, for many decades, class identity was clearly aligned with political identity. What has changed today is that to each political identity is attached a whole assortment of social identities. While throughout American history it was common to have many voters with cross-cutting identities—those who mixed and matched from the range of social identity components—such cross-cutting has become an exceedingly rare phenomenon.

The conclusion that Mason draws from her analysis is only logical. In order to revitalize a democratic public—to make it possible for Americans to come into contact with members of the other team, and to find compromises with them—the aggregations of social identity clusters into "mega-identities" need to be loosened. Only when political identity no longer determines the whole set of a person's social identity components will it be possible for people to reach across the aisle. For under these conditions, the aisle will merely be a political aisle that has already been crossed on a regular basis in many other dimensions of everyday life. Psychologically, this disaggregation will make it easier to interact and deliberate with people from the other team since what is at stake—what is potentially threatened in a confrontation—is no longer the totality of a person's identity, but only the position on a given issue.

At first glance, it might seem as if Hochschild could agree with this assessment. As she writes, "should the grievous day arrive when President Trump declares progressive and liberal citizens as 'enemies of the American people,' let it fall on the deaf ears of those who have already broken bread with them."[30] The grassroots movement she cheers on could be seen as driving a wedge into identity blocks compactly opposing one another.

At the same time, however, Hochschild's investment in empathy works against the centrifugal forces that might break open the identity clusters that compose the polarized camps. "Getting in the spirit of things," "coming to see the world through their eyes": approaches such as these are prone to reify overarching mega-identities, rather than break them open. Instead of contributing to making politics less a matter of culture, she ends up furthering the culturalization of politics. Instead of working towards a disidentification

---

29   Mason, 14.

30   Hochschild, "Response," 423

of politics, she pursues as cultural politics of recognition, on the basis of which she hopes to mount a new democratic culture. Tellingly, even her best hope for such a democratic revival remains identity-bound. Rather than envisioning a public sphere in which people come to find compromise through debate, she hopes to bring people from opposite camps into coalitions over issues about which they in truth already agree. Democracy, for her, isn't about conflict, deliberation, and compromise, but about communities of agreement. Hoping to climb the empathy wall in order to undo polarization thus turns out to be an ill-fated effort. The goal is not to climb the empathy wall. The goal is to tear it down by dispersing the identity you could empathize with.

The best hope to overcome polarization, then, would be a politics of disidentification, in which the bundle of sorted identity components becomes disaggregated. The task may be herculean, but it does not require going to Louisiana to see how the other half feels. One might instead begin by driving a couple of wedges into one's own sense of self.

15. Thick Redescription
Narrating Sociocultural Forms with Matthew Desmond's *Evicted* (2016)

Alexander Starre

I first read *Evicted: Poverty and Profit in the American City* while on fellowship at Brown University in Providence, Rhode Island. The year was 2017, and, I seem to recall, I started reading Matthew Desmond's bestseller right around the time Donald Trump was inaugurated over the course of a few bleak winter weeks. I'm not a sociologist, neither do I work on urban poverty in the United States. Aside from the many books and essays that form my daily pile of professional reading in literary and cultural studies (somehow always growing, never shrinking), I like to have a handful of non-American novels and general interest books around my place that I can pick up at odd hours to let my thoughts run elsewhere. Desmond's book was in that latter category, having little to nothing in common with my ongoing research at the time. I was also grateful, I remember, to escape from the daily television coverage and online news feeds chronicling the first fits and starts of a disastrous presidency into a coherent and forceful narrative that tackled and made sense of profound social problems in America.

I always like to think of books, even academic works, as material objects in the world. With the book at my side as I write these lines, I am struck by the way my paperback copy of *Evicted* literally comes wrapped in cultural capital: the covers of the book proclaim it a "book of the year" as selected by the *New York Times*, the *New Yorker* and the *Washington Post*, as well as the winner of the Pulitzer Prize, the National Book Critics Circle Award, a Carnegie Medal, and the PEN / John Kenneth Galbraith Award for Nonfiction.[1] An endorsement by

---

1   I admit that the inclusion of *Evicted* on the *NYT* "10 Best Books of 2016" list was probably what prompted me to pick up a copy at the campus bookstore.

Barbara Ehrenreich establishes the book's academic credentials on the front cover, while short blurbs on the back by authors Ann Patchett and Jesmyn Ward lend a certain literary cachet to this ethnographic work. In his study, Desmond follows eight families in post-Great Recession Milwaukee who try to escape the vicious cycle of poverty, eviction, and homelessness, while also portraying the strategies that landlords, city courts, the police, and other actors employ to manage and often exploit lower-class renters. Desmond contends that the bottom portion of the private housing market is not distinct from the capitalist excesses in prestige real estate development; if anything, the immense potentials for profit and the structural exploitation in this market segment lend themselves to even more predatory behavior.

The book's enormous success, both popular and academic, speaks to the fact that it qualifies in the eyes of many current experts and readers as an ideal type of epistemic artifact. *Evicted*'s massive impact on the cultural conversation in the United States certainly stirs the type of "sociology envy" that Rita Felski recently diagnosed in herself and in the wider discipline of literary and cultural studies.[2] Traditionally, literary criticism and media studies have turned to sociology for framing theories and concepts that locate aesthetic objects within larger social domains (think Bourdieu's "literary field," Luhmann's "social systems," or Williams's "structures of feeling"). But the attempt to analytically connect micro-phenomena (e.g., a literary text) to macro-phenomena (e.g., capitalist Western society) needs to draw upon various registers of critical practice, with theory being only one of them. It also requires forms of narrative redescription that follow connections between domains, relations between people, institutions, and artifacts. Taking the reflexive stance of *Culture*^{2} as my cue, I inquire less into the content of Desmond's book (i.e., less into *what* it tells us about American culture) and more into its form: *how* does *Evicted* become such a supremely effective account of urban, race-inflected poverty? A great part of its appeal lies in the public-facing nature of its written prose, which is not only more empirically grounded and more directly political than today's literary and cultural criticism—as one should expect from good sociology—but also more assertively literary in style. I read *Evicted* as a late outcropping of a submerged strand of American sociology associated with the pioneering, but often professionally sidelined work of early activist sociologists such as W.E.B. Du Bois and Jane Addams. With Desmond's study as my

---

2   Rita Felski, "My Sociology Envy," *Theory, Culture & Society* (blog), July 25, 2019, https://www.theoryculturesociety.org/rita-felski-my-sociology-envy/.

companion text, I aim to make a case for sociological *narrative*, rather than sociological *theory*, as a useful interdisciplinary resource for cultural studies. Furthermore, this short essay sketches how Desmond's intervention in *Evicted* rests on a foundation made up of a network of co-texts that firmly anchor it in a midway position between the scholarly publication sphere and the wider domains of mass media discourse.

*

In *The Racial Order*, their ambitious work on social theory and an important companion text for *Evicted*, Matthew Desmond and his co-author (and erstwhile doctoral adviser) Mustafa Emirbayer link their sociological outlook to a peculiar American genealogy of the field. In the closing paragraphs of the book, they refer to a "primordial diremption" in the early years of professionalized American sociology, which split apart a "reformist, public-minded" type of inquiry from what would become the "discipline-building, professionalizing" mainstream.[3] This rift between positivist and normativist schools of thought, they argue, needs to be overcome: "The way forward requires affirming, as Addams and Du Bois sought to do from the outset … that reflections on the kind of society and racial order one wants to have—and considerations as to how it might be brought about—do not have to be relegated to the realm of arbitrary speculation. These moral practical inquiries also can be reasoned, systematic, and open to empirical testing in much the same way as substantive knowledge about the racial world."[4]

Indeed, Du Bois's early work, which emerged from his research activities as an enterprising social scientist trying to break into the white-dominated academy, struck this balance between empiricism and didacticism with care—and sometimes with flair. As such, *The Philadelphia Negro* (1898), Du Bois's first professional study after his doctoral dissertation, carries as its first footnote the following pronouncement regarding the word "Negro": "I shall, moreover, capitalize the word, because I believe that eight million Americans are entitled to a capital letter."[5] This is quite a prescient opening salvo, considering how publishers and newsrooms in America are only now opting for

---

3   Mustafa Emirbayer and Matthew Desmond, *The Racial Order* (Chicago: The University of Chicago Press, 2015), 358.
4   Emirbayer and Desmond, *The Racial Order*, 359.
5   W.E.B. Du Bois, *The Philadelphia Negro: A Social Study* (New York: Oxford University Press, [1899] 2014), 2.

a capital B in "Black" after the groundswell of Black Lives Matter activism in 2020. Bracketing the many pages of measured prose and innumerable statistical items, the final chapter of the book ends with urgent rhetoric within two sections of moral-practical advice titled "The Duty of the Negroes" and "The Duty of the Whites." Having staked out a claim to identity and citizenship in its first footnote, the book ends with an earnest, poetic admonishment of Philadelphia's white citizenry. Du Bois calls for a "polite and sympathetic attitude" and a "desire to reward honest success" on behalf of the whites, and ends with the exhortation that "all this, added to the proper striving on their part, will go far, even in our day toward making all men, white and Black, realize what the great founder of the city meant, when he named it the City of Brotherly Love."[6] Coming on the heels of the publication of his doctoral thesis as the first monograph in the Harvard Historical Series, *The Philadelphia Negro* constituted Du Bois's full-fleshed attempt to establish himself in the professional field of sociology. In a larger context, this turn-of-the-century sociological publication partakes of the foundational identity crisis of this very field, which wavered between, as Wolf Lepenies has written, "a scientific orientation which has led it to ape the natural sciences and a hermeneutic attitude which has shifted the discipline toward the realm of literature."[7] Within Du Bois's early oeuvre around 1900, *The Philadelphia Negro* gravitates toward the domain of science, while *The Souls of Black Folk* (1903) marks the author's entry into *belles lettres*.

As recent scholarship has examined, this mixture of hard science, activist interpretation, and literary style—pioneered by Du Bois but also by Jane Addams and her associates at Chicago's Hull House—was relegated to the sidelines throughout twentieth-century professional sociology, with race- and gender-based discriminatory structures engulfing and curtailing its impact.[8] With explicit references to this shadow history of American sociology included in *The Racial Order*, Desmond's widely read work in *Eviction* also be-

---

6   Du Bois, *Philadelphia Negro*, 275.

7   Wolf Lepenies, *Between Literature and Science: The Rise of Sociology* (Cambridge: Cambridge University Press, 1988), 1.

8   With regard to these two underappreciated founding figures of American sociology, see Aldon D. Morris, *The Scholar Denied: W.E.B. Du Bois and the Birth of Modern Sociology* (Oakland: University of California Press, 2015); Mary Jo Deegan, *Jane Addams and the Men of the Chicago School, 1892–1918* (New Brunswick: Transaction Books, 1988).

comes implicitly aligned with the trajectory of a more narratively engaged and interventionist approach of social inquiry.[9]

*

In her essay on her "sociology envy," Felski contends that sociology has a bad rep among literary and cultural studies scholars because it is often caricatured in one of two ways: either "as being synonymous with quantitative and statistical methods" or "as associated with broad synoptic theories of modern or postmodern society." She reflects on the value of sociological writing for her own career as an academic: "Looking back over my own writing, for example, I'm struck by how often I've been helped out of intellectual jams and dead-ends by sociological thought."[10] She goes on to list Georg Simmel, C. Wright Mills, George Herbert Mead, Max Weber, and Luc Boltanski as important sociological interlocutors to her thought. Reflecting on this small canon, Felski holds,

> None of this work drew on quantitative methods; nor did it turn to sociology to bolster broad claims about the nature of modern or postmodern society. What I found instructive in sociology, rather, was its sharply honed attentiveness to the many kinds of phenomena that make up social existence. While sociologists continue to assume a concept of society—a concept that Bruno Latour, for example, would question—they cannot help being conscious that this society is highly variegated and differentiated: made up of many kinds of institutions, communities, norms, and behaviors.[11]

If I were to reflect on the genesis of my own conceptual thinking on the interrelation between "culture" and society, I would likewise highlight the influence of theoretical sociology by writers such as Niklas Luhmann or—more recently and going along with many in the field—Bruno Latour. At the end of the day, however, one returns to the writing on the page, the practical medium that

---

9   Consider Morris on the way Du Bois innovatively combined research methods in his early work as a freshly minted Harvard PhD: "Du Bois emerged from *The Philadelphia Negro* as the first number-crunching, surveying, interviewing, participant-observing and field-working sociologist in America, a pioneer in the multimethods approach" (Morris, *Scholar Denied*, 47). While the relative proportions are different, Desmond's account in *Evicted* is based on all these methods as well.

10   Felski, "My Sociology Envy."

11   Ibid.

has to lay out a narrative path connecting various levels of analysis—from a literary character or a specific metaphor, say, via genres and institutions, all the way to "American culture" or "neoliberal ideology."

So how does *Evicted* do this?

*

While you shouldn't judge a book by its epigraph, the paratextual addendum of a signifying quote often establishes a meaningful framing, with snippets from literary source texts frequently used to open accounts of a non-fictional nature. Desmond chose Langston Hughes's poem "Little Lyric (Of Great Importance)" for this purpose. The framing achieved via Hughes's poetic hope for a "heaven-sent" solution to poverty among urban renters highlights, first, the durability of the housing problem in the United States and, second, its peculiar relevance to non-white communities.

After this opening move, the prologue of the book starts in medias res, with the simple sentence "Jori and his cousin were cutting up, tossing snowballs at passing cars" (1).[12] The reader will get to meet the adolescent Black boy Jori, his mother Arleen Belle, and his little brother Jafaris in more detail in the chapters to follow; but first we see Jori's snowball spinning through the air on a cold January day in 2008, landing on or close to a passing car; the car stops, the driver gets out and runs in pursuit of the two boys; he doesn't stop at the front door the boys had thrown shut behind them but kicks the wooden barrier down; this small incident triggers a chain of events resulting in the landlord's decision to evict Jori and his family. What does this opening establish? A very common narrative strategy, such a beginning *in medias res* grips the reader's attention right at the get-go before leading over to a more thorough introduction to the storyworld: drama before exposition. A reviewer for a sociological journal would likely write this off as mere decorative prose distracting from the scholarly core of the argument. But is this paragraph not also something more? We could say, with Latour, that Desmond here manages to enlarge the sphere of actors by showing the interactions of humans, structures (car, street), and objects (snowball, door) as they bring about a surprising result that needed the active agency of each to come about. We could also say, against Latour, that the affordances of snowballs and doors really do not matter much in such a scenario but that this passage merely illustrates a

---

12   All parenthetical citations in the text refer to Matthew Desmond, *Evicted: Poverty and Profit in the American City* (New York: Broadway Books, 2016).

principle in which certain human behavior (youthful shenanigans) results in specific social outcomes (repercussions for parents).

In the larger scope of *Evicted*'s narrative, the opening scene manages to provide an apt metaphor—the snowball—to illustrate how little it takes in the precarious situation of poor Americans for their home to be lost and their daily lives to be upended by eviction. As the reader begins to follow the characters, the opening image of the snowball remains in the background. Which small action, which inconsequential transgression, which damaged or lost item will precipitate the next tragic eviction?

In multiple cases, Desmond injects a positive tone into scenes of despair. For example, here is the invisible narrator-sociologist observing Arleen and Jori on the day of yet another eviction:

> At sunrise on Thursday, the sky was the color of flat beer. By midmorning, it was the color of a robin's egg. The still and leafless tree branches looked like cracks in the sky's shell. Cars rolled slowly through the streets, caked with salt and winter's grime. Milwaukee Public Schools canceled classes because of the cold advisory. Arleen's boys weren't going anyway. She needed them to help her move. Jori loaded a U-Haul truck that a family friend had rented for them. The cold gripped him. His fingers and ears began to sting. Icy air filled his mouth, and it felt like his gums were hardening into one of those plastic molds of teeth in the school nurse's office. His breath was a thick gauze circling his face. He smiled through it, happy to be useful. (211)

If I understand Rita Felski's description of her sociology envy correctly, what she has in mind is a more direct form of accessing literary and cultural fields as sites of social action as well as a specific kind of thinking on interrelations between social spheres and institutions. Now, would not a literary scholar also envy the way that Matthew Desmond gets to write the above paragraph—a beautifully thick redescription of what he observed in the field? (The beauty of it deriving from the way that the prose style coordinates social setting and aesthetic expression, as when he associates the morning sky over one of the poorest parts of Milwaukee with "the color of flat beer.")

Desmond unsettles the expectations that many readers (among them reform-minded, liberal urbanites who buy books recommended by the *NYT*) will bring to this narrative. He humanizes his subjects in a way that, on the one hand, illustrates how they are entangled with systems of oppression and exploitation but, on the other hand, also lends them a narrative space to feel, think, and act outside of the stereotypical social positionality they are in. The brief glimpse into Jori's head in the quote above—surely not backed up by much empirical data—gestures at the reference frame of a child thinking about the school nurse's office while also showing the pride of agency that can emerge within the oppressive and depressing scenario of being evicted.[13]

Desmond's characters stand in for the statistical norm but also include several outliers. As a Black single mother trying to provide a home and a livelihood for her family, Arleen Belle serves as a representative for an important social group in the lowest segment of Milwaukee's housing market. Her landlord Sherrena Tarver is an outlier, one of the very few Black female landlords in the city, who expertly navigates the market and accumulates enough property and capital to afford extended vacations and prestige professional events. While Sherrena's success story shows the complexity of the race-biased economy, Arleen's multiple evictions speak to the supreme precarity of Black female tenants in the American city. Spending time in the Milwaukee County eviction court right before Christmas, Desmond briefly zooms out of his chronicle of various characters, who try to prevent eviction, and presents a macro view of the structural racism hardwired into these institutions: "If incarceration had come to define the lives of men from impoverished Black neighborhoods, eviction was shaping the lives of women. Poor Black men were locked up. Poor Black women were locked out" (98). This is a stark pronouncement, but also an eminently quotable phrase that begs to be shared far beyond the networks of scholarly communication. Not surprisingly, Barbara Ehrenreich latched onto this statement in her *New York Times* review, calling it an "epiphany."[14] It *reads* like an epiphany, that much is true. But the passage

---

13   The most instructive instance of this comes in a longer passage about how the poor white woman Larraine spends her entire monthly food stamp allowance on a lobster and shrimp meal after toying with the thought of buying a large TV set (217–220). Desmond pairs this up with a series of longer footnotes which include a transcribed conversation between him and Arleen. Desmond asks her: "When I write about this, it's going to be a little hard for people to understand," (377), referencing the potential reaction even of well-meaning readers to such careless frivolity. Larraine replies: "Well, they don't have to understand it. I don't understand a lot of things other people do, but they do it" (377). After a literature review on US mainstream reactions to perceived luxury items in US households, Desmond affirms his stance: "There are two ways to dehumanize: the first is to strip people of all virtue; the second is to cleanse them of all sin" (378).

14   Barbara Ehrenreich, "Matthew Desmond's 'Evicted: Poverty and Profit in the American City,'" *The New York Times*, February 26, 2016. www.nytimes.com/2016/02/28/books/review/matthew-desmonds-evicted-poverty-and-profit-in-the-american-city.html

is of course *carefully constructed* to appear as such. In a pair of accompanying footnotes that stretch across several pages of fine print, Desmond performs the epistemic heavy lifting: first, he outlines the results of his own statistical number-crunching based on close to 100,000 eviction records of the county of Milwaukee; then, he adds statistical and critical literature on Black incarceration.

In a way, what holds for Desmond's work as a whole—more on that below—also holds for the internal structure of *Evicted* as a monograph: it resembles a lean edifice (the main text) erected on top of a broad and multi-voiced foundation (paratexts such as afterword and footnotes). Why multi-voiced? On the one hand, we find in the footnotes the typically restrained voice of the academic, documenting research activity and surveying the critical literature in the field. Even in this professional voice, the book has its convention-breaking moments, as when Desmond recommends Elie Wiesel's *Night* and Tim O'Brien's *The Things They Carried* as "accounts of human behavior under extreme conditions" (376)—both of which are formally experimental accounts of trauma and war. (Note also that he simply writes "accounts" and not "literary accounts.") On the other hand, the footnotes also feature a more reflective, if not exactly personal voice that bubbles up occasionally. In one of the final footnotes, Desmond writes: "There's this idea that ethnography is a 'method.' ... I tend to think of ethnography as a *sensibility*, a 'way of seeing' as the anthropologist Harry Wolcott once put it. This means that ethnography isn't something we go and do. It's a fundamental way of being in the world" (403-04). This is a bold declaration, hidden in a very out-of-the-way place. Many casual readers will never notice this passage. And yet, it exerts influence and lends stability to the entire structure, in its supportive role as part of the reflexive foundation of *Evicted*.

*

After these stray comments on narrative style and structure, I want to look at one last formal aspect of Desmond's *Evicted*: narrative voice. In the afterword "About this Project," the reader receives a thorough making-of, as Desmond chronicles his days in the field, in this case split between a few months spent in a trailer park home and a longer stretch of time during which he trailed several of his sources while based in a rented apartment on Milwaukee's North Side. In the main narrative, however, there is no "I." The person Matthew Desmond does not seem to exist as a character in his own narrative. This stands in marked contrast to other recent public-facing sociology books. To give just one example, Arlie Hochschild's *Strangers in Their Own Land* (2016)—one of the bestselling books during that year's post-election search for meaning—makes extensive use of the first person, as Hochschild combines the story of her rural white subjects with a chronicle of her own ethical and ideological positioning in the field.[15] Desmond remains mum on this and only introduces such questions in the paratextual foundation of his text. Why?

In the afterword, Desmond rationalizes his formal decision in the following way:

> Ethnography has come to be written almost exclusively in the first person. It is a straightforward way of writing and an effective one. If ethnographers want people to take what they say seriously, the cultural anthropologist Clifford Geertz once observed, they have to convince readers that they have "been there." "And that," Geertz said, "persuading us that this offstage miracle has occurred, is where the writing comes in." The first person has become the chosen mule for this task. *I was there. I saw it happen. And because I saw it happen, you can believe it happened.* Ethnographers shrink themselves in the field but enlarge themselves on the page because first-person accounts convey experience—and experience, authority. (334)

Seen from the vantage point of the large-scale reckoning with issues of race and anti-Black racism in the wake of the police murder of George Floyd, it seems plausible that this stylistic and formal decision on the part of Desmond, the white author, also transports a political message in a narrative centered on predominantly Black actors. Desmond attests to his unease with the public embrace of the white expert by the larger public:

> [A]fter almost every academic talk I have given on the material in this book, I have been asked questions like: "How did you feel when you saw that?" "How did you gain this sort of access?" ... I am interested in a different, more urgent conversation. "I" don't matter. I hope that when you talk about this book, you talk first about Sherrena and Tobin, Arleen and Jori, Larraine and Scott and Pam, Crystal and Vanetta—and the fact that somewhere in your

---

15   See the essay on Hochschild by Johannes Voelz in this volume. On the use of first-person narrative in feminist theory and cultural studies, also see the essay by Maria Sulimma on Clare Hemmings.

city, a family has just been evicted from their home, their things piled high on the sidewalk. (335)

Lots of elements are at play in this scenario. Especially in an academic setting, such talks generally draw very privileged crowds, if not solely in terms of economic capital, then definitely in terms of symbolic capital. There will be a certain amount of voyeurism when such audiences are presented with the unsavory details of lower-class lives on the brink in the inner city, as reported by one of their own social set. Given this situation, people in the audience will likely empathize more with the researcher than with the researched—out of sheer professional proximity, but also because this is the much safer position. Yet, as Desmond well knows, his professional position allows him to actively consecrate the life experiences of people like Arleen and Sherrena, transfer them into "knowledge," and thereby build his symbolic capital in the academy.[16] In a crass sense, then, the exploitation critiqued in the book would be reenacted in and through its circulation.

There is no ethically pure way out of this situation. It is to Desmond's credit, I believe, that he realizes that narrative itself has agency in this communicative process (co-incidentally a base assumption informing the fields of American Studies and cultural studies at large). To distribute agency in a scholarly text—to really, fundamentally ask "who is doing what here?"—and then to compose sentences accordingly: this is a strategy that I take to be the essence of actor-network *practice* in the social sciences and humanities.

*

Moving on from the narrative structure(s) of *Evicted*, I wish to make a brief point about its positioning within Matthew Desmond's oeuvre. His publications in multiple venues also take on something like a larger structure—a structure that certainly contributed to the strong effect of *Evicted* on American public discourse and on policymaking in the housing market. *Culture²* focuses on singular works, on standalone monographs that shape our thinking. As I have tried to show with regard to Jane Addams and W.E.B. Du Bois, as well as in a different register with regard to Rita Felski, Desmond's book needs to be contextualized within larger intellectual conversations spanning more than a century.

---

16   In Desmond and Emirbayer's *The Racial Order*, the field theory and the notion of symbolic capital by Pierre Bourdieu hold a central position.

Nevertheless, the description I used for this book—the lean edifice erected on top of a broad and multi-voiced foundation—also applies to the relationship between *Evicted* and Desmond's other writings. As I already mentioned, Desmond co-wrote the magisterial tome *The Racial Order* (2015), which proposes a comprehensive frame theory for race studies. This book came paired with the textbook *Race in America* (2016), also co-written with Mustafa Emirbayer.[17] Add to this several essays and journal articles. Like any academic, Desmond publishes study results in increments across a variety of academic journals. Among his essays, I would single out two that do more than regular papers. These two position pieces stake out Desmond's disciplinary position, one in a more methodical fashion, one in an almost philosophical manner.[18] They establish "relational" and "reflexive" as key terms for his style of academic inquiry; remarkably, however, these terms and their attendant scholarly posture hardly ever appear in the register of *Evicted's* narrative. Instead, *Evicted* is relational and reflexive without rubbing your nose in it.

In this light, we can perhaps think of Desmond's bestseller as a distributed work. The book is assertively a work, a standalone artifact that has made an enormous impact in the form of a self-contained analysis. It is also and at the same time a distributed object; it rests on a broad foundation of texts in different registers and formal tonalities. The book would be a different artifact without these foundations. It can afford to be lean, precise, and narratively immersive because the gaps that it leaves have been filled elsewhere. In turn, the prestige garnered from *Evicted* gave Matthew Desmond authority and reach when he contributed a widely discussed and also fiercely criticized piece on the historical crosscurrents between capitalism and American slavery to Nikole Hannah-Jones's 1619 Project, published in 2019 by the *New York Times*.[19]

---

17   Matthew Desmond and Mustafa Emirbayer, *Race in America* (New York: Norton, 2016).

18   Mustafa Emirbayer and Matthew Desmond, "Race and Reflexivity," *Ethnic and Racial Studies* 35, no. 4 (2012): 574–99; Matthew Desmond, "Relational Ethnography," *Theory and Society* 43, no. 5 (2014): 547–79.

19   Matthew Desmond, "American Capitalism Is Brutal. You Can Trace That to the Plantation," *The New York Times Magazine*, "The 1619 Project," August 14, 2019, 30–40. For an opinionated discussion of Desmond's essay and in the context of research in "the new history of capitalism," see John Clegg, "How Slavery Shaped American Capitalism," *Jacobin*, August 28, 2019, https://jacobinmag.com/2019/08/how-slavery-shaped-american-capitalism.

*

So what is a humanist to learn from Desmond? As I tried to show in the beginning, the standard mode of practicing "sociologically enhanced" literary and cultural studies looks almost exclusively to sociological theory that can in some way or another be applied within readings of cultural artifacts. This is a tried-and-true technique that has resulted in robust interdisciplinary conversations and in multiple historical and cultural reframings and rereadings. Conversely, the recent tendency to treat Bruno Latour as another master theorist, whose works need to be quoted in every ambitious piece of research and will thus enter an inevitable boom/bust cycle, leads me to think that this overall procedure is somewhat exhausted.[20]

I will not enter the extensive debate on postcritique in my last few lines here—several other chapters take up this conversation. However, I will note that one of the pre-eminent critics currently assembled under this moniker had very kind words to say about Matthew Desmond. In her reply to a recent forum piece in *American Literary History* by Winfried Fluck, Caroline Levine defended the central claim of her recent scholarship, namely that literature, and especially realist literature, already does a better job than much cultural and social theory in accounting for "how the structuring of the social world works." Yet it's not just literature in the Dickensian tradition that achieves this effect. "It seems to me," she continues, "that many ethnographic sociologies, from Henry Mayhew's *London Labour and the London Poor* (1851–1861) to Matthew Desmond's *Evicted: Poverty and Property* [sic] *in the American City* (2016), also offer convincing accounts of the complex interaction of multiple social forms. These too, like *Bleak House*, are multiplot narratives with many characters interacting with overlapping institutions, including homeless shelters, schools, and the legal system."[21] In the best of scenarios, the intersection of postcritique and Latourian thinking injects a healthy dose of humility into the field of cultural studies. To extrapolate from Levine, we can try to align our scholarly interests with finely plotted narratives in the hope of saying something new and noteworthy and perhaps emancipatory about social structures.

In the current moment, in which basic tenets regarding the "right" register of speaking about aesthetic artifacts and the basic units of narrative—think

---

20   See Jesse Ramírez's chapter in this volume for a critique of Latourism in the humanities.

21   Caroline Levine, "Not Against Structure, but in Search of Better Structures: A Response to Winfried Fluck," *American Literary History* 31, no. 2 (2019): 255–259, here 259.

of David Alworth's reconceptualization of literary setting or Rita Felski, Toril Moi, and Amanda Anderson's recent ground clearing regarding literary characters[22]—converge with an unprecedented urgency of social problems that Americanists are called to address, it would be a mistake to only stray into sociological territory to look for "theories." Desmond's *Evicted* presents a thick formal lesson in how to tie social domains together, how to responsibly treat human beings as characters, and how to chip away at capitalist exploitation while still telling a good story.

---

22   David Alworth, *Site Reading: Fiction, Art, Social Form* (Princeton: Princeton University Press, 2016); Amanda Anderson, Toril Moi, and Rita Felski, *Character: Three Inquiries in Literary Studies* (Chicago: University of Chicago Press, 2019). See also Laura Bieger's essay on Alworth's *Site Reading* in this volume.

Contributors

Laura Bieger, Chair of American Studies, Political Culture & Theory, Rijksuniversiteit Groningen, The Netherlands

Dustin Breitenwischer, Junior Professor for American Studies, Institute of English and American Studies, Universität Hamburg

Ulla Haselstein, Professor of American Literature, John F. Kennedy Institute for North American Studies, Freie Universität Berlin, Germany

Katja Kanzler, Professor of American Literature, Universität Leipzig, Germany

Frank Kelleter, Professor of American Culture, John F. Kennedy Institute for North American Studies, Freie Universität Berlin, Germany

Philipp Löffler, Assistant Professor, English Department, Universität Heidelberg, Germany

Stefanie Mueller, Lecturer, Institute of English and American Studies, Goethe-Universität Frankfurt, Germany

J. Jesse Ramírez, Assistant Professor of American Studies, Universität St. Gallen, Switzerland

Christoph Ribbat, Professor of American Studies, Department of English and American Studies, Universität Paderborn, Germany

Kathryn S. Roberts, Assistant Professor, American Studies in Political Culture and Theory, Rijksuniversiteit Groningen, The Netherlands

Alexander Starre, Assistant Professor of American Culture, John F. Kennedy Institute for North American Studies, Freie Universität Berlin, Germany

Maria Sulimma, Postdoctoral Researcher, Research Group "City Scripts," Department of Anglophone Studies, Universität Duisburg-Essen, Germany

Johannes Voelz, Heisenberg-Professor of American Studies, Democracy, and Aesthetics, Institute of English and American Studies, Goethe-Universität Frankfurt, Germany

Sarah Wasserman, Associate Professor, Department of English, University of Delaware, USA

Samuel Zipp, Professor of American Studies and Urban Studies, Brown University, USA

Cultural Studies

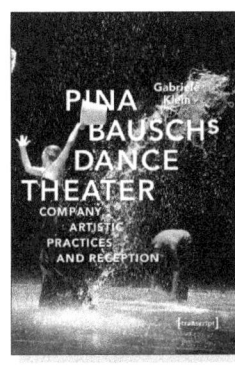

Gabriele Klein
Pina Bausch's Dance Theater
Company, Artistic Practices and Reception

2020, 440 p., pb., col. ill.
29,99 € (DE), 978-3-8376-5055-6
E-Book:
PDF: 29,99 € (DE), ISBN 978-3-8394-5055-0

Elisa Ganivet
Border Wall Aesthetics
Artworks in Border Spaces

2019, 250 p., hardcover, ill.
79,99 € (DE), 978-3-8376-4777-8
E-Book:
PDF: 79,99 € (DE), ISBN 978-3-8394-4777-2

Nina Käsehage (ed.)
**Religious Fundamentalism
in the Age of Pandemic**

April 2021, 278 p., pb., col. ill.
37,00 € (DE), 978-3-8376-5485-1
E-Book: available as free open access publication
PDF: ISBN 978-3-8394-5485-5

**All print, e-book and open access versions of the titles in our list
are available in our online shop www.transcript-publishing.com**

Cultural Studies

Ivana Pilic, Anne Wiederhold-Daryanavard (eds.)
Art Practices in the Migration Society
Transcultural Strategies in Action
at Brunnenpassage in Vienna

March 2021, 244 p., pb.
29,00 € (DE), 978-3-8376-5620-6
E-Book:
PDF: 25,99 € (DE), ISBN 978-3-8394-5620-0

German A. Duarte, Justin Michael Battin (eds.)
Reading »Black Mirror«
Insights into Technology and the Post-Media Condition

January 2021, 334 p., pb.
32,00 € (DE), 978-3-8376-5232-1
E-Book:
PDF: 31,99 € (DE), ISBN 978-3-8394-5232-5

Krista Lynes, Tyler Morgenstern, Ian Alan Paul (eds.)
Moving Images
Mediating Migration as Crisis

2020, 320 p., pb., col. ill.
40,00 € (DE), 978-3-8376-4827-0
E-Book: available as free open access publication
PDF: ISBN 978-3-8394-4827-4

GPSR Authorized Representative: Easy Access System Europe, Mustamäe tee
50, 10621 Tallinn, Estonia, gpsr.requests@easproject.com

www.ingramcontent.com/pod-product-compliance
Lightning Source LLC
Chambersburg PA
CBHW061609120626
46550CB00004B/1666